The Shores of Heaven

Based on a true story

Fr. Joseph Gill

First Printing: May 2020

ISBN: 978-1-71694-258-7

Printed in the United States of America

Cover Illustration and Design by Ewa Krepsztul

The Shores of Heaven

A Novel, Based on a True Story

Begun February 1, 2019

Table of Contents

"We spring up in greater numbers the more we are mown down by you: the blood of the Christians is the seed of a new life."

Tertullian, _Apologeticus_ (c. 197)

Prologue

The end of the third century was marked with political and spiritual turmoil within the Roman Empire. The emperor Diocletian, who reigned from 284-305, grew progressively weaker and less interested in ruling such a vast empire, which stretched from Hadrian's Wall in England all the way around the Mediterranean to North Africa, Turkey, and Egypt. In 286, he split the Empire in two, sharing his power with the co-emperor Maximian who reigned in the West (spending most of his time on campaign as a military commander, putting down rebellions across the Empire), while Diocletian himself retired to the East. Finding the administrative challenges more than he could bear even with this dual-emperor system – and hoping to make more political allies - Diocletian split the Empire further in 293, forming a tetrarchy ("rule of four"). He named his son-in-law Galerius to be the Caesar in the East (a title distinct from Emperor by this point), while Maximian named his son Maxentius to be Caesar in the West, ruling over England and Gaul (France).

Galerius was a bloodthirsty ruler who used any means necessary to subdue rebels within his territory. He was known to slaughter entire cities that threatened rebellion. In addition, he was the driving force behind the persecution of Christians in the Empire. They had lived in relative peace under Diocletian until Galerius convinced the Emperor to pass an edict in February of 303 which ordered churches destroyed and Christians executed. He personally oversaw the execution of a number of Christians in Nicomedia (modern-day Turkey). Because of the backlash from these executions, Galerius fled Nicomedia and came to Rome for safety in the summer of 303.

The Christian faith was new and unfamiliar, and many rumors grew up around it, leading to widespread rejection and persecution. The Emperors needed to unite the Empire both politically and religiously – but this new sect had arisen which pledged allegiance to a higher Kingdom, and was therefore a threat to unity and peace. Although around the year 300 almost ten percent of the Empire professed the Name of Jesus, they were still very much outcasts. Thousands of martyrs died in this last persecution, which stretched on until 311. Some of these saints became well-known and beloved in our Church. But others remain more obscure: Saint Pancras, Saints Nereus and Achilleus, and Saint Domitilla.

This is their story.

PART ONE: The Voyage

Waves crashed upon the boat, sending a misty veil into the air, obscuring the slowly-shrinking coastline. It was colder out here, on the water, with a salty spray that cut like a dagger through the cloak, penetrating through bone and marrow. But this wind would hasten the journey, favorably pushing the seaworthy craft further out across the Aegean Sea. Squinting into the wind – and blinking back tears – Pancras snatched a final glimpse of his homeland, with the port city of Miletos fading in the distance.

The journey from the boy's homestead to this seafaring town had been arduous. He recalled the way his *bulla* had bounced around on his chest as the cart traversed uneven ground, as it methodically worked its way along the cobblestone roads that led from one city to another. It was winter's end now, the muddy streets pockmarked with holes from the freezing-thawing cycle. But the days stretched longer, and the breezes contained a hint of the warmth to come. According to the calendar, the journey took but a few days. But it seemed interminable in the regions of the soul where the grieved dare not explore.

The resonance of grief was still as raw as the cold Westerly winds that blew down from the Taurus mountains. Those long nights on the land-journey, safely ensconced in the inn or beside the campfire, were none too easy on the lad, aching as he was to recover what was lost. With the rhythmic snores of his uncle Dionysius as a background, Pancras found sleep elusive. There was an ache in his heart, a grief he could not yet comprehend at his tender age.

Daybreak brought no relief. As the cart would round a bend or summit a hill, the landscape would change, and with the ever-changing scenery, the finality of death sunk in yet again. His hometown was a distant memory. Nevermore would Pancras see his father, now lying silently as ash in a necropolis. The pyre consumed, and he was no more. Cleonius now rested in awful silence beside his beloved wife who had preceded him into the underworld.

The underworld – a fearful thought for a ten-year-old boy. As he would lay there by the fire at night, struggling to suck at the last bit of warmth, the glowing embers casting frightening specters to dance upon the trees, Pancras pondered silently the eternal fate of men. Will we be like these shadows, a cold reflection of what once had life?

And yet, as he stood on the bow of the ship, gazing out to the land being consumed by the sea, all he knew was the pain of loss.

This was supposed to be an exciting experience, his first-ever nautical journey. A chance to see different lands, to adjust to a new culture. Ever since he was young, Pancras had desired to see the world beyond his estate and town, to breathe new air and meet men of different upbringing. But now, with all that had happened, this journey had none such savor. Even the gently undulating floor, rising and falling with the tides, was disorienting. He missed his wooden house, his donkey, his father. A sigh shuddered in his lungs, a stifled sob of pent-up grief.

He could hear the distant call of the seagulls, hovering close to land which was quickly becoming a memory. Their squawking, almost drowned by the sloshing waves, was another part of his past that was disappearing. Tears sprang unbidden to his eyes.

As the grey and misty evening began its slow descent into night, he heard his name called from beneath the deck. Presently a ruddy and rounded face appeared at the base of the stairs, flush with the warmth of the galley fire.

"Pancras!" the man called. "We are eating now."

Pancras turned back to the sea. "I am not hungry."

His uncle stared, appraising him. In the weeks in which the boy had been in his care, the lad had become drawn and gaunt, losing the vivaciousness of youth. It was understandable, he reasoned. But he had given his word to his late sister's husband, and he would see to it that Pancras grew to be a man!

"You must, son. You have a long journey ahead of you."

Pancras turned, and in the dimming dusk Dionysius could see that the moisture on the boy's cheek was not entirely attributable to the mist of the sea. He ascended the stairs and looked out over the whitecapped water.

They stood silently for a moment, until Dionysius raised his voice above the tumult of the waves. "You need to let it go. Phrygia is the past. We are headed to a new life."

Still Pancras did not respond. How could he? Phrygia contained the only home he ever knew. His ancestors lived and farmed there. His playmates, his school. His father.

His uncle rested a reassuring hand on the boy's shoulder, but with firmness in his voice said, "All of us have lost loved ones. We must move on."

In the fading shadows he could barely make out the thin contours of land before they vanished out of sight.

"Will I ever see them again?" Pancras barely whispered, hoping his words would be lost to the wind.

Dionysius didn't respond, but could sense in the boy's silence the subtle pain of mourning.

The two of them stood on the deck for a while longer, watching the dusk turn to night. Clouds parted, and a few stars began to radiate their piercing light in the firmament.

"Come, Pancras," his uncle led, guiding the boy down into the galley.

~~

A small rivulet of wine ran down the face of his uncle, with whom he shared the heavy woolen blanket. Enough wine can help a man sleep in the most uncomfortable locations, no matter the circumstances. A wooden plank and a covering, and a bed is contrived. The peaceful countenance of Dionysius showed a man drugged beyond the cares and concerns of a child.

The gently swaying hull and the rhythmic lapping of the waves should have provided a peaceful lullaby. But once again, staring into the dying coals of the galley fire, nestled atop a bed of sand and iron, Pancras found sleep elusive.

Perhaps it was the lingering odor of wheat in the hull of the ship that sparked his memory, as the past summer's harvest was coming to mind. It had been a particularly good harvest, the first one in which Pancras was allowed out in the field with his father and their hired workers. He could still see the sun glistening off their scythes as they whipped them through the standing grain, cutting it down. The older men would then follow and gather the wheat into bundles, laying the burdens on the cart pulled by one of their many donkeys. That had been a happy summer, a time of playfulness and joy.

Presently his father paused in his labors, laying down his harvesting tools and drinking from a skin slung around his body. He then turned to his son, who had been following, helping to gather small bundles in his arms.

His father had smiled, and offered Pancras a sip from his water. The boy gratefully accepted and paused his work to drink.

There was a gaze of affection as the father picked up the boy and hoisted him upon his own broad shoulders, moist with the sweat of hard work. Cleonius was a tall, broad-shouldered man, his bronze face glistening with the evidence of his toil. His dark features lightened by the summer sun, he was the living god of Pancras' adoration. Gazing at him with the squinted eyes of a laughing face, Cleonius was his protector, his rock, his only living family.

As he lay in the dungeon of the ship, his father's face came back to him in clear focus. Vivid memories washed over him, and he wondered why this particular summer's day was recalled to his mind?

"All of this, Pancras," his father had mused, as his breathing became less labored from the exertion. "All of this will be yours."

Everything that could be seen belonged to his father; this he knew. Golden fields of wheat undulating under the autumnal breeze, the distant foothills of the Pontic mountains, the azure river that flowed down just past the pasture for the flocks. A rich man's estate, he knew, even as a young boy.

"But Pancras, know that this was given to you as a gift from the gods," he continued, with a smile. "You must treat it well, and give to those who go without. A generous heart will please the gods and they will bless you abundantly."

Pancras had nodded solemnly. He knew from his father's tone that this was serious, although he did not fully

11

understand what he meant. All he really knew is that he was so happy to be here, on the shoulders of a great man who loved him unconditionally. In the uncomplicated way of children, Pancras looked about him and was filled with contentment, knowing that this joy would never end.

No matter how hard he shivered, he could not get warm in the damp hold of that ship bound for Ostia. Or perhaps the cold was coming from within, from the sobs choked back or the tears he tried in vain to hold. No, his father was never coming back. No, he would never see him again. The underworld had claimed him, and there would be no more visits from his beloved Papa until he joined him in the city of the dead.

~~~

The journey stretched interminably. There were no other children on the ship, and very few passengers. A few other sailors busied themselves with their tasks, keeping the merchant ship on course. Casks and casks of olive oil sat untouched in the hold, to fill the insatiable appetite of Roman consumers. A tall pile of dried meats, taller than Pancras himself, stood in the corner, to be sold in the marketplace. Kegs of salt, baskets of dried apricots and figs and raisins, and bundles of wool filled every nook of the underbelly.

The days turned sunny, the warm Sahara breezes bringing good tidings from the South. From the prow, Pancras watched as the islands of Graecia rose from the sea as mountains from a plain. But these passed by as they continued down southeasterly. The scenery changed little. At a certain point the captain, taking pity on the lost and lonely boy, invited him to gaze upon the gleaming city of

Athens, visible only to the squinting eye. Pancras could only make out a small white man-made bump on an otherwise nondescript island, but it brought back memories.

It was early winter, when his father was still well. A light snowfall had dusted the roof of their house, but they were warm enough with the dung-and-firewood blaze that roared in their fireplace. Cleonius was reclining on his wooden couch – the one with the dyed woolen covers, Pancras remembered - stitching together his good tunic which had developed a tear beneath the arm. Near him on the same couch was Pancras, sitting with legs folded, poring over his papyrus reader. A charcoaled stick served as his writing implement, as he traced the Greek letters onto the page next to his father's handwriting.

A comfortable silence stretched between them. These cold winter nights lingered on, and his father was not much of a talker. He liked to think before he spoke.

"How does it go?" his father finally inquired.

Pancras put his stylus down with a bit more force than he intended. "I do not understand why this is important. You do not need to read and write to grow wheat."

Bemusedly, Cleonius chuckled. "Ah, yes, but neither does a donkey need to read or write. It is our education that makes us a man."

He knew that his father had studied, indeed. His grandfather had sent his father to school, and after a while he had served as a pupil of a sophist, until Cleonius' father's untimely death necessitated a return to the administration of the family estate.

"Do you not have any ambitions, Pancras?" Cleonius inquired with a smile.

Pancras looked up at him with impish eyes. "I want to be just like you and take care of this farm."

"But what if you have the talent to be an orator? I know how you like to argue," he bantered.

"You cannot eat words. We need bread and meat to live."

"Yes, but money can buy bread and meat," his father countered.

Pancras thought a moment for a response. He had never met an orator, or a senator, or a philosopher. These could well be mythical creatures, for all he knew was the life of the farm and the small village of Synnada. "You told me that all this would be mine. I want to be a farmer like you."

"Ah yes, I did say that," he mused with a smile. "You are just like your name: Pancras, *he who holds everything*. It will all be yours…and more." He turned his attention back to his tunic, indicating the end of the conversation.

Taking up his papyrus in hand, he tried to focus on the symbols, but he considered what the *more* might be. What might his father have in mind? He could not fathom. There could be nothing happier than to be here on this farm, raising a family. Pancras looked back to his father, noticing that his sun-dried face had seen much, but still had hope and kindness within it.

Without losing his focus on his stitches, Cleonius took up the thread again. "Have I ever told you of my time in Athens?"

Pancras had heard the story so many times he had lost count, but eagerly wanted to hear it again.

"It was a beautiful summer, that year. I had finished my twentieth year, and was still young enough to hold the world in my hands. My teacher had recommended me to study at the University of Athens. He thought I had talent

14

enough to serve as a public orator, or perhaps in some form of law or government. I knew I wanted out of this backwater town, to see the world. A little education is a dangerous thing, I always say. Broadens your horizons, yes, but it can also make us dull to the grandeur already around us. In any case, I was ungrateful to my loving parents and the life they had provided, and I suppose I wanted to make a name for myself. Here in Synnada, I would forever be known as the son of Patricius. The glamour of the big city drew me.

"So I set sail across the sea. It was quite a journey. I was on a ship which was transporting slaves from the East, conquered peoples from Indus and beyond. They were men quite unlike us in tongue and custom, but when I gazed into their eyes I saw they were just like us with their hopes and desires.

"Their treatment was so poor. My heart was moved, for we were the barbarians, they the noblemen. They carried themselves with such dignity, though we treated them like criminals condemned to die. I would often sneak into their quarters late at night to offer them water and food, for days would pass without any relief being offered to them. Never did they see the sun until they saw it at the slave market.

"But the journey itself taught me many things. For one, I tasted their foods and their spices. The holds were filled with treasures from the East – elephant tusks of pure ivory, aromatic balms, gold-woven silk. The plunder of a conquered people. Whether right or wrong, I cannot say, but I am not sure the gods would approve."

His story was interrupted by the scratching of footsteps leading to the door, followed by a knock. Rising, Cleonius went to the threshold and warmly welcomed the visitor, one of their hired servants, a bald man with gnarled hands and a weathered face.

"Forgive me, master, but our fire has gone out," said the servant, dusting the snow coating from his shoulders as he bowed low. "We humbly beg your mercy for an ember from your fire."

Encouragingly, Cleonius clutched the man's shoulders to straighten him. "Yes of course, my friend. Did you bring a vessel?"

"I am sorry, sir, I did not."

"No matter, I have one for you," Cleonius smiled. "Pancras, please take the terra cotta dish – no, not that one, the smaller one up on the shelf on your right – yes, that's it. Scoop a generous ember for our visitor." The boy complied and brought him a glowing ember in the terra cotta pot.

"Many thanks, many thanks," the visitor intoned, bowing copiously as he backed away from the door.

When the house was securely shuttered once again to preserve the warmth, Cleonius reclined a second time on the couch. "So where was I with the story? Oh yes, we had just reached Athens.

"It is hard to describe the Pearl of Antiquity to anyone who has not seen a city. She is more than a city; she is a triumph. A living testament to all that humanity can become. The columns rise to heights unknown here in the provinces. To walk up the stairs to the Temple of Athena was akin to climbing Mount Olympus itself. It is a gateway into another world.

"And the people! The tones on the skin are as varied as the colors of the earth. Every tongue of man sent a representative to that city. There were more people gathered in the agora than I had ever seen in my life. Some may claim that the glories of Athens have dimmed with the rising of Rome, yet for a young man like me, not accustomed to venturing far from our family's homestead, this was a shock to encounter. I was speechless, simply taking it all in as I wandered about the town.

"You should see it, Pancras. After an hour or two of wandering I happened upon the Parthenon, the temple dedicated to Athena. It was majesty, pure majesty. I ascended the steps and felt as if I were ascending Mount Olympus, about to step into the throne room of Zeus. Doric columns of marble, white as snow. Gilded interior shining in the sunlight. It was so bright I had to shield my eye. 'Tis a shame it was destroyed in a fire the following year; it will never be the same.

"And the Athena Parthenos! A finer statue I have never seen…"

At this point Pancras interrupted. "A statue?"

"Yes, you know what a statue is! It was as if she were alive and reigning as patron, waiting to receive the petitions of her humble beneficiaries."

"Yes, Papa, I know what a statue is. But can statues really hear our prayers?"

His father looked pensive. "Well…" he lingered, formulating a response for his ten-year-old questioner. "I suppose not, as they are mere figures of marble and gold. But it is who this statue represents that instills it with power."

"Like my bulla?" He fingered the talisman around his neck, a simple disc three-fingers-wide, with inscriptions of Greek prayers to the gods on its faces. It dangled from a simple leather cord, and Pancras never took it off, unless he was bathing in the river.

"Yes, much like that," Cleonius replied, gently stroking the leather cord around his son's neck. "It is just a symbol, but a powerful one, promising protection from the gods."

Pancras smiled up at him.

"So, as I was saying, I stayed in the Parthenos for the afternoon sacrifice until the time for the evening meal, when I reported directly to the University. They had prepared an unbelievable feast for the first-year students. Roast pig, duck, lamb, wines from every corner of the earth. I soon found myself engaged in a conversation with a fellow first-year from Thermopylae, who was telling me the fascinating history of his city. Did I ever tell you how a thousand men held off an army of a hundred thousand at the small pass of Thermopylae? No? Well, that is another story for another day!

"We feasted that night until late. The main aula was lit by more candelabras that I have ever seen. It was a veritable bonfire, as bright as midday, although the darkness outside had fallen. We had a few speeches, none notable or worth remembering. But what a chance to get to know our fellow students! They were a fascinating assortment of characters – some from humbler backgrounds like myself, but some very cultured and interesting young men. I found myself drawn in to hear their stories – histories of war and peace, of famous men whose names I had never heard.

"Yet as the night stretched on, from outside the aula came the noise of revelry. It was some feast specific to Athens; I cannot yet remember the reason for it. But people were singing and dancing in the streets as we departed. Drunkards everywhere, with music and raucous laughter and dancing. Such a shock to me, for as you know in our small village, everyone is in bed by nightfall! Yet this party lasted far into the night. I stayed a while there, dancing to this foreign music and falling in love over and over again with the pretty girls who mingled with us first-years.

"We went to sleep in a dormitory large and broad, all seventy-five of us. The snoring was terrific! Yet the journey had so exhausted all of us that we fell into a dreamless sleep.

"The following day, arising early, we headed quickly to the university where, after a meal of bread and milk, we began our classes. Philosophy, medicine, theology, and literature from past ages filled our day. The debates were vigorous and satisfying, and I found it both fascinating and, at times, difficult to keep up. My former education had left me stunted compared with the other first-years, and my mind was continually opening to new horizons because of the topics."

"Like what, Papa?"

"I remember on our first day discussing the philosopher Heraclitus, one of the Greeks from time immemorial. He had said that a man can never step into the same river more than once, because it is not the same river, and he is not the same man."

Pancras' furrowed brow brought a chuckle to his father's lips. "You do not understand?"

"No, I don't. I swim in our stream many times. What does he mean?"

"That's all right, I found it difficult at first, as well. He means that life is constant change. Nothing stays the same."

Pancras felt a sudden current of nostalgia sweep through him. "But what if I don't want it to change? I like things the way they are."

Putting his arm around his son in the ancient gesture of paternal love, Cleonius said, "Ah, my son, but change is how we grow. You cannot stay young forever. I want you to travel far, see the world, find the truth."

"But I want to stay here, with you, on our farm."
There was some desperate, unnamed fear slowly arising within him, as if everything might be taken away.

"But a truly rich man is he who knows about more than cows and chickens," Cleonius concluded. "Before you can inherit all this, you must learn much and seek the truth. Then, all this will be yours…all this, and wisdom, too."

"You cannot eat wisdom," he retorted, not wanting to be wrong.

"Is eating what makes you a man? If so, then our pig must be a man, because he eats a lot!"

They both laughed an easy laugh, dispelling the hints of gloom that had crept in.

"Anyway, I stayed in Athens for only a week. The third day there, I saw a sight I will never forget. We had just been dismissed from afternoon lectures when a commotion on the street caught our eye. Being young and foolish, we wanted to see what was causing such a row. We joined the gathering throng surrounding two men. One seemed to be a prisoner of the other; he was grasped around the neck to the point that he could barely breathe. The stronger man had drawn his sword and was shouting to the crowd.

"'Let it be known by all!' he cried out. 'This man has stolen a purse of coins from my wife. I caught him in the very act of carrying away the purse.' With that, he grabbed the constrained man, caught his arm in a vice grip, and placing the arm on the table, proceeded to cut off his right hand with a pass of his sword."

Pancras continued to stare, eyes wide with horror and fascination.

"The man cried out and fell to the ground, in agony, clutching his wrist. All of us were struck dumb as donkeys standing there. Yet no man thought to intervene, for this was justice, we knew. It was a sober warning that justice would be dealt, and great suffering awaited those who were wicked."

"But what if the man was innocent?" Pancras interrupted. This seemed unfair to him – no chance to defend himself from such a charge!

"If the man was innocent, then may the gods repay the injustice done to him."

This answer did not satisfy the boy. "What if they do not?"

"They must. The gods are just."

"But he has no hand. The gods will not provide him with one."

"No, but they will repay him in other ways. Perhaps he will amass good fortune. Perhaps he will live to see the downfall of the man who injured him."

"Perhaps he will die homeless and poor," Pancras retorted, surprising himself with his boldness.

Cleonius too was surprised. He was silent for a moment, considering the thought. At length he murmured, "Alas, my son. I can only hope that the good are repaid and the wicked are punished. Otherwise, this life is nothing but a…a game played by fools."

An uncomfortable silence reigned. Outside of their solitary window, the flakes of snow were as so many shooting stars plummeting to the earth. Pancras pondered whether he believed his father. Oh, he *wanted* to believe him – that right is always rewarded and evil is always punished. All he had ever known has shown him thus. When he would fall into one of his childish pranks – like when he would put dried pigs' dung in the fire, which would smoke the house terribly, or when he would steal the honey for him to eat in secret – oh, he would be punished all right. Nothing serious, of course, for the consequence befits the crime. But was this always so?

And was it so with the ways of the gods? He had heard of the *Moirai*, the Fates that determined the lives of men. Capricious and random, these Fates spun the webs of life, weaving a tapestry tragic or glorious. Are we at their mercies?

Disturbed by these thoughts, Pancras shook his head to clear his mind. Not the kinds of thoughts that should be pondered on a cold winter's night!

He broke the silence. "Finish the story, Papa."

His father was slow to respond. In a low voice, he continued, "You know the ending, my son."

"Tell it anyway."

"In my seventh day in Athens, I received a message from home, that my father had taken ill. I hurried back home and took care of him for a year before he died. At this time my siblings and my mother relied upon me to care for them, so I was forced to abandon my studies and learn how to farm." He looked at Pancras with a grave and loving gaze. "I wish for you to succeed where I never succeeded. I want you to win the world. But more than that, I want you to be a man I can be proud of."

Pancras felt a lump of emotion coming to his throat, so he looked away. They fell lost to their own thoughts.

Finally he squeaked, "Will you take me to Athens?"

"Even better, my son," he replied. "I will go with you to Rome!"

The captain noticed that the boy's eyes had grown red and teary. Surely this was from squinting into the summer sun, trying in vain to make out the Parthenon as it towered over the city. "Maybe you ought to go underneath for a spell," he suggested with compassion. "I will summon you when we draw near to Kithira. Now *that* is an island to see!"

Pancras wiped the tears from his eyes and silently departed.

~~~

The coastland arose, looking much like the many islands they had passed on their journey. This time, however, they drew closer to the land, until it was clear they were near to landfall. The buildings grew from specks to miniatures to regular-size. Soon they could hear the voices of men carrying over the waters, bringing hope that the journey would finally reach its completion.

Gently, as a mother laying down her sleeping baby, the ship sailed into harbor, approaching the dock with a splash as the anchors dropped into the deep. The passengers were jolted as the ship came to rest against the thick wooden pilings, with crew leaping off the ship to tie its mast down. A small plank was produced to disembark the passengers, and Pancras saw Ostia for the first time.

This bustling port city was abuzz with activity. Even from the docks they could hear the echo of commerce, money changing hands on the streets as merchants hawked their wares.

A few trunks and crates, and a woolen bag each, were the only possessions of the travelers. With haste they had unloaded their cargo onto the dock. Dionysius quickly found a man with a cart who could be persuaded to take them to Rome for a couple of *sestertii*, some of the profit from the sale of Cleonius' estate. Loading the crates onto the cart, they began the journey, with the driver and Dionysius seated in front, Pancras balancing precariously on the cargo in the

23

rear. A solitary horse pulled the small wagon along the bumpy cobblestones, through the center of the town.

"Won't be long now!" Dionysius called back to his nephew. He was clearly in a jubilant mood, grateful to be back on dry land. "Only about one hundred and thirty stadia to Rome. Not long at all. We shall be there by nightfall, right, my friend?" A clasp of gregarious friendship was offered to the driver, who smiled broadly.

"As long as ol' Dorceus here will cooperate," he replied jovially, giving the reigns a light snap. "She has a mighty temper, you know, and is skittish like a mouse. She can throw the finest rider, but we might get lucky, eh?"

Dionysius glared at him. "Truly? I pray that you will get us to our destination in safety. Or I might have to request a refund."

The man laughed brightly. "No worries, friend. We shall arrive, in one piece or several."

Dionysius smirked.

But Pancras took no notice of this banter, for he was entranced at the new sights. For a moment he forgot his troubles, absorbed as he was in the streets and insulae of the city. The buildings rose all around, red-brick edifices with painted awnings and porches stretching into the street. Large open windows pockmarked the dwellings, wide enough for the boy to peer into, revealing women performing their domestic chores. The narrow street was lined on either side with stalls and booths, selling foodstuffs and wool, bread and jugs and pots, jewelry and dyed clothing, dried herbs and livestock.

The men and women dressed similar to people in his native village, he thought. They were speaking his familiar Latin but with an accent specifically Roman. Many were clothed with tunics belted about the waist, cream-colored and stained from their employment. Some wore over-cloaks to guard against the early morning chill, but the day had warmed sufficiently for many of them to lay aside their outer garment. Sandals shod the feet of most, though some of the small children ran around barefoot.

The dray passed through an intersection, and down the side street Pancras could see three white-haired men in blue-rimmed togas engaging in an animated discussion. Doubtlessly they were leaders of the city, magistrates of some sort.

"If Rome is the Eternal City, Ostia is the gate," Dionysius mused, himself drawn into the uniqueness of the experience.

"Aye, perhaps it is, but this is a mere pittance compared to the glories of Rome!" replied his driver.

Pancras could not remove his eyes from the sights and sounds and smells of this new town. It was greater and grander than anything he had ever imagined. His small hamlet of Synnada was a mere backwater compared to this teeming metropolis. Up ahead were a few slaves sweeping the porch of a domus; through the window he could see bread being removed from a giant clay oven, warm and fresh and issuing forth wonderful odors. A woman to his left was pounding olives in a great pestle and mortar, the light green oil dribbling out into a jug. A few of the poorer children sat in the dust just outside of the public baths, drawing with sticks in the dirt and playing some foreign game with dried nuts in a circle.

All of a sudden, a dog bolted out from an open doorway, barking furiously at the passing cart. Startled, their horse bucked once and took off down the main thoroughfare, swerving in and out of the stalls and forcing merchants to dive out of the way.

To escape from the pursuing canine, the horse and cart took a sharp left turn. The next thing Pancras knew, he was hitting the ground with a startled "Oof!", watching the cart and horse run off without him. Pain shot through his back and side where he hit the cobblestones, and momentarily his vision blacked out. He cried out in pain and lay there, stunned and unable to move.

When he opened his eyes a moment later, a small group had gathered around him. A matronly woman knelt on the ground with her warm hand on his forehead.

"Marcos! Bring him water, and a wet cloth," she called out to her son. Looking down at the injured boy, she cooed and clucked her tongue. "Now, now. Do not move. We will fetch the doctor. Where does it hurt?"

A far-off moan escaped his lips, unable to speak.

The woman began to poke and prod his back and neck, to feel for any broken bones. At times the gentle touch would elicit a sharp pain, causing the boy to whimper.

The scuffling of sandals on cobblestone drew everyone's attention to the man who had hastened to the scene, hovering over the injured youth.

"Well!" Dionysius gruffly began. "You should have been holding on. Look where it has gotten you. Hurry to your feet – we have to make Rome by nightfall." His arms were folded, his face set in disapproval, and Pancras felt a pain in his soul deeper than the pain in his flesh.

The woman continued to massage his neck and ribs, which were sore and bruised but not broken. The moistened cloth was brought and applied to his forehead, which considerably lessened the pounding in his head. She helped him to sit up, all the while muttering comforting words.

"Now you are one lucky boy. Seems like nothing was seriously broken. The head? Oh, that will mend in a few

26

days. You knocked it hard against these cobblestones. They ought to strap you into that cart – the driver doesn't know how to control his horse! A horse like that should be accustomed to dogs, it's not like we don't have enough of them around here.

"Do you think you can stand? Not yet? All right, let's wait just a moment, let you catch your breath."

Pancras looked around, his head still feeling like the anvil in a blacksmith's shop – pounded again and again by a ceaseless hammer. The crowd around him had started to dissipate, mildly disappointed that the injury had not been anything exciting, he was sure. Against a far wall stood his uncle, leaning back, looking perturbed at this unexpected delay.

"Help me up," Pancras murmured, still unsure if he could walk, but fearing to disappoint his uncle.

The woman gave him her arm, and he was able to struggle to his feet. His shoulder and neck screamed in agony – something was wrong with them, he was sure – but on unsteady feet he was able to stumble a few steps forward.

"Good," grunted Dionysius. "Let's go. The dray is just up ahead, a hundred cubits – the driver has been trying to settle the horse."

He took his nephew from the care of the matron and began the trod down the road, with Pancras falling behind as he limped his way to the cart.

The driver was glad to see them coming. "My deepest apologies, young master," he said as he helped Pancras back onto the wagon, nestling him deeper in the nest of crates and carpetbags that filled the wagon bed. "I pray this will not happen again."

"An inauspicious start to our journey," Dionysius added dryly, climbing back into the seat. "If we meet with a

27

similar mishap, it will be you who will be injured, not my nephew."

"Aye, my friend, no need to get testy. I make this run twice per day, and have never had much trouble."

"Then let us be off," he concluded impatiently, in a foul mood.

The driver quickly snapped the reigns and the horse began its faithful trot toward the Eternal City.

~~~

The landscape changed from urban to suburban to the rolling and undulating hills of Lazio. The fresh air and the fields, now fallow, reminded Pancras of home. He closed his eyes, letting the sun warm him. The jolts and bumps of the uneven road caused continual pain in his head, but he was unwilling to complain lest his uncle grow harsher toward him.

It was the smell, the smell of earth and manure and cypress trees, that brought him back home. He always loved this time of year, when the snows had receded to the peaks of the mountains and the fields had just begun to grow wild grasses, before they were tilled and prepared to receive the grain. It was the end of the cold and the winter, the promise of a warmer season yet to come. Hoping, aching, pining, Pancras thought this might be a metaphor for his life, that the season of cold was beginning to thaw and a warmer season might be dawning.

But for now, as he lay in the cart, jostled like so much cargo, he was still grieving. Even after all these weeks, the memories would accost him unawares, drowning him once again in an ocean of sorrow.

He reached up to grasp his bulla, the one lifeline he still had to his father, and could not find it on his chest.

Eyes flying open, he sat up and looked around. Indeed, the medallion was not around his neck anymore. Panic began to rise within him as he started searching among the crates, anxiously hoping to find that it had fallen between them. But to no avail – it was not to be found.

The sounds of wooden crates shifting behind him caused Dionysius to turn around. "What is the ruckus?"

Stricken, Pancras looked at him. "My bulla. I cannot find it."

His uncle shrugged and turned back around, unconcerned. "Oh, I am sorry. We will purchase a new one in Rome."

"No, you do not understand. This was the one my father gave me."

"Yes, yes, that's unfortunate," he replied distractedly, looking at the scenery.

"It must have fallen off back in Ostia. We must turn around and look for it."

Dionysius turned around, piercing him with a severe look. "We are not turning around."

"We've only traveled three or four stadia…"

"It's only a trinket – it means nothing. This journey has been wearying already – let us continue so we can rest in Rome."

"It means nothing? It is protection of the gods!"

Dionysius snorted. "The gods? Hah! A magic amulet cannot protect you. That is a myth."

"It is true! My father told me so."

"Yes, your father believed in the gods and the Fates and the omens. Myths, all of them. We make the world as we want it, Pancras. We are not controlled by the stars or anything else. No, we make our own destinies."

"Yes, but…" The words died on his lips. How could he share that his bulla was his lifeline, his last and firmest connection to his home, his father? To hold this amulet, as his uncle derisively called it, was to reach across space and time and hold his father's hand, but no one could understand this. This secret box in his heart was not to be shared with anyone – it was his alone. And his bulla was how he accessed these hidden memories.

He looked back up to his uncle, grumpy and greedy and altogether selfish, and then looked back to the town now fading further and further in the past. And he knew what he needed to do.

As quietly as he could he climbed over the wooden chests and bags, standing on the rear edge of the wagon. Mustering the scraps of his courage, ignoring the pain in his head and the fear in his heart, he leapt off the cart and onto the cobblestone.

He did not land well. With a roll, he hit his head once again, feeling sharper and more blinding pains resounding through his whole body. But he had only one thought on his mind, which drove him to his knees and then to his feet – he must find his bulla, the one tangible memory he possessed of the only one who ever truly loved him.

A quick glance back showed that his uncle and the driver had not noticed his departure. He set off on a run back towards the accursed town of Ostia, but the pounding of his feet on the cobblestones exacerbated the pounding in his head. He was forced into a rapid walk, driven onward by his memories and his sorrow.

A furlong, then another. His throat was closing with anxiety, fear of never finding the bulla, fear of never finding his uncle again if he continued onward to Rome, fear of his uncle's anger if he did. Fear of loss. Fear of despair.

He was cold all over, despite the warmth in the air. He did not have the courage to lift his eyes from the road. The voyage seemed endless. Perhaps it would never end until he reached the underworld. His heart was being wrung out, choking on everything – sorrow, exhaustion, hunger, grief, terror. One foot in front of the other – no need to go insane now – just reach the destination, reach Ostia, never mind the future. Just keep moving in the present.

He was almost to Ostia when he noticed his tears splashing on the pavement. They were not tears of physical pain, considerable though it was. No, his tears gave vent to the frustration building up inside. There seemed to be no scrap of hope that he could cling to, grasp as he might. For what is there to hope for when your past is gone, your future is empty, and your present is suffering?

There stood the walls of Ostia, just up ahead behind the grove of cedars. He passed through the city gates, grateful to finally return. Hastening, Pancras turned down the labyrinthine streets, turning left and right until he found the spot where he had fallen.

The bulla was not laying there. The dust had been kicked up, evidence of the boy's earlier fall, but the talisman was not within sight.

Panicking, he leaned against the wall and surveyed the scene. Abandon the search? Return to Rome, ashamed of his impulsive behavior? Continue looking, looking, looking…?

For what? The bulla could not bring his father back. Why was he so obsessed with his trinket? He shook his head, disgusted at himself, his childishness, his own sorrows, the misfortunes that continually befell him. Time to grow up and face the harsh reality like a man. No time to get sentimental, to keep wallowing in…

A flash of light darted across the agora, the sun's reflections off of a locket made of polished lead. There, around the neck of one of those poor boys he had seen earlier, dangled a bulla.

He quickly crossed the open space, his legs churning faster when he saw that it resembled his own bulla.

"That is mine!" he called out, approaching the seated boy, who was surrounded by three compatriots playing knucklebones on the dusty street.

The boy looked up with the hostile stare of a dog about to lose its bone. "What are you speaking of?"

"The bulla around your neck. Where did you get it?"

"I found it on the street, that's where," he spat back, a foul attitude lacing his words.

"It's mine."

"Then you'll have to fight me for it," he replied, returning to the game at hand. "It's nicer than mine, so I'm keeping it."

An inordinate rage seethed through Pancras' mind. He could not control everything that had been so cruelly ripped from his grasp: father and homeland – but this one would not be taken without a fight.

With a cry of anguish and fury, he attacked the boy with fists blazing, landing punches on his face and neck.

The other boy, despite being older and stronger, was taken by surprise at the ferocity of the attack. Quickly he regained his senses and returned the beating, landing a fist on Pancras' eye and another on his nose.

The cheers went up from the other boys, always glad to watch a fight. They stood in a circle, hooting and delighting in the bloodshed.

The tussle went on and on. A kick in the ribs, an elbow to the throat. Both boys landed jabs on the other in an even fight. Their bodies were intertwined as they rolled around on the dusty ground, locked in each other's unrelenting grasp. Despite the older boy's size, he was not driven by the same desperation that fueled Pancras.

The noise drew even the attention of a few adults in the vicinity, who shook their heads in disapproval or smiled secretly, remembering their own youthful contests.

Blood from Pancras' nose dribbled down his face, and his eye was beginning to swell, but he quickly threw the older boy off of him and, flipping over, put a knee in his chest, pinning him to the ground. Before the boy could react, Pancras grabbed the bulla and tore it from his neck with a snap.

Clutching it in his hand as a lifeline to sail across the underworld, he scrambled to his feet and began to run, as fast as he could, away from the scene. He found what he wanted, and now wanted to put vast distance between himself and the thief. Dodging in between the vendors and customers, he darted in between the marketplace stalls, heading toward the road to Rome.

It wasn't until he was outside the city walls a good distance that he finally believed he had not been followed. His pace began to slow, his heartbeat returning to normal.

Was it worth it? He tied the leather straps in a knot and slipped the bulla around his neck, willing himself not to think about such questions.

He could barely breathe or see, as his nose and eye were swollen. The pain in his head was now a thunderous roar, constant and piercing to the point that the sunlight felt like knives in his eyes.

It would be a long, long walk to Rome. One foot in front of the other. The sun was now high in the sky, beating down incessantly as he walked along. Overhead, the clear blue sky was dotted with a couple of crows, calling their desperate caws and longing for prey.

The basalt cobblestones, heated up in the sunshine, radiated warmth and distorted the view ahead, which appeared to shimmer as a mirage in the desert.

An hour passed, slowly progressing towards the city of kings and peasants like himself. At a certain point a man on a horse passed by, but Pancras did not raise his head to notice him. He was a sack of pain, a living contradiction. An escapee from hell, heading back to another hell. Dragging himself reluctantly along the path, there was nothing else to do but keep moving, for to stop would be to stop moving for eternity.

He acutely felt every suffering. The hunger pecked away at his stomach. His physical torments were unbearable, with the gong inside his head and his face smashed in. His soul despaired of ever finding hope again.

A few homesteads passed him by, but he took no heed. They weren't Rome; they weren't his uncle; they did not interest him.

A jutting cobblestone caused him to stumble, but he caught himself and looked up. The milestone to his left gave the distance to Rome. He stopped briefly to read it, and heaved a tremendous sigh, doubting that he would reach the city by nightfall.

The way did not vary from its arrow-straight track, without a single curve or landscape feature to draw one's eye. Just one foot in front of the other, on an endless journey from nothing to nothing. Pace by pace, furlong by furlong.

Rome might have been the other side of the world for all he cared.

Then, looking up, he saw a wagon stopped by the side of the road, and a man reclining beneath the shade of a palmetto tree.

Hesitatingly, but knowing he must face his fate, he continued on until he stood beside the wagon.

"We had left you for dead," the man said mirthlessly, his eyes closed.

Pancras stood there for judgment.

Dionysius rose slowly and came over to him, standing a pace away and sizing him up. Intense shame flooded the boy, for his bloodied nose and bruised face, signs of a fight he should never have begun but for his disobedience.

Dionysius slapped him across the face, so suddenly that Pancras was unable to react until his face stung from the blow.

"Do not ever disobey me again," his uncle concluded coldly, before turning away and embarking.

The driver had been fiddling with the harness, and now climbed in himself. Pancras, too, dragged himself onto the wagon, collapsing into the crevice between the crates, wishing for death.

~~~

The sun had dripped towards the horizon slowly, until it cast long shadows across the empty fields.

"A mere five stadia until we arrive!" the driver crooned with a forced cheerfulness.

Drowsily, Pancras had been passing in and out of the realm of sleep, motionless in his agony for the past several hours. Gingerly he raised himself up to a seated position, noting that the landscape had not changed in the intervening time.

"Let us stop at a tavern for supper, if we may," Dionysius requested.

"Ah, yes, I know just the one. A fine place for hot food."

"Something quick, no need for fine dining."

Up ahead, there was several tall tree trunks shaped oddly, lining the roads at regular intervals. He considered it odd that they were in such a perfect arrangement, as if they were planted purposely by a civil engineer. But the trees had no leaves and only two branches, perfectly perpendicular to the trunk.

As they drew nearer, the odd outgrowth on the trunk came into focus.

It was a human body, stripped and naked, hanging from the tree.

A gasp escaped his lips. Why would someone be hanging there?

They passed by one, then another, then another. Some of the bodies were clearly dead and in various stages of decomposition. A few had been nailed to the crossbeams, while most were tied with ropes. Deathly moans issued forth from a few of those still living, though they were more like breathing corpses than men. All of the men were completely naked. Dozens and dozens them lined the street, putrefying the air with the foul stench of death and excrement.

Dionysius remained silent, clearly nonplussed.

"We Romans," the driver sought to jest, "We love our spectacles…and our fellow countrymen."

A word was written above some of the crosses.

"Insurrection," Pancras read aloud. "What does that mean?"

Dionysius turned around. "Means these men rebelled against Rome. Always a dangerous idea. Rome will defend the Empire at all costs."

"But these men…" his voice trailed off. How could one man do this to another?

"Life is brutal, Pancras," his uncle added, his voice hard. "Brutal and short. Enjoy life while it lasts – one day this will be you and me."

Despite the grotesque demonstration, Pancras could not remove his sight from these pallid men. The cadaverously white faces of corpses and the tortured grimaces of the dying evoked a strange admixture of disgust and pity. He irrationally wished to take food and water to the men still living, or to grant a proper burial to the dead, lest they decompose right here in the open, their bodies as so much carrion for the birds. So much death on parade…

But deeper beyond the pity was the realization of how much he had been protected from. Never in Phrygia would a scene like this be reenacted. He had not so much as seen death, save for his father's untimely demise. How could men treat one another in this way? Was it true that life was brutal and short? His young and idealistic heart rebelled against the thought. No - in Phrygia, men loved one another. They were always quick to meet each other's needs, to celebrate life in all its various forms. Surely death mustn't be the paradigm.

Yet there, crucified before him, was the response. Death reigned everywhere he looked; death and violence. His own blood flowing from his face; these men's blood flowing from their hands and feet. A body lying prone on a bier, his father's face turning from flesh to white to ashen grey. The body of a boy beaten on a street in Ostia, these bodies hanging from leafless trees.

Shocked and silenced, Pancras sat back, closing his eyes, hoping against hope that these images would not be burned upon his imagination. Yet there they were, in his mind. Likely they would follow him to his dreams, as his father's face had followed him, haunting him, plaguing him.

They continued their somber procession past the dozens, hundreds of crosses until the walls of the City of Rome came into view.

~~~

The air was growing rather cold as darkness settled upon the city, though the lights glowed brightly within the tavern. Yet Pancras knew better than to try to fetch his uncle, who dined – or more likely, drank – within. He would sit, shivering, in the wagon until Dionysius came out, whenever that might be.

Oh, they had gone in over an hour ago, with promises to be just a minute, to purchase food and drink and bring it back to the starving boy. But the raucous laughter spilling out onto the sidewalk and the patrons still mulling around showed a celebration without indications of slowing down.

So he sat, and waited, looking around and trying not to think too much.

The passers-by spoke a unique dialect, he realized. He understood it all but their accent was distinctly Roman. They were dressed somewhat better than he, with a toga to cover their tunic and hammered gold jewelry dangling from their wrists. A gaggle of dignified ladies pranced by, dressing their hair in unfamiliar patterns. An argument had broken out further ahead between two men in fine linen togas, evidently on some obscure point of law that Pancras was unfamiliar with. In all, though, the streets were quiet in this downtrodden part of town, the inhabitants likely retiring for the night. Various oil lamps speckled in insulae windows, signs of life within.

The sound of a swinging wooden door, rusty on its hinges, brought his attention back to the tavern. His uncle and the driver stumbled forth, laughing and belching their way back to the wagon. They climbed aboard, clearly in good spirits.

"Here you are," Dionysius offered, passing back a small loaf of bread and a few dried fish, the odor of alcohol wafting back with the food.

The meal wasn't enough, but grateful for the pittance, he accepted it without complaint and began to devour it.

"Where is your destination?" the driver slurred, snapping the whips.

"Via del Gianicolo. I have a friend who has reserved a room for us."

"Transtiberim?" the driver verified with upraised eyebrow. "Nothing but a swamp and some Jews over there."

"You are forgetting Caesar's Garden."

"True, it is not the trash-heap it once was. But nothing like the Palatine Hill."

"Aye! But who can afford that? This residence is only temporary, anyway. Once my business is prospering, I will find a more upscale neighborhood."

Around a few narrow streets the cart continued to wander, crossing a bridge over the Tiberis River, until finally coming to rest beside a three-story brick insula tucked away in a narrow side street.

"Alas! We have arrived. An eventful journey, to be sure!" crowed the driver.

Dionysius was without even a smirk as he disembarked. A knock on the heavy oaken door produced the sound of scampering footsteps behind it. A deadbolt lock was drawn, and the door opened gingerly.

"Good sir, what is your business at this hour?" asked a man from within the darkness.

"I am Dionysius of Phrygia. Cassius has arranged a room for me and my nephew here. Surely he has informed you."

The door swung wide open and the man stepped into the alleyway, his smile dimly visible in the half-moon. "Ah yes, of course. We have a room reserved for you. Welcome to Rome!" He extended the handclasp of friendship, which Dionysius gratefully exchanged.

They worked in relative silence to unload the cart, hauling the crates down a narrow hallway, up a flight of stairs, to a room at the rear of the building.

Pancras was considerably underwhelmed at its size. A mere four paces across in either direction, it featured a small fireplace and rough concrete floors. Illuminated by a solitary arched window framed by brick, without glass or even oilskin to separate them from the chilly night air, it provided them with a view into a small central courtyard of a few trees and overgrown grass. The room was otherwise unfurnished and bare. The boy felt a stab of nostalgia for his relatively spacious homestead back home.

Home? What was home? Was Rome to be his home now? Would he ever feel for Rome what he felt – still feels – for Synnada?

No matter – these were questions for another day. Right now there were more crates and carpetbags to haul.

Two more trips emptied the wagon, and as the wagonmaster departed into the night, the door to the apartment was shut, and they had arrived at their new residence.

Dionysius found a crude broom out in the hallway, and quickly swept their floor which had accumulated a layer of dust and rat droppings in the intervening time since its last tenant. Pancras could only stare in shock, still trying to process the newness, feeling as a butterfly having shed its chrysalis but unsure if the wings would fly, or if he would forever remain stillborn.

Quickly, his uncle threw his mat and blanket on the floor. "Tomorrow, we will purchase furniture." He lay down his corpulent frame, exhausted by the journey, throwing his knapsack beneath his head as a makeshift pillow. Pancras followed suit.

"Tomorrow shall be a grand day," his uncle murmured, fatigue setting in. "We shall find you a school, and I shall go about establishing my trading business. We must rest."

Within a minute, Pancras could hear the snores that signaled a sleeping man. But his own rest was elusive. He stared at the moonlit shadows dancing on the walls, the moon playing with the trees who were swaying in the wind. Few sounds filtered through the window, save the moaning of the breeze and an occasional animal crying out. Carts, prohibited within the city limits during the day, rolled by, clattering on the cobblestone, but their sound was muffled as the window faced the courtyard and not the streets.

It wasn't that he wasn't tired – oh, he was. Still sore from the day's battles, his head's pounding had slackened somewhat, though his swollen face pulsed with a dull ache that reminded him of failures past. But he feared that to drift into the arms of sleep would be a journey into pain, to memory, to misery, to the underworld. For the ethos of death in which he lived might follow him into his dreams.

But as much as he tried to avoid it, his eyes grew heavy and he eventually drifted into a fitful sleep.

And thus began his first night as resident of the greatest city on earth, the city that crucifies her children.

~~~

Morning dawned with dusky pastels stretching across the sky. Pancras stirred first, rising to gaze out the window at the courtyard as the sky turned from royal blue to the color of a bluebird's wing.

His silent observation of the world, beyond the realm of thought and sorrows, was interrupted by the rustling of his uncle, sitting up and rubbing his eyes.

"No chamber pot, eh?" he remarked crassly, looking around. "Guess I'll head to the street. Meet me down there in a bit?"

Pancras nodded, happy to be free from his uncle for another five minutes.

Oh, it wasn't that he wasn't grateful for what his uncle had done. In the time of his greatest need, Dionysius had stepped in and served as a surrogate guardian. Guardian, but not parent. Pancras could always sense the subtle annoyance that he caused his uncle. Simmering just below the surface, he knew that he was a burden to the man, who had been content to live his life as a trader, without a family to care for. Who would want to have a ten-year-old boy thrust upon him, let alone a boy who was unsure if he was losing his mind?

In truth, Pancras feared his uncle. Dionysius could, at any time, abandon him to the streets. So many children were left to the elements – he had seen it before, the feral boys and girls who wandered the alleyways, searching for a scrap of food or a dry place to sleep. One step away from death or slavery, they seemed afraid of everyone and everything, like a skittish dog beaten harshly by its master.

He remembered one time he was helping his father take the wheat harvest into Synnada. The two of them were walking side-by-side behind the cart, hauled by a team of oxen. A couple of their indentured servants walked up ahead, leading the beast. The monthly deliveries of wheat to the market was always a day of much excitement to the young lad; a chance to see the world beyond the farm and homestead.

The city was nothing like Rome or Ostia, but it featured a wonderful array of sights and smells. He knew almost all of the merchants, who waved at him cheerfully as they passed by the stalls. The olive merchant would always give him a handful of pickled olives, he knew, and he could count on a warm embrace from the scarf lady, who liked to make a fuss about how big he was growing.

There, up ahead, almost hidden from sight along the western wall of the temple, were two children about his age, a hunted look in their eyes. They wore nothing but a thin loincloth to cover their emaciated nakedness. Squatting on the ground, they were picking up specks to eat, glancing furtively around lest they be found.

Cleonius stopped walking upon catching sight of these sorry orphans. A dark and troubled look overshadowed his countenance.

"Pancras," he gently ordered, "Take this food and give it to them. They are more likely to trust you than an adult."

Pancras took the package with uncomprehending eyes. "But Papa, this is our meal!"

"We have more than enough," he replied, emanating compassion. "Come now, go to them." With a little push, he sent Pancras away.

Trembling and nervous, the boy approached the other two. Even from his distance, he could smell foul odors coming from their unwashed bodies.

When the orphans noticed him, they immediately froze. Unblinking eyes stared at him, ready to fight or flee if the situation warranted. Pancras could see their muscles tense in terror at being discovered.

"Would...would you like this?" he offered, his hands shaking.

Without warning, the boy and the girl turned quickly and fled. Pancras could notice the stripes across their back as they disappeared down the lane, out of sight.

Pancras looked back at his father, who was stricken with a mysterious sorrow.

"Just place the food down on the ground...there, that's it. They will come back to it."

His son did as he was told and quickly returned to the safety of his father's side. They continued through the marketplace for a time before he summoned the courage to ask, "How do they become like that?"

Cleonius' sigh, from the depths of his spirit, contained the fullness of grief at the injustices of the world. "Likely exposure. Parents do not want their children. Or perhaps the parents died, leaving them without the care of relatives."

"There were stripes on their back."

"They had been slaves, then. The horrors they must have endured..."

"But our slaves do not have stripes."

"We do not have slaves, Pancras. These are free men who are in our debt, but they are our brothers and we must treat them as such."

"But these children…"

"They have suffered more than we can comprehend. We must always be merciful to them, for this is what the gods desire."

Pancras asked no more questions, but not for lack of interest. He would never forget the image of those children, who could have been himself. Or rather, this could still be his lot if Dionysius should so choose.

He shook these thoughts from his head, breathed deeply from the fresh morning air, and went downstairs to meet his uncle.

~~~

A light meal of bread made from millet and fresh water from one of Rome's many public fountains served to break their fast. They began to walk through town, to find the school that Dionysius' friend had recommended to them.

The city was laid out in a maze of streets, narrow and winding. After crossing the Tiberis River, they passed through the Forum, which was sleepily stirring as few merchants had begun their day's labor in setting out their wares. Pancras' eyes grew wide, overwhelmed at the vastness of the entire enterprise. The brick-and-concrete shops were far more sophisticated than the small wooden carts that would have served as the traveling marketplaces in Synnada! It was almost too much to absorb at once – such sights were only a far-fetched rumor in his home country of Phrygia.

There it was! The Colosseum, one of the great wonders of Rome. It lived up to its name, glistening white marble in the early morning sun. He wondered when he would be able to spectate the games. They walked past, mouths agape at its grandeur. Surely this city and these people were the greatest on the earth!

The street began to slope upward, as the streets became more occupied. The quiet tinkling of morning pots and pans gave way to the sustained bustle of conversations, the tramping of feet, hammering and sawing and roosters' crowing: rich noises of human activity.

The chill of the night had evaporated, and a bead of sweat appeared on Pancras' forehead. His uncle, unaccustomed to strenuous physical labor, was out of breath by the time they had crested Capitoline Hill. From there, a stairway rose to the Temple of Jupiter, standing watch at the zenith.

"Come, my boy," Dionysius panted. "I will show you a sight."

Ascending the marble stairs to meddle in divine affairs, Pancras was overawed at this Temple. It made the Temple back in his hometown look like a mere juvenile toy, in scale as well as in materials. This Temple, capping the Capitoline Hill, shone with radiant gold tiles on its roof, making one believe that they were approaching the surface of the sun. Marble columns, as brilliant as fresh snowfall, arose before them, beckoning them welcome. These were carved with intricate leaf-and-vine patterns by the finest sculptors of the day. The gold-plated doors separated the inner sanctum from the vulgar street below, inviting guests to leave behind the world and enter the heavens. Statues of the deities rested upon the peak of the temple roof.

Pancras was beyond belief. This was a world never dreamt of. Finer buildings did not exist in the whole of the earth; the greatest art, the purest gold, the most costly marble and stones combined with the genius of the finest engineers and architects to produce a temple fit for the highest god alone.

"This temple, we will visit later. The daily sacrifices have yet to begin. But this is not why I brought you here, Pancras. Now, turn and look."

From the uppermost step, he turned and beheld, before his eyes, the greatest and grandest sight of his life.

From the perch atop the highest point on Capitoline Hill, he could see the entire city of Rome stretched out before him. Terra cotta roofs stretched to the horizon, thousands of buildings housing a million souls. Here, they towered over the immense Colosseum, and the Forum appeared as a mere toy beneath their feet. They could see the Tiberis winding its way down the watercourse to the sea. There – the Baths of Caracalla! Over there – the great Imperial Palace! Trajan's Column appeared as a mere blade of grass, hidden beside his great market. Dwarfed by the view, the Arch of Septimius Severus!

The entire city seemed to rest in the palm of his hand. He wanted to reach out and touch it, to fall in love with it as he had fallen in love with Synnada and his little house and farm. He might, in time. But for now he was content to fall silent, in awe at the capital of the world.

"All of this will be yours, Pancras," Dionysius intoned solemnly, and Pancras immediately felt a dart of regret. He should have been standing here with his father, who had already promised him the world and all that is in it. This surrogate guardian could offer nothing more than Cleonius could offer.

"I solemnly swear to you this, in the presence of Jupiter and his temple," Dionysius continued. "We will be living here on Capitoline Hill in a fine villa within the year. May the gods smile upon us with good fortune."

"I thought you…" Pancras' voice trailed off. *I thought you didn't believe in the gods*, he finished in his mind.

"This is the beginning of a new life, Pancras," he replied with uncharacteristic gentleness. An arm around his nephew's shoulder, and he added, "I know you must be frightened. But you mustn't be. This will make us far more prosperous than we could be in Phrygia. We were limited there – but here, a pauper could become the son of an Emperor!"

Pancras responded with silence. If the Fates allowed…but who knows what the Fates will allow? They have only allowed death and destruction thus far. Why should he believe that the future would differ? He shared little of the hope that filled his uncle. Only resignation.

"Come, let us bring you to your school. It isn't far."

~~~

The red brick building was teeming with life. They could sense it as they climbed the few stairs leading up to the schoolhouse. Here in this *ludus* he would spend the next several years of his life, learning to read and write, to speak and debate, to think and to grow.

Dionysius swung the door open and the two stepped in, seeking to remain hidden as the lesson progressed at the front of the room. Pancras silently observed from the rear – there were twelve children seated on benches, eight boys and four girls, listening to the tutor: a thin, balding man with a ring of grey hair surrounding his temples. One by one, they approached the front, where they read from a single copy of the *Aeneid*, unrolled upon a podium of wood.

The smell of baking bread wafted through the door. This school, like many others, shared a building with a business. Pancras began to salivate and found it hard to concentrate.

The boy currently reading, a tall and ruddy fellow with a mop of curly unkempt black hair atop a face both earnest and sincere, concluded his sentence with confidence. He looked expectantly at the tutor.

"Yes, Antonius. Well done."

Antonius flashed a quick smile before resuming his seat.

The tutor looked up, and for the first time noticed Pancras. "Good morning, and welcome. Class?"

The twelve students arose and turned to greet the newcomer in unison. "Good morning." Pancras noted that some seemed pleased to see a new face, while others responded with suspicion or contempt.

"Welcome to our school. You are most welcome here. I have been alerted to your arrival by Cassius. Your name, master?"

Still overwhelmed at the rapid events of the past few days, he managed only a whisper. "Pancras, sir."

"You must speak aloud if you wish to be part of this class. Your name, sir?"

"Pancras!"

"Good," he grunted. "I am Master Lucius Rufus Ludinium. You are welcome in this school. Please be seated on a bench as I discuss the matter of your tuition with your uncle."

The two adults stepped outside for a brief word, as Pancras found a bench and sat down, unsure of himself. He looked at his hands, not wanting to engage in conversation at this time. Too much to take in. An unnamed anxiety, his frequent friend and companion, arose within him once again. Wringing his hands, he shut his eyes and hoped for the best.

There was low tittering among the other students, a myriad of fingers and glances pointed in his direction. A new student was a rarity for this school, and already he was the subject of gossip, doubtless.

Presently the teacher reentered and quieted the class. "Now, class, please take out your stylus and wax tablet. We will be copying quotes from the Aeneid, and you will be translating them into Latin."

Rustling, then the removal of twelve wax tablets and styli. Pancras again looked down to his empty hands.

"No tablet, master Pancras?"

Pancras noticed the severity in his voice. He shook his head dejectedly.

"You will be granted leniency today, master Pancras, as this is your first day. But all here are familiar with the consequence of neglecting one's studies."

The class as one looked nervously to the switch in the corner, knowing the answer.

"You know Greek, master Pancras?"

"Yes, sir," he mumbled. "A bit."

"Good. I will ask you to come forth and read the passage these children will transcribe. Come forward, let us see your mastery."

The dread within him was paralyzing, suffocating. He willed himself to stand, forced himself to take one step after another until he stood at the center of the room, with twelve sets of young eyes affixed upon him.

He took hold of the text, unrolled before him, and with quivering voice began to read.

"The gates of Hell are open night and day,
Smooth the descent and easy is the way…
But to return, and view the cheerful skies,
In this the task and mighty labor lies."

Such words were not merely text on a page. In those inked markings, Pancras saw his past, his present, his future – the yawning chasm of grief that threatened to drag him down headlong, and the struggle to push ever onward, in the dim hope that he could escape the shadows and dwell in the sunlight.

His interior pain choked the words in his throat, barely able to finish.

"Well done, master Pancras. You have a fluency that belies your young age. You may be seated." Still, the tutor did not reward him with a smile.

Pancras bowed stiffly toward him and returned to the seat as the other children began diligently copying the words he spoke. To them, it was a poem written centuries ago. To Pancras, they were words that reminded him of all he had lost.

~~~

Toward midday, the students were granted a reprieve for lunch and recess. Like children of every time and place, they flung themselves outside, grateful for the freedom.

Pancras found himself sitting alone on a tuft of grass as some of the other students went to purchase lunch from a vendor. He had no money, so despite his hunger he had to content himself with looking longingly at the *prandium* of others.

One of the other students wandered over. Rail-thin and drawn, he looked like a ghost of a boy, of similar age. Carrying a chunk of flatbread and cold salted pork, he came up and kicked dirt on Pancras.

Pancras tried hard to ignore it.

"Why are you such a *stultus*?" he demanded.

Silence. In his mind, he was home, in the fields, running his hand along the tops of the wheat ears, happy once again…

"Where are you from, anyway? You have a strange accent. And why is your face bruised? You get beaten in a fight, you weakling?"

He would not be drawn in, no, he was impervious to these insults. He will not cry, no, he must not…

The skinny boy scoffed, taking a gratuitously large bite of his bread. "So you can talk in front of the teacher, but you are a mute out here? What kind of sissy are you?"

"Stop that at once!" came another young voice from behind him. He looked up and saw Antonius coming forth, food in his hand and fury written on his features. "Why must you treat everyone like they are your inferiors? You're nothing but a…"

"Come now, Antonius," the skinny boy replied, looking up at his taller opponent, his bravado dissipating quickly. "I don't mean any harm. I just wanted to meet our newcomer."

"Yes, I've seen how you 'meet' people. Get out of here and leave us alone."

Grumbling, the boy backed away and went to join his other friends.

Antonius sat down on the dirt beside Pancras. "Don't pay him any attention. He is a stupid pig, but a harmless one. I'm Antonius."

Pancras noticed his outstretched arm, the first friendly gesture he had received since his arrival. With some suspicion, he grasped it firmly and shook.

"Would you like bread? I have extra."

Despite himself, Pancras nodded. He was feeling faint with hunger.

Antonius gave him a large portion, and seeing how voraciously Pancras consumed it, silently offered him the rest as well. He then held out his skin of water, from which Pancras drank gratefully.

They sat in silence for a while on the grassy hillside. Other small groups of students gathered in circles to share their midday meal, but none approached the two boys seated together.

The silence stretched on. Pancras knew he should think of something to say, lest he lose his new friend, but his mind felt like sludge. He could think of nothing.

Finally Antonius broke the uncomfortable silence. "So where are you from? Your accent is not Roman."

"Phrygia."

"Ah. Recent arrival?"

"Yesterday."

"Welcome to Rome. I am not from here, myself. I was born in Antioch, but raised here since I was two."

Pancras nodded, not sure what to say.

"Whew, you certainly know your Greek! Did you study back in Phrygia?"

He shook his head. "My father taught me." My father, oh my father!

"Well, you will have to give me lessons. I struggle to read it like you do."

Pancras shrugged.

"How old are you? I am twelve years."

"Ten." Or ninety-three, as he felt.

"So what brought you to Rome?"

Silence. This interior chest would not be opened.

Antonius seemed to read the implications of his silence. Softly he began, "Everyone has a story. But I hope you like it here. After school I want you to meet my two best friends, I think you would really like them. You like playing ball games?"

Of course! What rightly-constructed boy does not! He nodded.

"Excellent! Daily we gather for something – ball games, or exploring the fields outside of Vaticanum Hill, or finding some way to raise trouble in the market." There was a twinkle in his eye, and with a smile, he added, "Do not fear, it's not *real* trouble. We're just having fun."

A spark, long-dead, was rekindled in the younger boy. He noticed he finally had something to look forward to. Perhaps he would not always be alone.

"You are very kind," Pancras replied. "Why?"

Antonius laughed. "Oh, I am not that kind…ask my little sister!"

Pancras smiled.

They passed the time chatting about inconsequential things until the hour drew nigh for class to resume.

~~~

True to his word, Antonius brought Pancras to the outskirts of town, just beyond Transtiberim, where the swamp began and the marsh of Vaticanum Hill rose in the near distance. As fortune would smile on them, Antonius lived in a domus not far from the insula of Pancras, just across the bridge. They passed both houses on the way out of town, each pointing out their own residence.

"What is there to do, out here beyond the Tiberis?" Pancras asked, stepping on tufts of grass which provided a way through the swampy ground.

"Anything we wish!" Antonius replied with ebullience. He began to leapfrog one tuft to another, scattering birds nesting in the rushes.

Pancras followed suit, treading the path marked out by his friend. Up ahead, he could make out the figures of two more youth, squatting down over the mud, seemingly searching for something.

"Ah, my friends arrived first," Antonius commented with a smile. "Come, I will introduce you."

Their thin path through the reeds rustled the vegetation, causing the squatting boy to glance up. "Oh, Antonius, it's you."

"Salve, Decian," the tall lad replied. "Catch anything?"

"Almost. We almost snatched a frog, but not yet."

"I want to introduce you to my new friend, Pancras."

The boy named Decian stood upright and smiled. Pancras noted that he was covered in mud up to his elbows, with streaks of dried dirt crisscrossing his face. He seemed about Pancras' own height and age.

"Pleased to meet you," Decian said formally with a slight bow.

"And this, over here," Antonius began, gesturing to the compatriot frog-catcher who was intensely focused on the water, "is my friend…"

All of a sudden, that yet-unnamed friend let out a quick whoop and plunged his hand underwater, coming up with a fistful of mud in which a single small frog writhed and wriggled.

"Got one!" The friend stood up, and for the first time Pancras saw that it was a girl. "And you said that women cannot catch frogs! You have not even caught one, and this is my second!"

"I never said women couldn't catch frogs," Decian defended. "I merely said that it was not ladylike."

"Oh who cares about that! I am better than you at it!"

Decian grew haughty in mock offense. "At frog-catching, perhaps, but in everything else I am better! Swordplay, wrestling…"

But Pancras could not hear anything else. The girl turned to face him, and Pancras was immediately, irrevocably smitten. He had never seen a more beautiful sight than this goddess before him. Beneath the mud and dirt caked on her face, she glowed as a lamp at midnight, and the boy felt a flame grow within himself, a new and unexpected feeling. Her rough woolen tunic could have been made of gold itself, her flaxen hair shone with the late afternoon sun, and her bashful smile melted away any coldness in his heart. She was a ray of sunshine, her dimpled face luminous – a perfect admixture of sincerity and beauty, love and courage. Forever and forever, Pancras would be in love – he already knew it.

He puffed out his chest slightly, and with a trembling voice masked by confidence, he introduced himself. "My name is Pancras."

She nodded her head demurely. "I am Daphne. Where are you from? You speak like a foreigner."

"Phry…Phryrigia," he stuttered, utterly captivated by her beauty. Could such a one exist outside of Olympus? He knew he was staring, but he was unable to tear his eyes from her face.

"Welcome to Rome," she said. "This is what we do for fun around here. It's not much, but I bet you cannot catch more than me!" Gently she knelt on the ground and released her captive amphibian. It gratefully returned to its home.

Antonius had been watching this exchange with some amusement. Girding his loins, he jumped into the ankle-deep water, letting out a yowl as the cold pierced his flesh. "Come on, Pancras, let us show you how!"

Reluctantly but with a secret smile, Pancras turned back to his new friend.

"Here, I captured one! Look at its size, too!" Decian called out from a stone's throw away. Everyone went to look, appropriately appreciating the size and skill of the catcher, and then fanned out to search on their own.

In this manner they passed a pleasant afternoon. Decian quickly surpassed Daphne in the skill of frog-gigging, having had more experience. He and Pancras found themselves near each other as they stealthily stalked their prey, hiding among the reeds and last years' cattail stalks.

"Do you attend a school?" Decian asked softly, so as to not alert nature of his approach.

"Yes, I began today."

"Huh. Just came to Rome?"

"Yesterday. Do you attend school?"

"Of course. But I hate it."

"You hate it?" Pancras stood up, stretching his back from the strain of remaining hunched.

"Oh yes. My father is an artisan, a blacksmith, but he gets by well enough. He wants more for me than to labor. So he sends me to school."

"And do you want this too?"

"No, I want to lay on my back in the Forum and have birds drop figs into my mouth!" He cackled.

"That seems unlikely," Pancras offered, still trying to decipher this new fellow and his personality.

"Is that any more useless of a life than reading Epicurus?"

"Who is Epicurus?"

"One of the ancient philosophers. Dull, dull, dull. Whether I read philosophers or become a layabout, both are quite meaningless."

"So what do you want to do?"

"Whatever is easiest. Maybe I'll spend my life catching frogs," he concluded, plunging his hand deep into the mud. His face contorted angrily as he pulled up his hand, empty of any living cargo.

"Well, you'll have to do better than that!" Pancras offered, a little timidly, not sure if this comment would elicit laughter or rage.

Thankfully, Decian chose the former. "You're all right, Pancras," he laughed. "So why did you come to Rome?"

Pancras' eyes searched the mud carefully, looking for the small bubbles that signified the presence of an underwater creature, trying to pretend that he didn't hear the question.

"Did someone die? That's why a lot of people move here."

But this story must remain sealed, untold. No one must know.

"Life is short. That's why I try to enjoy every day – no use wasting my time on school! There are frogs to be caught, enjoyment to be had, life to be lived!"

They could hear a cry from Antonius – whether it was of victory of defeat was unclear.

"Luckily, I have only one more year of schooling," Decian continued. "Then, I apprentice with my father. Then, I work for a few years. Then, I retire to a villa in Tivoli, and enjoy the good life!"

"Where is Tivoli?"

"It is a place up in the mountains, near here, a few hours' journey. I will show you someday. Hadrian had his villa there; it is magnificent!"

"I look forward to seeing it," Pancras said, noncommittally. He was unsure if he trusted this boy, but he certainly was an intriguing sort of fellow.

They worked aside one another in silence for a while. Poor fortune was looking down upon Pancras. At times a bubble would arise, a blade of grass would stir, or a ripple would cause the water to tremble, but none of his quick lunges and desperate grasps could produce the requisite prize. All he succeeded in doing was splashing his tunic and eliciting harmless chuckles from his compatriot.

"I cannot understand what I am doing wrong," he sighed in frustration as he watched Decian take another frog from the water.

"Hey, Pancras," he called out. The boy looked up just in time to see Decian toss the frog in his direction. It landed on his shoulder, where it quickly jumped off when Pancras leapt out of the water, brushing it off with a cry of surprise.

"See? You can't even catch a frog when I throw it at you!" Decian crowed, hooting with laughter. Antonius and Daphne, who had seen the whole exchange, added their amused chuckles.

Sensing no animosity in the laughter, Pancras allowed himself a smile.

The afternoon wore on, with a few triumphs and a few failures. The chill of the water was beginning to soak into their bones, as the sun began its slow descent over the Vaticanus. By mutual agreement, they decided to return home and meet up again the following day for more adventures.

"See you all tomorrow," Decian said, heading north toward the banks of the Tiberis. Daphne also took her leave, stealing a quick glance at Pancras over her shoulder as she departed, who returned a longer gaze with a heart-felt ache.

Antonius and Pancras walked across the bridge that spanned the mighty river, reentering the metropolis. They said little, but no words were needed. He had begun this day in the very pits of hell, but knowing that he was no longer alone reinforced his steps with a strength he had not felt since the end of his world. It was premature to call it happiness – no, the wound still gaped and gushed forth blood, but there was something else in his spirit now. A mysterious hope.

At a certain point they had to part. Antoinus offered him a handclasp, readily returned, with the words, "It was great meeting you today. I hope you will join us tomorrow."

"Yes, of course. See you at school!" And into the hastening twilight his friend departed.

To the rest of the world, it seemed an afternoon filled with frivolity and the silly pastime of children. But it is no small thing to rescue a boy from the shores of the underworld.

~~~

Weeks later. A southerly wind brought surprisingly welcome warmth to the season. The rhythm of life began to settle into Pancras' soul. A distance grew within him, the distance between his past and his present. As long as the past remained hidden, locked amidst the unthinkable memories, he was able to rise each morn and go about his daily business, finding sparks and flashes and moments of happiness amidst the melancholy. No longer did a pervasive sense of doom plague his every waking moment. No, it had mellowed into a routine that he performed, as if he were an actor in a play. As long as he did not think of the darkness, he was all right.

His new friends helped with that. They knew almost nothing of his past; merely a silence here and there, a dodged question with an answer avoided, caused them to piece together a bit. Pancras knew that they probably suspected what he was fleeing from – but he would not bring it up with them, no, never. They were the distraction that allowed him to live as a human being, rather than as a boy condemned to the deepest pits of sorrow.

It had become a custom to meet, the four of them, after studies had concluded, in the marshy fields just outside of the necropolis on Vaticanum Hill. They were able to fill their afternoons with adventures of every sort. At times they played tag, or tossed a ball made of old rags tied with twine. Other times, it was explorations of nature that kept them occupied – Pancras was fascinated to learn the different flora and fauna that was present in the temperate climate of Rome, much of which he had never encountered in Phrygia.

Decian liked to fill the silence with humorous banter, which made him the natural storyteller. The other three would lay on the dry grass on the edge of the hill, as he would begin a lively story about a one-armed man fighting Orcus, the god of the ancients who fed on human flesh, or perhaps a made-up tale of the Etruscans, a mysterious people who were his ancestors in Italia. He had a brash way about him which even broke down Pancras' stoic defenses. Although unable to completely abandon himself to the carefree laughter of his friends, he would smile and offer a chuckle, grateful for the humor to push back the clouds in his soul, if even for a short time.

Most of the time, though, as Decian would be waxing long on some absurd legend, Pancras would try to steal as many glances as he could afford at his Daphne. His Daphne?, he chided himself. Who said she felt the same soul-fire that he felt for her? But then again, his glances were sometimes exchanged furtively, as a stolen treat would be shared among friends. He would catch her looking at him with a sweet smile that they seemed to share exclusively.

It was in the midst of one of Decian's stories about the mighty feats of the Oracle of Delphi that Pancras caught his muse smiling back at him. Who needs a Delphic oracle? He had the genuine one, the priestess who offered him a sacrifice of beauty to brighten his mortal soul. He was a willing victim at her altar. Like a goddess she was, a statue of a Platonic form (Pancras had been learning about that in school) that existed only in the realms of ideas. But no, this girl – this princess – was true flesh and blood, sitting a mere pace away. A beauty that transcended the ugliness of the city of Rome, a beauty that was a pinprick of light amidst his everlasting darkness.

A funny gesture from Decian brought him out of his reverie. He noticed his raconteur had a mischievous gleam in his eye, and Pancras was unsure if he was able to interpret the secret glances passed between him and his hidden beloved. He needed a distraction, and quickly.

Abruptly, Pancras found his feet and declared, "I am bored. Let us do something else."

Bemused, Decian shrugged. "Fine with me. I did not have an ending to this story anyway – I was just making this up as I went along!"

"All right, then," Antonius concluded with a smile. "Pancras, I challenge you to a wrestling match."

Pancras looked at his opponent, who was two years his senior and at least a hand taller, with no little trepidation. "But I have never wrestled…"

"It is easy! Come, I will teach you," he concluded, crouching down for the initial attack.

Not having another avenue of escape, Pancras followed his example and crouched, circling his foe with alacrity. His last tussle leapt unbidden to his mind – in Ostia on the march from hell – and just as quickly, he forced it away.

Antonius danced nimbly on his toes, as the two orbited each other in anticipation of the first move. Dust began to rise on the heat and expectation. The afternoon sun glistened on the beads of sweat materializing on their foreheads.

Decian and Daphne began to chant and cheer as they waited for the initial strike.

It was instantaneous, and Pancras was blind to its coming – a lunge towards his abdomen, knocking him backward on the ground. His breath came out in a muffled groan.

Gathering his strength, he squirmed out of the crush-hold. On his knees, he sought to pin Antonius, but the older boy's arms were too strong and he was quickly able to send an elbow into Pancras' sternum, throwing him back into the dust.

On and on it continued, to the delight of the two spectators. Knees were skinned on rocks protruding from their makeshift arena, faces were ground into the gravel, but still the vanquished managed to rise again. Antonius, with his superior strength and age, was able to keep Pancras beneath him, but the younger boy was agile in a way Antoinus was not. The hard farm work had given Pancras a wiry grit that refused to admit defeat. Squirming and struggling, Antonius could not pin his adversary to the ground, as he was always able to force his limbs free.

With a heave, Pancras curled into a ball and then exploded forth, knocking Antonius back. The younger boy then sought to immobilize his opponent's head, wrapping his small arms around his neck, but Antonius fought back with a swift elbow to the stomach and was able to extricate himself. Throwing himself back on his friend, he was about to immobilize his arms when he was stunned by a sudden cry from the vanquished.

"Stop! Stop!" Pancras cried out, his eyes afire with panic.

Antonius immediately leapt off, concern lining his face. "Are you injured? What happened?"

In desperation, Pancras grasped at his chest. "My bulla! What happened to it?"

The older boy looked quizzically at him. "I'm sure it fell off during our tussle. We'll find it, do not fear."

But Pancras was already on his hands and knees, searching the tufts of grass and weeds that lined their playing-ground.

His friends began their search as well.

"You seem quite attached to it," Decian commented. "I lose mine all the time. The one I wear now is my third one; I had lost the other two. My father says that if I lose this one, no more bullae for me!"

Pancras wanted to hear nothing more of such mindless banter. Find the amulet, keep his soul from shattering into pieces. It was a search for so much more than a talisman – this was his very sanity that he was seeking.

"Oh, here it is." Daphne held up the bulla with its leather string, now snapped in two.

Leaping to his feet, Pancras snatched it out of her hand and began to tie the loose ends together. His fingers fumbling in their haste, in their near-panic, he took a deep breath. Glancing up from his frantic action, he was humbled to see understanding in her eyes.

"Thank you," he whispered, ashamed. Ashamed that he cared more for this piece of metal than the girl who handed it to him.

She smiled a simple smile. Did she read his secret fears?

"All right, we found the bulla. Who is next?" Decian brusquely demanded. "Pancras? I should be a suitable opponent for you."

Pancras shook his head. He had enough for one afternoon, thank you.

"I'll accept your challenge, Decian," Antonius threatened with a laugh. "Let's see if you can do better than our friend Pancras. Do you want to take your bulla off first, or will you need that for a good luck charm?"

Decian scoffed. "I need no luck!" he boasted, handing the amulet to Daphne before the contest began in earnest.

It took a couple minutes before Pancras' heartbeat returned to normal, his asthmatic gasping for air subdued. Standing next to Daphne – close enough to touch, but, no! Never! – helped to restore his sense of calm.

The other two boys continued to scuffle, but it held no interest for Pancras. His thoughts were simple – gratitude for this goddess' simple kindness, and the masterful dodging of the old anxieties that continued to plague him – anxiety that he would lose forever this one lifeline to everything else that had been lost. Anxiety that he was truly alone in the world, that everyone he loved would go the way of all flesh.

"I have noticed," Daphne began, breaking his silent reverie, "that Antonius does not wear a bulla like you and Decian."

Pancras had not noticed before this, but yes, it was true. "Perhaps he has taken the toga of manhood."

"At his age?" she asked, glancing askance at him.

He shrugged.

"He is different, that Antonius," she returned. "I do not know why, but he does not act as the other boys."

"In what way?"

"It is hard to explain. Small things, as you will see. But not in a bad way. He is the most noble of them all."

"He was the first one to be kind to me in Rome," Pancras whispered.

"Yes, he is kind," she said, her fingers grazing his. "Very few are like him."

Her gentle touch restored peace to his heart. Yes, he had lost a great many things. But along the way, there had been blessings from the gods, as well.

~~~

Sounds of dusk washed over Pancras, lying on his thin mat, listening. The clinking of pots, the echo of a horse's whinny, the clatter of a cart rolling over the cobblestones. It was the sound of life; it was the sound that reminded him that he was not alone.

66

Once again Dionysius was absent. Whether cutting deals with his brokers or drinking away the profits, his nephew often drifted into the land of dreams before he returned home.

Slowly, slowly, the room was being filled with furniture, turning it from a tenement into a home. Just last week two *klinai* appeared, purchased at some cost, where they could recline like civilized men, instead of squatting on the floor to eat their supper. Only the poorest of the poor – the man-beasts that could be seen haunting the Forum – squatted to eat. Pancras thought it far beneath his dignity and was very grateful to see the couches, simple though they be.

Now in a small wooden cabinet on the floor, opposite the hearth, was a small larder – pickled olives in a jar, last year's dried figs, desiccated meats and seafood of various types, and bread which was refreshed on a semi-weekly basis. Just enough for a growing boy to eat on his way to school, or to stave off the hunger pangs when he returned from his afternoon jaunts with his friends.

A smattering of pots and cast-iron pans hung on the walls, remnants of his former life in Phrygia. They seemed to fill only a decorative purpose, however, as Dionysius had never used them.

The window, now covered with a thin linen sheet, billowed and danced in the light breeze. Vernal winds blew a comforting coolness into the room. Staring at the ceiling, Pancras wondered when his uncle would return for the night. He was alone – not as alone as he was when he first arrived, but the inner ache was still there. Dulled, but still arising within his heart on these fresh spring nights.

With a creak, the door slid open, and Dionysius clomped in. His nephew closed his eyes, pretending to sleep.

He could hear his uncle slip off his sandals, and heave himself down onto his mat, throwing the blanket over him.

"I know you are awake," he growled, his words slurring together.

So the tavern it was. Pancras did not acknowledge the statement.

He could hear his uncle's labored breathing become more rhythmic, as he settled down to rest for the night.

"Master Ludinium was pleased with you today?" his uncle murmured.

Pretending to sleep might elicit an unpleasant reaction, he realized. Whispering, he replied, "Yes…yes, sir. It was a good day."

"Good," he grunted. A long silence ensued. Pancras hoped his uncle had drifted off, but instead he pursued the conversation further. "I too had great success today. My friend came through for me."

Pancras did not know what he meant.

"He was able to put in a word of recommendation, and I am now the clerk to the *curule aedile*. We have hope now, Pancras. In time I will be able to begin importing the grain for the public dole; perhaps as soon as this summer. But the money is not in public service, no. Fixed pay. This is only until I can begin private importing. The world must eat, as you know. He who owns the grain owns the world. In a year, maybe two, I have plans to become the largest importer of wheat to the greatest city on earth. Today was the first step."

The boy didn't know what to respond. This meant more luxuries, to be sure. But could luxuries bring back what was lost? He stared into the blank ceiling, feeling as blank as it looked.

"Just wait…" Dionysius mumbled, drowsiness overtaking him. "It will be a new life, our dreams…" Within a moment, his snores could be heard.

Pancras turned over and waited to drift into the peaceful land of dreams.

~~~

There was an excitement at school. The typically-subdued boys were animated by the anticipation of something mysterious. As soon as Pancras crossed the threshold, he noticed the tittering like so many sparrows, the boys leaned in close and conspiratorially with one another.

Uncomprehending, he took his usual place on the bench beside Antonius. Alone among the classmates, Antonius refused to engage in the discussion. His face betrayed a barely-disguised disgust as he sat, staring intensely at the floor.

Unaccustomed to his friend's severe attitude, Pancras dared not ask him any questions. He took out his wax tablet and pretended to trace lines of Greek text, all the while trying to overhear the snippets of conversation.

"…games tomorrow…"

"…last year's gladiator…"

"…thrown to the lions…"

"…wonder if the Emperor…"

"…try to go. What about you?"

The curiosity grew with each tidbit that floated through the air. What sort of games? Lions, gladiators, the Emperor…

He desperately wanted to ask Antonius, but he seemed unapproachable for some unknown reason. So he continued to listen hungrily for any other clues that invited him into the inner circle.

Something about the Colosseum. Names were bandied about, names that Pancras did not recognize. There was talk about the weather for the following day, and whether that would affect the charioteers and their ability to navigate the sharp curves of the circus. A spectacle of spectacles, from what he could infer.

His interest grew, having never seen the class stirred up quite like this. Feeling as if he would burst if the fullness of truth wasn't revealed, he whispered to his friend, "Antonius, what are they speaking of?"

Antonius' pursed lips angrily spat out the words. "Bread and circuses. Bread… and circuses." He pronounced the final word as if it were a curse.

"Why are you angry about…"

"Pancras, I will discuss this with you after school," he grumbled. "Do not listen to them. They are entertained by filth and bloodshed."

Pancras leaned back on the bench, intrigued. He did not understand his friend's anger. Surely games could not be anything more than a harmless diversion, an enjoyable way to pass the time. In Phrygia, they would have footraces between countrymen, and the whole town would come out to watch at the amphitheater. There was that one day, a few years ago, when a man had come from Africa to race. Cleonius had taken his son that day, and Pancras was amazed to see a man with skin the color of burnt bread. He was fast – faster than all of the native Phrygians. After he had handily won the race, Pancras remembered, they feted that man with garlands of olive branches and bouquets of roses. The governor was even in attendance, handing the man a golden necklace as a prize. These games were always a wonderful chance to see his friends, to dream about athletic prowess. Even Cleonius loved to attend, spending those afternoons in animated conversations with other noblemen. From the pauper in the street to the governor himself, the entire town would enjoy these events together. For one afternoon, the divisions between rich and poor, free and slave, men and women disappeared. All partook of the enjoyment; all delighted in the games.

He was sure that it was the same in Rome, but on a grander scale. So why was Antonius so vehemently opposed?

Amidst the considerable hubbub, the teacher abruptly stood up and attempted to begin class. "Boys, I know we are all thrilled by the announcement of the games resuming on the morrow. I, too, eagerly anticipate them. But let us not grow slack this day, as we have our studies to attend to."

The boys paid him heed, some glancing nervously at the switch in the corner. Just yesterday one of their own had suffered the punishment for a minor infraction; his cries for mercy went unheeded as he was scourged, forty lashes.

Although their fidgety bodies were stilled by an icy glance from their stern master, their thoughts were across town, in the Colosseum. And Pancras was no different, his curiosity growing like an unscratched itch.

When eager anticipation tickles the mind, the day trickles along in agonizing sloth. An eternity, perhaps two, had passed before the boys were released for the day, flinging themselves heedlessly into the streets for their afternoon play.

Antonius and Pancras headed out, to meet their friends at the customary spot.

"Antonius, let us take a different route," Pancras suggested to his still-sullen friend.

"Where shall we go?"

"Let us pass by the Colosseum. You can explain to me what these games are, and why you dislike them so intensely."

Antonius shook his head, his black curls bobbing up and down. "Never," he said resolutely, angered at the suggestion. Without another word, he headed off, leaving his friend standing there in wonder.

"Antonius!" Pancras called out, catching up to him. "I do not understand. Have I offended you?"

"Rome offends me," he replied. "They say this is entertaining. They never get enough blood, do they? Thirsty, always thirsty."

"Blood? These games involve blood?" Pancras felt ashamed by his naïveté, but he needed to know.

Abruptly, Antonius stopped, and whirled to face his younger friend. "All right, Pancras. Let us go by the Colosseum. As we pass by it, you can see what will take place there tomorrow."

Their footprints led them in a new direction. Passing through the narrow streets, they could see in the distance the upper echelon of the grandest amphitheater in the world. A colossus it was, indeed. A marvel of the world. Although Pancras had seen it before, it never ceased to draw his gaze in wonder.

They came to the Forum, which abutted the Colosseum. They began to walk in a large arc around the building, taking in the gleaming white marble, the magnificent arches, the banners snapping in the wind. There was a different silence between them – for Pancras, it was the silence of awe. But he could sense his friend's silence was more a sign of mourning.

They stopped when they arrived at the Arc of Titus, gazing at the two monuments to the triumph of Rome.

"I do not know what your public games were like in Phrygia, but this is a spectacle seen nowhere else in the world." Antonius looked up to the upper reaches of the Colosseum, blinking back tears.

"This I hear. Why may I not see it with my own eyes?"

"This place is evil – and holy ground."

"I do not understand."

"Have you ever seen a man torn apart by lions?"

Pancras shook his head, eyes wide.

"Or a man fight another man to the death, only to please fifty thousand demons who feast upon this bloodshed with their eyes."

"You have seen it, then?"

"Never. I do not wish to."

"Then how do you…"

"I have seen men and women and children – boys and girls our age – enter the arena, and never return."

They resumed their circuit around the monument. Pancras was troubled by this revelation. Surely death was to be feared, not celebrated. How could one man kill another for sport? His friend must be exaggerating. He had never seen it with his eyes. This is a legend, much like the legend of Cronus who devoured his own children. Only in the realm of myth did such cruelty exist.

"I am not sure you are speaking truth," Pancras muttered timidly, not wanting to infuriate his friend, who seemed to be in a fouler mood than ever before.

Shaking his head, Antonius replied with a profound and mysterious sadness, "Promise me one thing, Pancras.

Promise me that you will never go in there, as long as you live."

Not wanting to make such a promise, he tried to redirect his attention. "Come along, Antonius. Let us go meet our friends. They are waiting for us."

"Promise me," he insisted.

"All right, I promise," he replied lightly, not wanting to further this discussion. "Now, let us go meet our friends."

"Today, I shall not come," he replied sadly. "I wish to go home. But will I see you tomorrow? At the third hour?"

Pancras realized this was when the games would begin – a ploy to keep him away from the Colosseum. But there was something plaintive in Antonius' eyes, boring into his soul with a sincerity and somberness not often found in a youth of twelve.

Shrugging, he replied, "Yes, I will see you at the third hour. At our usual place?"

"Yes. Bring Decian and Daphne with you."

"Daphne will come, but Decian might need to be tied up and dragged!"

Antonius chuckled mirthlessly.

Pancras could only wonder as Antonius headed away. It was only natural for a man to desire to live, and to see others live. He had tasted death already, and found it disgusting, repulsive. Who could rejoice in death? Only the most depraved of men. It did not make sense. Is it possible to find fifty thousand men so depraved, even in this city? Certainly his friend must be wrong. Yes, that must be it.

He turned to look at the Colosseum. Bare-backed workers made ready, sweeping the concrete floors through the arches. Some put out more banners and flags, triumphant and colorful. Carts overloaded with bread and jugs of water were brought through the large iron gates leading into the structure.

A noise drew his attention to the south. Ten men shackled together, stripped to the waist, filthy and bronzed and chiseled as one who had spent weeks in the field without rest. Lash marks crisscrossed their back – some red and oozing liquid; others white scars. Their legs were linked together with heavy iron chains. Driven onward by two imperial soldiers with imposing scourges, they slogged onward toward the arena.

Pancras could only stare, mouth agape, though the men paid him no heed on their devastating march. They passed by him, heedless of the world outside of their own miseries, their feet dragging and hope absent from their eyes. The soldiers had no need to use their discipline, for these men had no possibility of escape. There must have been some doom awaiting them, the boy realized; a doom greater than he could fathom.

When they were out-of-sight, Pancras turned away and himself headed home. Perhaps there was more to this world than what he had experienced. Despite all that he had suffered, he had been protected from so much. This realization filled him with a pall of dread. There was far more evil and suffering in this world than he could ever have imagined.

The memory of crucifixes lining the road haunted him all the way home.

~~~

Sunrise. The sun had made its circular trek across the heavens yet again. How many sunrises has he seen in this city? Had it reached a hundred yet? He didn't know. Oh, no matter. The routine must begin afresh daily, a routine that is settling into…if not happiness, then contentment.

As long as he was not given too much time to muse on the darkness which stayed hidden within him - locked in an impenetrable fortress which no one, including himself, dared to breach - then he could face each day with aplomb. His studies, while tedious to an active ten-year-old boy, were a continual source of distraction. He didn't mind it, learning about Pythagoras and geometry, or Hippocrates and his study of medicine. The Greek philosophers were more difficult to slog through, but provided a good mental challenge. Pancras would always feel worn out after reading such convoluted arguments, but it was a good sense of tired, as a man might feel after a vigorous day in the fields.

After the solitary incident on his first day, Pancras found no more trouble at school. He mostly kept to himself, occasionally spending time with Antonius or fooling around with the other boys who regarded him as no threat to their schoolyard regimen. Though cordial, these other boys made no overtures to become more familiar with him; and for his part, Pancras did not seek out their friendship. They were pleasant acquaintances, nothing more. He had his friends – the foursome that would meet daily after school to romp and roam.

Daily his uncle would bring home more and more food for the boy, whose appetite had returned with a vengeance. Once wasted away in grief, he now filled out his frame, as he looked less like a refugee and more like the middle-class lad he wished he was. The wages must have been good, too, for the food increased in quality as well as quantity. No longer was it merely millet bread – here and there, a loaf of white bread, blanched and soft, would appear, accompanied by a round of fresh cheese, some eggs, and fruit as the seasons provided.

In all, it was not an unpleasant life, as long as he allowed the dead to remain dead. One had to move on, he reasoned. The past cannot be changed, so it ought not to be examined.

But at times, waves of sadness would unexpectedly wash over him. This was one of those days.

As he walked through the marketplace, Pancras would pause to observe the faces of his fellow city-dwellers. He knew he must look *delirus* – foolish – for doing so, but he was enamored at the stories he could read in the eyes and the wrinkles. He wondered if his own eyes, the lines of his own face, betrayed the journey he had made.

The creases on the face of that old man, yes, the one with the leathery skin that looked like a turtle's extended neck, he must have seen many things in his years. His hat loose on his liver-spotted head, he would look up from his perusal of dry goods to catch Pancras' glance with a mirthful eye. Though his best years were behind him, he certainly kept a youthful vigor in his spirit, if not in his flesh. Pancras wondered what land he called his home, for he had the deep bronze of one who lived under the sun, in the fields or on a boat.

There was that poor waif who always roamed the agora, a young man whose gaunt face and hollow eyes flickered with the fear of being hunted. Pancras had seen such furtive glances in the fieldmice who would anxiously search the sky for a sign of their predators. What secrets did this man contain? What tragic past followed him? Or, was it his own choices that he never wanted to face?

That one time, yes, he could remember it clearly: the day the princess visited the common folk. A matron with golden hoops in her ears, her hair was styled in a way that flaunted her wealth. Her face set in a lightly-disguised sneer, she picked over the produce with a manicured hand, allowing her fingers only the briefest rest upon the apples on the stand. Much to Pancras' chagrin, she looked up and caught him staring at her finery. The boy took it as a challenge to stare her down, never minding the cold arrogance shooting forth from her eyes. With a huff she turned away, her silk scarf – imported, doubtless - flapping in the breeze of her upturned heels.

And then he was called forth from his reverie by an elderly woman crying out in the marketplace.

"You there!" she called, pointing to Pancras. "Come here, son."

With trepidation, he approached the booth where she sat. It was a small tent selling dyed wool and its accoutrements, with the earthy odors of a fresh shearing still clinging to the merchantwoman.

"Do not stand there like a lout!" she barked. "This woman needs help. Take this spindle and distaff, along with this wool she has just purchased, to her home."

For the first time he noticed a bent woman, advanced in years, leaning heavily on a staff and standing off to the side of tent. She was so hunched that she stood shorter than Pancras himself. But she had kind eyes and a humble smile as she looked up at the boy.

"She lives not far, on Via Cassia, up the hill." The brusque merchant forced the goods into Pancras' arms. "Walk with her. She totters sometimes and needs assistance."

With no choice, Pancras accepted the armful and turned to the elderly woman. She nodded, still grinning toothlessly, and began to shuffle off, obediently followed by the boy.

The pace was slow, compounded by the woman's unintelligible chatter and periodic gestures. Pancras was content to walk beside her, nodding appreciatively despite not understanding what she was saying. It was a babbled sort of Latin, spoken by the fragile of mind. Though it did not make sense, she rambled with such enthusiasm that Pancras was entertained.

And, perhaps, he was grateful for a bit of human contact. In a city such as this, the anonymity could be overwhelming. And Pancras had been aching with loneliness lately. Yes, he had his friends…but apart from their afternoon adventures, he had long stretches of time every day all by himself. His heart ached during those times, when he allowed himself to reflect on it. Was it the grief of his loss, or a new emptiness that caused the pain? He would awake to an empty house, take his meals in solitude, and drift off to sleep by himself. His uncle was not worth the name *family*, and his neighbors in the insula lived their own separate lives. It was the two hours every afternoon with his friends that barely kept him sane; apart from them, no one would care if he lived or died.

So he found a scrap of happiness in this strange woman's delight in him, as they dragged themselves up the hill at a snail's pace. Like a grandmother, she continued to smile at him, slurring unintelligible words until they reached her home. He offered his arm as they had three steps to climb, entering into another faceless insula in a city of faceless insulae. Down the hall they shuffled, until she reached a heavy wooden door. A rap on the door, and it creaked open to the face of a younger version of the old woman.

"Ah! My sister, you have returned!" she crowed with pleasure. Quickly grabbing the armful of wool and spinning tools, she set them on her table, saying to Pancras, "Thank you, young man. I am grateful for your help. Now we can continue spinning our yarn."

The older woman turned to him and grabbed his face in her hands. Still smiling with glistening eyes, she pulled him in and gave him a kiss on both cheeks. Pancras was both embarrassed and grateful, and smiled back in return.

As soon as he stepped out onto the street and his eyes adjusted to the sunlight, he was greeted with a smirk.

"Finding a girl in the city?" Decian jested, as they started in the direction of their usual field.

Pancras' face flushed red. "Just an errand for an elderly woman."

"I hope she paid you handsomely."

A subtle smile grew on his face, remembering her kindness. "One could say that."

"Well, we've been waiting for you. School has been out for an hour – you are late!"

"Sorry. I needed to think."

"Yes, I know. You're in one of your moods, aren't you?"

Was his lonely melancholy that obvious? No! If he didn't acknowledge it, it doesn't exist!

"I just like to be in the marketplace sometimes, that's all."

"Better than being with your friends? Come now, do not offend us!"

Pancras could tell that his friend was joking, but he had no laughter within him. "How did you know I would be near the Forum?"

"It was easy. You like to drool over the things you can't have; it's your favorite pastime."

Pancras looked sidelong at him, and caught his impish grin. The young fool had a talent at making the most brooding soul break down his walls. He looked up, a cloud lifting. The streets became a maze as they approached the Tiberis, but Decian knew the way.

"My uncle promised me a domus on Capitoline Hill," Pancras replied after a while. "He is a clerk, you know. And hopes to start his own business."

"Ah, the city of a million dreams!" Decian groaned with a smile and an eye roll.

Pancras smiled back and gently punched him in the arm as they strolled across the Milvian Bridge. "You will wish you were kinder when I am rich and you are my servant."

"Your servant! Never! I would rather eat worms!"

"I would happily feed you worms, if you prefer. No need to waste precious food on a worthless slave like yourself."

"Worthless, am I?" he gave him a playful shove. "You will see, Pancras. I will someday be famous!"

"There are not too many contests for the laziest boy alive," Pancras remarked drolly. Decian cackled.

They soon reached Antonius, who had been sitting on the hill weaving field grasses into a braid. Further along, Daphne was picking crocuses and putting them into her hair. She looked up and smiled at Pancras, her flowers crowning her brow.

Pancras smiled and nodded, gulping hard to still his hammering heart. How does she grow more beautiful every day?

"Pancras, where did you go after school?" Antoinus asked, rising. "I was looking for you but you darted off."

"He was near the Forum, finding a lady friend," Decian responded.

Noticing Antonius' bemused look, Pancras began to stutter. "Mm...Mm...n-no, of course not."

"Everything all right?" The sincerity emanating from his older friend was disarming. But no, Antonius needn't know about his loneliness or melancholy or the hidden places within where no man dares to trod.

Looking away, he tried to think quickly and lied, "I...I just wanted to see the Ludus Magnus."

Antonius looked wary. "The Ludus Magnus? The school for training gladiators? You promised me..."

"No, no, I haven't gone to the games. But I was curious what they did there, how the gladiators trained."

"A future warrior, eh?" Decian remarked, picking up a stick. "All right, my friend. I challenge you to a duel. Let us see what type of gladiator you will become – a victorious one...or a dead one!"

Pancras smiled and picked up a stick of his own to begin the joust.

Upon seeing the action, Daphne cried out, "Oh! I want to play!" She quickly grabbed her own fallen branch and joined the fray. Antonius stood off to the side, watching with amusement.

The three warriors began brandishing their sabers, striking with agility and deftness. But after a few blows, Decian's sword snapped in two, being rotted on the inside. A cry of dismay, and he was forced to forage for a new tree limb.

Daphne and Pancras went back and forth, exchanging thrusts and blows. Pancras tried a high strike, but was blocked by Daphne's sword. In return she tried to swing from the side, but Pancras jackknifed out of the way.

On and on the two parried and dodged, attacked and fended off the blows. Dust began to rise from their sandaled feet. A thin rivulet of sweat trickled down Pancras' back. As he continued to strike to no avail, and was constantly forced to defend his position, he began to gasp for breath.

"You are very good at this," Pancras panted.

"I hope to be a warrior princess," she replied with a surprising intensity, plunging her weapon directly at his chest. Pancras nimbly leapt back, trying to retain his footing.

"Really?" he verified, unable to go on the offensive. Her rapier flashed through the air and attempted to land on Pancras' thigh, but he blocked it again with his own blade.

"Boys are not the only ones with courage," she shot back, lunging forward with a swift left-handed swing.

"You certainly possess it," Pancras said. This unexpected fierceness did not take from her beauty; no, there was something entrancing about a flowered maiden who was skilled with the sword.

Another sharp upward jab, and Pancras' stick came flying out of his hand, landing three paces' distance away.

Daphne held her stick to his throat. "Surrender!"

"You win," he sighed. From the sideline, Antonius and Decian cheered appreciatively.

She stepped back and smiled, the ring of lavender on her forehead shining in the afternoon sun. "You are quick, Pancras. Do not waste your talents on the arena. You would make a good Praetorian Guard."

"What is a Praetorian Guard?"

"The Praetorian Guard? They are the guardians of the emperors. You see them marching through the street sometimes."

Vaguely he recalled seeing phalanxes of men marching in step through the Forum. They had appeared to be in training of some sort. Their scale armor clinking in sync as they traipsed, the glimmering helmets and bright red shields had made for an impressive sight.

Pancras shrugged. "Maybe. Who can be certain where the Fates will take me?"

"If you serve in a cohort, maybe then you will finally have your domus!" Decian laughed. "Four hundred denarii each year!"

"That is a generous salary," he remarked, impressed. "It sounds like a grand adventure, too."

"The only unfortunate part," Antonius added, "is that you must work for the Emperor. Ugh."

Decian shrugged. "He gives us bread, and games. For that, I am thankful."

"He is a bloodthirsty monster," Antonius retorted severely. "And those games of yours..."

"Be silent!" Daphne declared. "The hills and the trees have ears."

Anxiously they glanced around, but upon the glade and the hills only the breeze was stirring.

Antonius looked down. "Sorry. I must be cautious, you're right."

"I will never understand your opposition to the games," Decian shot back. "Have you attended? You would enjoy it."

"What you enjoy, I find disgusting."

"Well now! Aren't you the arrogant bastard! Too refined for the entertainment of us poor folk?"

Antonius merely shook his head. With a sadness of the ages, he sighed, "Someday we will discuss this. But not today. I'm going home."

His abrupt departure filled Pancras with wonder, and a certain sadness himself. Antonius' head bowed low, he seemed burdened. Pancras knew the feeling acutely – an inner millstone dragged around the neck, a weight too heavy to bear. His own interior sadness was understandable, but what afflicted his friend so much? Perhaps every man has his own grief.

He turned back to his friends. Decian was still seething, not much in the mood for further play. With an unspoken agreement, the parties disbanded.

~~~

Thick sheets blanketed the sky, as a steady rain drummed upon the city. Pancras was grateful for the rain; it was a late spring shower that felt good when one ran through it on their way to their destination. The cleansing tide would wash away the muck in the streets, the detritus of human existence – and it would temporarily dampen the stench that hung about the city.

It was a foul city, to be sure. Nothing like the clean air of Synnada. No, this city smelled of the sweat of a million people, mixed with the manure tossed carelessly in the streets. Very little was pristine or clean – the buildings featured a layer of soot caking their exteriors, while the streets ran with used dishwater.

But the rain! It brought about a cleansing, a rebirth. Surely the flowers and trees would be drinking thirstily today!

As school dismissed, Antonius and Pancras made a frantic dash through the rain. There was a terebinth not far from their usual gathering place; it would be dry there, beneath the new-leafed branches.

Their feet dashed through puddles, splashing cascades of water into the air. They hastened along but as they approached the Milvian Bridge they caught sight of Decian approaching, calling out.

"My friends! Come with me!"

They turned and greeted him, eager to see what plot he would contrive this day.

Decian led them through the streets, circumventing the Colosseum in a wide arc. A narrow alleyway emptied into a large and spacious piazza, containing a tall marble building inscribed "Thermae Traiani" – Trajan's Baths.

The rain continued to streak down their faces, matting their hair and soaking their tunics. "What are we doing here? We are too young to enter," Antonius pointed out.

"Oh, we will not enter," Decian replied. From within a fold of his garment he produced two hardened tufts of wool, thick and matted. "We will merely have a bit of fun."

"Where did you…?"

"From the frightening mind of Decian!"

"So this is what you do with your leisure?" Antonius laughed, as they crept closer to the building.

"Concoct pranks? No, I do that when I'm supposed to be studying. My leisure is when I *pull* the pranks!"

Pancras came along, unsure of what he intended to do with the two woolen clods. They slinked along the side of the building to where the sewers emptied in a river of waste. The murky water, thick with excrement, was stagnant and stunk.

"Just remember," Decian announced, "Water flows both directions!" He hunched over to shield the dry wool from the rain.

"Come along, Pancras," Antonius bemused, turning away. "Let us watch this prank from a safer distance. One never knows who or what might erupt from inside Trajan's Volcano!"

They took shelter beneath an overhang across Via Tiburtina. From their safety of twenty paces away, he could see Decian striking a handheld iron instrument onto a flint stone, throwing sparks into the damp mud. Expertly he was able to land a few sparks onto the wool, which required only a few breaths to come to life as a flame. The flame started to spread, until half of the wool was engulfed.

"Ah, he used oil," Antonius realized with a chuckle. "Oh, he is going to be beaten for this one!"

The two lit flaming balls were gently placed upon the stagnant river of human befoulment, and given a gentle push until they sailed like tiny ships into the baths, entering directly into the wastewater channel of the public restrooms.

They could see Decian laughing and laughing, doubled over, as he waited for the reaction.

The first scream was loud and shrill, echoing across the piazza. It was quickly followed by more shrieks. Men's voices were reaching higher than a woman's in quick, piercing cries, all coming from within the baths. There was a tumult inside, the noise spilling out - an epic commotion, as if a battle were taking place within the walls. The rancor and shouting was enormous.

Meanwhile Decian had slunk down against the walls of the baths, still uproarious.

"So he sailed that flaming torch beneath the bottoms of the patrons?" Pancras asked incredulously, his eyes wide. Never one to make trouble, he had never met anyone as brash as this.

Antonius was barely able to stifle his mirth. "It has been done before!"

The row continued, but much of it was drowned out by the steady tapping of a ceaseless rain. Still, across the courtyard, they could hear the shouts and muted angry curses of men who had been made to be fools. Decian had melted into a pile of laughter. With each cry from within the bath, a new hilarity overtook him.

At length the noise began to dissipate. The projectile must have lost its flame.

Around the corner of the bathhouse came a man, his toga flying in fury, heedless of the downpour. He quickly caught sight of the culprit and flew in a rage at him.

Instantly Antonius' humor evaporated. "Come, Pancras, we must leave."

Without waiting to see the fate of their friend, Antonius led Pancras away on winged feet, flying through the city. They ran, seemingly unconcerned about where they were going – just away, away from any reprisals or punishment. No one could catch them; they were rats in the street, birds taking wing.

The absurdity of their situation soon caught up to them, and they stumbled into a doorway, laughing uncontrollably.

"I am amazed!" Pancras exclaimed. "Decian is a genius!"

"Oh, but how he will pay for this, dearly! I would hate to be him when those men catch him!"

"It was worth it!"

"So says the boy who *wasn't* caught!"

Pancras leaned back against the dry brick, soaking in the warmth radiating from it. "Come now, Antonius. Tell me this was not a brilliant plan."

"Most certainly brilliant!" he laughed, shaking the water out of his black curls. "I would never have thought of it!"

"Or had the courage to execute it."

"You use *execute* very well – Decian will certainly be executed for this one! I don't know if it was courage, or just not having a brain between his ears!"

"The two are often the same!"

"We must tell Daphne about this. She will be sorry to have missed out."

~~~

The following day, the world awoke to a thick humidity that blanketed the city, as if a free steam bath had been granted to all the fine citizens of Rome. Pancras paused his sweeping, gazing out the window of his one-room apartment into the hazy courtyard, abuzz with the hum of insects. Summer was fast approaching, and with it came the oppressive heat that he despised.

There was no school that day, for games were scheduled for the afternoon. What feria was it today? He could not keep track. It may have been the second *Tubilustrium*, perhaps – that great day which celebrated the military and its many conquests. These festivals did not interest him much, except that they provided a pleasant respite from the monotony of school. He rarely attended the civic displays, the parades and speeches, that marked these holidays.

There would be sacrifices, too, at various temples in the city. Twice since his arrival he had attended such a ceremony – it was a sobering thing to see a living calf or lamb lain upon the altar, struggling for breath as its life-blood formed rivers flowing down upon the sanctuary. It always filled him with awe, even when he was back in Phrygia and would attend the semiannual feasts with his father. To think that a living thing would give its life for another! Such innocent beasts, knowing no wrongdoing, now brutally murdered so that the gods would be appeased and look with blessing upon those ritually cleansed by its blood. A mysterious feeling overtook him every time he beheld the sacrifice – a feeling of unworthiness and wonder, reverence and gratitude.

His uncle had departed at daybreak to a location unknown. As clerk, it might be important for him to be present at the games and sacrifices, Pancras reasoned. Surely he must make an appearance at the main civic event of the city. But his uncle rarely told him of his whereabouts, and seemed rather unconcerned about knowing the boy's.

But this little act of service, of sweeping and tidying up, was an attempt for Pancras to be less of a burden on his uncle. He knew he was another mouth to feed, a school tuition to pay, a bother and an annoyance to a man who once enjoyed complete freedom. Although Dionysius never mentioned it, Pancras knew he would rather not have the responsibility of a child, let alone a child as troubled and moody as himself.

But he could not help it! He could not help the grief that plagued him night and day. He could not stop the feelings of sadness, the secret desires of walking out into the night and never coming home, just walking wherever his feet took him, in a futile desire to escape the hidden memories. As much as he hated himself for it, he could not stop the tears that flowed when no one was around, for he would never, ever, share that sorrow with anyone. Everyone carried a burden, and he had to carry his own.

Punctuating his thoughts with a particularly vigorous sweep, he was startled by a knock on the door. Upon cautiously opening it, he was relieved to see Daphne there, wearing a bashful look. Her hair was swept up in a beautiful braid, with two lonely strands framing her shy face. She was ornamented in a golden necklace, with interlocking gold rings cascading from her earlobes. Clearly she was dressed in her finest garments, as her tunic shone with a luster not seen in their afternoon play. A simple blue shawl draped her shoulders, despite the heat.

She smiled sweetly, and Pancras became aware of his mouth agape. Quickly gaining his composure, he greeted with a squeaky voice, "Hello Daphne, how are you?"

"Salve, Pancras. Are you going to the games this afternoon?"

He shook his head wistfully. "I wish I could, but I promised Antonius I would not."

The answer seemed to please her. "I understand. I am wondering, then, if you would accompany my family and me to memorialize my mother's *dies natalis*?"

Why did she say *memorialize* and not *celebrate*? "The day of her birth? Well, that is kind of you to ask. I am thankful. Yes, I will come. To where are we going?" Pancras quickly locked the door behind himself as they walked down the hallway.

"The catacombs of Via Appia. She is interred there."

His heart stopped with a hard thud. The catacombs? The very shores of the underworld? Frozen, he ceased walking.

"I cannot. I am sorry."

She turned to face him, crestfallen. "Why not? I do not wish to face this alone."

Her voice was barely audible, with the interior noise of crashing waves echoing in his ears. He cannot go. He must stay far away from death, for if he goes near, he will be sucked into the undertow, and there will be no escape. It would surround him, consume him from the inside out. The inner trunk of memories, if cracked open, would be unstoppable. The darkness would drown him. He would crack, he would crumble, his very self would shatter into a million pieces. There would be no more future, no more hope. He could not set foot in the tombs, for he would never return.

"What about Decian?" he gasped, grasping vainly at his dissipating sanity.

"He is unable to come – his father has punished him most severely for yesterday's foolishness. And Antonius refuses to come. I do not know why."

Pancras looked up, his vision going blurry and darkening. The face of his beloved seemed distant somehow, fading into darkness. He felt faint, dizzy, overwhelmed with the anxious bile that was erupting within him.

"I...I can't..." he murmured, steadying himself against a wall, lest he fall and never rise.

His inner agony was visible to her, and in her kindness she reached out and took her hand.

Tears sparkled in her eyes. "I cannot do this alone. This is her first *dies natale* in the afterlife. Please come."

Her plaintive pleading moved his heart, but in his mind's eye the funeral pyre still burned brightly, taking life up to the sky and leaving behind only ashes.

He closed his eyes. No tears would fall, no. The trunk must remain locked, the room unexplored.

"We can do this, together."

Together. He had not had a *together* since his world ended across the sea.

Several deep breaths were exhaled. The anxiety did not dissipate, but they were now a *together*.

Opening his eyes, he looked deeply into the rich pools of hope in her eyes, deeper, perhaps, than the grave.

He nodded, the lump in his throat preventing speech.

There was a cart with a horse waiting for them. Introductions were made – Daphne's father shook his hand manfully, before mounting the horse. Her sister and grandparents already occupied the cart, greeting them as they climbed in.

Pancras tried to be polite but could only think of the mound of dirt in Synnada, a mound that covered his last *together*. He could still remember the day he stood by that mound, the wind cutting across the countryside and into his flesh and soul. The world had suddenly lapsed into monochrome that day, a grey sky covering a grey landscape. The mourners had gone, driven to seek warmer accommodations. But Pancras had been intending to freeze to death himself out there. What is one more death-mound in a world of death-mounds? It was the well-meaning Dionysius who dragged him away, the boy having no will to resist. No will for anything – eating, drinking, breathing. The days that followed were a suffering unlike any since the world began.

As the cart bumped and jostled along, he clutched his bulla and covered his face with his arm, unwilling to shed tears before inquisitive eyes.

The ride was silent, mournful. All those in the cart nursed their own private griefs.

It was good to leave the city and ride into the countryside. The wheat was sprouting now. Through the humidity, the sun beat down incessantly upon the travelers. They passed by cattle and flocks, fields and homesteads. Quiet homes sat as sentries by the road, unsleepingly keeping watch for those making their weary journeys. A pleasing odor of fresh-cut grass and manure scented their travels.

As they traversed further into the countryside, the provincial landscape began to allay the deep darkness of soul. Perhaps this *parentalia* tradition would not cause an inner eruption, merely an inner disruption of the status quo.

And then they arrived at the site.

It was a large field, with a small funerary chapel built out of stone in the center of it. Through it was the portal to the underworld.

Daphne's father helped the elders to the ground, then gathered the items for the ceremonial meal into a cloth knapsack. He led the trek to the grey monument, followed by the family. Pancras had to force his legs to move, for everything within him wanted to turn and run.

A small wooden door on the chapel separated them from the shores of the underworld. It opened with such ease! A blast of cold wind issued forth, as the smell of death hung heavy in the air.

His heart was racing, watching the father stride blithely down the stairs into the darkness, a solitary lantern lighting their way. How could he cross this threshold? It was the River Styx, with Hades lying in wait on the other side. Where was Charon, with his ferry? Where was the coin needed to pay for safe passage? He would never return, he would never return!

The lantern grew dimmer as they continued to descend, with Pancras still a statuary at the door. If he waited longer, he would not be able to find them in the labyrinth below. But could he take the step, cross the threshold, and enter the waters of the deep?

Yes. He must. Because he is a *together*. He gave his word.

Suffering every sort of revulsion, fear, and grief known to man, he stepped forth into the cold and darkness, down the stone staircase and into the catacombs.

They marched together through the corridors, lighting a series of oil lamps along the way, which provided a trail to return to the surface. In silence they went along, surrounded on all sides by tombs. Pancras tried to distract himself by reading the inscriptions.

To the Sweet Repose
And Innocent Piety
Of a Most Dear Youth, Augustinius
Of Ten Years and Four Months
Who followed the Shepherd
And Now Rests With the Angeli (Pancras was unsure of this word; it sounded like "angeloi" in Greek, which he knew meant "messengers".)

They continued deeper into the cavern, the floor sloping downward into more and more tombs. They were surrounded on all sides by death, drowning in it, at the bottom of an endless pile of death-mounds.

Another inscription read: "Domus Petri" with a fish and a man carrying a lamb around his shoulders, painted onto the stone.

He put his hand out to steady himself, feeling the walls sweat with perspiration. Only the dimmest pinpricks of light pierced the darkness, but nothing could pierce the darkness of his soul. He was choking, choking, choking. Gasping for breath but finding none. Hoping for life but finding only death. Longing for light but being plunged in darkness. Desperate for the sun but buried beneath layers and layers of earth, where he will rest for eternity.

Presently they came to the *triglia*, the room used for funerary banquets. It was not much more than an alcove, a niche cut into the tufa where a family could memorialize a loved one in comfort. Oil lamps were lit, casting an eerie glow of dancing shadows on the wall.

In profoundest silence, Daphne's father began to set the table. A jug of wine, a stack of flatbread on a platter, a series of cups and plates made their appearance. A bowl of fresh black beans. A small decanter of olive oil. Salt. Dried fish. They were arranged in a symbolic fashion, set out in the manner of the *Parentalia* festival. Every person had a place setting, with one extra for the deceased. With great ceremony, the man reclined, followed by the grandparents, and then the children.

The father poured wine for all, and the ceremony began.

"We commend our sister Aelia," he murmured gravely. "To Vesta, her mother. Join the righteous upon the Elysian Fields, may the gods have pity on you."

They drank in silence, reflecting. The red wine appeared as blood – and Pancras looked away.

"May the fears be banished from you; may the light shine upon you."

Each person took a handful of black beans to eat – black, the symbol of death! He was consuming it just as it was consuming him!

"Virtuous though she was, she went the way of all flesh. Her body returned to the earth; her soul passed on to the underworld. Go with the gods, Aelia, and reunite with the ancestors who await your presence. Enter the earth and make it fruitful; enter the afterlife and die no more."

The quiet ritual continued, with its proscribed eating and drinking, but Pancras could not focus. The words haunted him. Where were they now, the dead? They lived no more! This ritual was empty show, a panacea to the living!

He raised his cup again with trembling hands, shaking with suppressed sobs. He put it to his lips but could not swallow, for the screams were only buried deeper and deeper.

His bulla dangled above the table, as empty as these flowery words. Why did he not just rip off this meaningless emblem! It was an open wound; it was a ghastly memory.

Gone, gone. They were all gone. These bones in the tombs, these men buried beneath the death-mounds. To dust be they! To dust was he! And the utter blackness that surrounded him, filling him, oppressing him…

He longed for a precipice to throw himself off, for a poison to imbibe. There was no end to this pain, no relief to this grief. He would carry it until he himself became dead.

Meaningless.

It all mattered not; in the end there was only death.

He only became remotely aware of a quiet weeping, not coming from him. Daphne had begun to shed unashamed tears, splashing on the table, falling on the floor, cleansing no one.

His grief was now multiplied. For him, for her.

The father continued on, becoming only a voice in the background. He spoke lies of false hope, swept away on an ocean of despair. For Pancras knew the truth, turning in his heart like an endless knife. There was no hope. All are swept away in the flood of time. No one is remembered; not Augustinius, nor Petri. Their remains are a sign of futility, the emptiness of a life forgotten. It will be so for him, as well.

Nothing will remain of him but bones, and even these too will return to the earth to feed another meaningless generation. The days pass, the seasons pass, the years pass, and all is vanity upon vanity!

The ritual called for another drink placed to his lips, another shard of bread dutifully chewed. Why do we do this? We shall hunger again; we shall thirst once more. We shall seek after the wind, hoping to catch the breeze. And yet it comes again, unfulfilled, unreachable, and utterly void of meaning.

O death! It surrounds, it is within the heart, the mind, the very being!

And then Daphne rose and fled out of the room, a cry escaping her lips before she departed.

Pancras raised his downturned eyes, startled, to see her flee. He looked to the father, who had oceans of compassion in his face, but who did not move and continued the ceremony. The boy looked back to the corridor, where his friend had fled to. And he knew what he must do.

He rose and followed her, hastening down the dimly-lit passageways. She was fleeing back the way they came, heading to the surface and the bright sunlight. Torches lined the path, giving them enough light to traverse quickly. As much as Pancras had embraced the death within, she was fleeing from it.

Their feet ascended the stairway: Daphne's first, and trailing behind was Pancras. Then bursting forth into the sunlight, Daphne ran to a stone bench across the courtyard, collapsing on it in a pool of tears.

Pancras strode over and sat beside her, holding her in his arms. His heart was bursting with pain, exploding, erupting. He held her and held her, her head against his chest as her sobs wracked her body. Pancras was content to absorb the pain – hers and his own. For he was accustomed to it, had embraced it.

A long time passed, as her weeping began to quiet.

How much longer could he hold it in?

Something within him cracked. The inner chest was opening, the inner room was seeing the light of day. He felt a burst, and knew he must speak.

"Everyone has a story," he rasped. "May I tell you mine?"

PART TWO: Citizen of the World
(Three Years Later)

"Will that be all, Master Pancras?"

The talking, breathing statue in the tawny tunic was something to which Pancras had not yet accustomed himself.

"Yes, thank you," he replied. "That will be all."

The servant bowed crisply and departed. Always impeccably attentive. And impersonally distant. A sad fate, to be sure, although Pancras tried to treat them much better than his uncle, for they were men too, albeit of the lowest social class.

Only a paltry few more things to stash in his knapsack. A thick woolen blanket, for although the steamy days of Iulius sweltered on, he had heard that the mountains could grow cool at night. A skin of water, to be refreshed regularly from the generous breasts of the public fountains. A flint knife, useful for a thousand tasks – including defense from the brigands that had been known to prowl the countryside. A few coins in a leather bag. Bread and dried meats.

The banging at the door echoed throughout the marble hallways. Pancras continued packing, knowing that his servants would let in the visitor. Probably Decian anyway. Let him be impressed by the slaves!

"Master Pancras, your guest awaits."

He smiled at the aged servant, standing with dignity befitting his manhood. "Many thanks," the boy replied. "You may show him in."

As the servant departed, Pancras gazed out into the courtyard, towards the mountains. This was an adventure of the first order, one which mingled excitement and apprehension.

He was pulled out of his distraction by a cackling hyena.

"My liege, forgive the intrusion of such a lowly lad," Decian began, bowing low before he entered the room. "I do not deign myself worthy of your grace, but beg of you to admit me to your audience."

"Oh Decian," Pancras shot back, "I prefer to be called 'your excellency'. You'd best remember that, lest I have you sent to the gallows."

His old friend laughed, a familiar and welcome sound. "Forgive me, I always forget. I am so overwhelmed by your palazzo, I sometimes lose my manners."

It was true – Decian never stopped gazing lustily after the marble halls, the towering columns, the inner courtyard flanked by windows, with a covered well at the center. Persian rugs protected their feet from the chill of winter, and statuary – not originals, of course – dotted the alcoves and niches. The painted walls, the tiled roof. Since occupying the villa last winter, Pancras found it hard to adjust to such luxury. It was so foreign – even their servants in Phrygia did not cook and clean, anticipating their every need. They merely helped in the fields as hired hands – while these slaves, purchased at auction, took care of every need they could have. From emptying the chamber pots to sculpting the topiary, these four slaves managed the household without flaw.

"Are you ready?" Pancras asked, wrapping up the knapsack. "And by the gods, cease your jealousy of my domus."

"Jealousy? Nay, this domus is a disappointment. For you promised me you would live on Capitoline Hill, and here you are in the slums of Caelian Hill. Such a pity."

Pancras laughed. "Come, let us find Antonius and depart. Tivoli by nightfall!"

"Tivoli by nightfall!" he echoed.

Before the boys departed, Pancras paid a visit to the triclinium, correctly assuming his uncle would be there, reclining at table as he glanced over a sheath of papyrus spread open before him. Business receipts, doubtless.

"Uncle, we are off to Tivoli!"

Dionysius looked up, nodding gravely. "This is indeed a momentous moment," he said, straightening. "Young Pancras on his first journey away from home."

The boy shrugged. "Merely one night away. I will be back on the morrow by nightfall."

"Yes, but a hundred and forty stadia is no small trek. Many dangers lurk in the countryside, but you have proven yourself trustworthy."

"And I shall prove ever more so," he responded, feeling a swelling of pride.

"This I do not doubt. Go with the gods."

Pancras nodded. He could not help but feel the gratitude of such trust.

On their way out the door, Pancras paused in the atrium at the *lararium*, the shrine to the household gods. In silence he placed his hands on the statues of the Lares, the gods entrusted with the protection of his home, asking for their intercession for the journey.

"Truly, Pancras?" Decian impatiently commented. "No one believes in the Lares anymore."

He shrugged, leading the way out the door. "No harm in asking."

102

"Do you believe in them?"

"I do not know." A long pause ensued. Then, quietly, he added, "My father did."

Decian shook his head. It mattered not to him.

They met Antonius on Esquiline Hill. He had gotten tall lately, lanky but still sporting an unruly thatch of black curls on his head that bobbed when he walked. This day, he was carrying a sack of equal weight and size of Pancras'. Only Decian carried his smaller satchel to his side, suspended by a leather strap from his shoulder.

It was the third hour when they set off, the coolness of night fading quickly into the heat of the day. Via Tiburtinus was clogged with patrons entering the city for the first day of Ludi Victoriae Caesaris, the ten days of games to celebrate the victories of the Caesars. Those in the countryside who rarely visited the seat of the Empire would visit on these days, hoping to feast their eyes on the second-longest series of games and festivities in the calendar. Pancras could remember hearing about last year's Ludi, when the crowds packed the Colosseum with such unruly vigor that forty-four people had been trampled to death, and a few were pushed off the pinnacle of the edifice to meet their demise in the streets below. Stories such as this made him grateful for that oath he had taken to Antoinus all those years prior, of never setting foot in the games. Yet the curiosity never ceased…

Ahead loomed the Porta Esquilina, the passageway through the first and older wall surrounding the great city. A few more furlongs and they had reached the Porta Tiburtina, allowing passage through the more recent Aurelian Wall. The crowds were less now, a mere trickle, and they were headed upstream from them all.

It was a grand feeling, walking beneath the tremendous arch which separated the city from the countryside. This was the furthest he had ventured from home by himself since he arrived three years prior. Oh, he and Dionysius had taken an annual trip to the beaches of Antium, south of Rome by a considerable distance. He had enjoyed the sights down the coast, and delighted in frolicking in the sea. Such freedom! But this – this journey, up to Tivoli with no elders to pay heed to their goings or comings – this was a release and a freedom unlike any other. He relished the feeling of liberty, of excitement – and even the trepidation, tinged with pride.

Their trek was replete with the light-hearted banter of boys, high spirits at the ready.

"Have we arrived yet?" Decian whined with a smile as they passed through the gates.

Pancras plucked a green olive from a tree pregnant with them. "Here, eat this. It will pass the time."

Decian took it and placed it gently into Antonius' mane. "It will find a better home there."

Antonius shook his head, flinging the projectile onto the ground. "For what reason do you attack me? I have done nothing! It was my idea for this trip anyway!"

"Nonsense!" Decian shot back. "I recall mentioning this very thing to Pancras years ago. Do you not remember, Pancras?"

He feigned innocence. "I remember no such thing. Besides, none of your plans ever come to pass anyway, so if you mentioned it, I concluded it would be as valid as your plan to build a monument to yourself upon the Arc of Titus!"

"That still might happen!" he declared. "I just need to gather the stones and masonry, that is all. I will build it at night, and it will be grander than the arc itself!"

"What great deed will it memorialize?" Antonius poked. "You have done nothing worth remembering!"

"My birth itself has changed the world!"

"Yes, as much as the birth of Commodus changed the world too."

"He was insane."

"So are you!" Antonius jested, laughing.

"And like him, I am a demigod."

"I know not whether it is better to be an insane demigod or a poor man with his wits about him," Pancras offered.

"Probably a poor man," Antonius commented. "The demigods get murdered."

"Have no fear, I brought a knife," Decian explained.

"As did I," Pancras agreed, "But you *do* sleep..."

"Must I fear you two more than the brigands?" he cackled.

"Yes, of course. I seek revenge on anyone who puts an olive in my hair," Antonius said slyly. "I recommend sleeping with one eye alert tonight!"

And on it went, the teasing that could only exist between friends whose bond was closer than brothers. Pancras found himself grateful for these friends, who had pulled him back from the shores of the underworld.

The back of his hand wiped the sweat from his brow, as the road was empty save for the trio. Barely an umbrella pine interrupted the fields where the wheat stood tall now, waving its greetings to the travelers. This land – this *ager romanes* – provided a small portion of the bread to the hungry populous of Rome. It was his uncle, he thought with a secret smile, who provided the rest.

They stopped to take a draught from the River Teverone, which wound its way through the fields beside the road. They would be following this river all the way to Tivoli, where a majestic cascade filtered the water through a mountain pass. Farther along the field stood the towering aqueducts, bringing water from the distant Apennines mountains to quench the thirst of a million residents. It was a delightful place to rest, and Pancras splashed some of the river water upon his scorching brow.

But driven by a desire to see Hadrian's Villa in Tivoli, the three travelers continued eastward, by this time away from the sun. Periodically a village would arise – Tor Cervara, the Deer Tower where deer were hunted for the imperial palace; Settecamini, the village of seven chimneys. From there it was another three hours' walk to Tivoli, but they paused in the intervening towns. These provided welcome respite, where they would rest and drink from their waterskins, fortifying themselves with a bite of food.

And on they went, with the cry of "Tivoli by nightfall!" on their lips!

The conversation was more sporadic as they grew wearier. The day dragged on and the initial fervor of the journey waned, replaced by a resolute determination to reach their destination.

Along a particularly uninteresting stretch of arrow-straight cobblestone:

"Why did Daphne not join us?" Pancras asked, his breath in short supply.

"Her father would not allow it," Antonius replied. "He thought it not proper for a young lady to accompany three lads for an overnight."

"It is too bad," Pancras replied wistfully, thinking of his beloved. She had grown impossibly more beautiful as the years passed, their love deepening into an unspoken romance. Or at least Pancras thought of it as such. Never would he approach the topic with her, for fear of losing the friendship that floated on the surface of their undercurrent of intense love.

"Yes, I fear she may not join us for our adventures much anymore."

Pancras sighed. "I fear the same."

"But worry not, Pancras," Decian broke in. "For soon she will be of marrying age…and we know who has his eye on her!"

Pancras feigned innocence. "Who?"

"Oh, don't be coy. You and she make a perfect match."

"I am far too young. And so is she."

"Do not wait too long! She may be taken up by someone else first!"

"I am sure my uncle will want me to marry someone of noble status."

Decian looked archly at him. "Yes, but you *love* her!"

Pancras stared at the ground, reddening from embarrassment. Of course he loved her. In his quiet moments, he thought of her – her form, her face, her modest comportment, her inner beauty. He could not lie about this.

"Ah, leave him alone, Decian," Antonius rescued. "At least he has a girl to love him back. We cannot say the same for you – now or ever!"

"Well then!" Decian declared, mock-offended. "Girls find me *very* attractive. Just last week, a girl in my insula said I was not the ugliest boy she had ever seen."

Laughter all around.

The road began to incline gently, passing by the baths of Tivoli on the outskirts. Hours passed, as the sun began to cast shadows eastward. Into the foothills of the Apennines they climbed. By this time, at the eleventh hour, their legs were growing weary. Pancras, unaccustomed to such an exhausting march, could feel a burning between his toes.

And then, there it was.

It did not dawn suddenly, but gradually. As a child's plaything on the horizon, so miniscule that they felt like they could touch it, the Villa appeared. Even from such a distance, its grandeur was amazing.

"Look, my friends!" Antonius announced. "The eighth wonder of the world!"

Every step increased their feelings of awe as they progressed toward the terminus of their journey. The long stretch of buildings became more defined, perched on the apex of a hill.

The road wound its way through an orchard: fruits for the royal table! To their left stood a length of stone wall, too tall to peer over. A hundred paces further and the wall ended abruptly, opening to a hedgerow on either side of manicured topiary, impeccably sculpted in swirling twists of yew tree and boxwood. The grass in between the hedges was of a lush and even thickness unseen in urban Rome; to Pancras it appeared to be a luxurious carpet, and he was filled with a yearning to run around barefoot.

The hedges ended at another wall, into which was cut a grand marble arch. Stationed there were a pair of legionaries, seated on cut stone and looking terribly bored.

As the three boys approached, they stood without any urgency.

"Hail Caesar!" Pancras cried out, imitating the arm salute that he had seen the soldiers exchange in the streets.

"What business brings you to the palace?" one asked. "The Emperor is not here."

"We have traveled from Rome," he continued. "We wish merely to feast our eyes on the grandeur of the place."

The guards exchanged skeptical looks. "The day is nearly done, and this business of yours is hardly urgent."

"Please, sir. For we have journeyed far and have only this day to visit."

With a weary sigh, they relented. "You may enter into the courtyard, but nowhere else. Stay within sight." They drew back their spears, allowing the boys to pass through.

One world was left behind, as they were born to a new and greater one.

Speechless, their mouths agape, they took in a marvelous sight. It was as if they entered a town of its own right, a diminutive version of Rome. There were artificial ponds flanked by Greek and Roman caryatids, with an overflowing fountain at the center. Two authentic Egyptian obelisks stood sentry at the sides. An artificial grotto displayed statues of antiquity in a type of outdoor museum. These ponds were the foreground to the grander buildings behind – the Maritime Theater, the Thermal Baths, the Three Exedras which formed a sort of outdoor temple. All of these shone with a luminosity not seen on the cinder-and-soot-encrusted buildings of the Imperial City.

Breathtaking murals flanked the outsides of these buildings. Some included inlaid gold, a bolt of fire in the evening sun. The three youths simultaneously thought that this palace courtyard contained more beauty than they had ever seen.

"I want to live here!" Pancras cried out, overwhelmed. He began to dash down the central alley, between the reflecting pools.

"I claim this one!" Decian declared, wandering towards the spa. "You can go home without me!"

Antonius, for his part, was fascinated by the hieroglyphics on the obelisks, running his hand over and over them.

They wandered by themselves for a bit, all staying within eyesight of the guards, who had gone back to dozing off at their posts.

This dwarfed the palazzo that Pancras now enjoyed as a recent member of the upper echelon. To think this courtyard was just the vestibule to an estate larger than any he had ever seen…

In absolute wonder, he wandered around the grounds as far as he was allowed, taking in the sights in a stunned silence. What must it be like to live in such luxury? If he did not know it to be impossible, he would be filled with an envious desire to live here. But he knew that this was out of the question!

But still…he felt the ache of longing. There was a sense of the sacred here. Hushed in solemn silence, he felt like he had climbed Olympus and was at the threshold of the house of the gods.

He sat down upon the blanket of grass, to take it in. Oddly, he felt the presence of his father there, stronger than he had felt for many years. His words – *all this will be yours* – echoed in his ears, bringing him a strange sense of comfort and hope. He half-expected to see Cleonius striding down a garden path. Knowing that to be impossible, he merely basked in the memory of his father's love, enjoying this beautiful day in a stunning location.

Some time passed. There was too much to see, too many sights to be impressed upon the mind. He rose and made rounds again and again, seeing the beauty from other angles and discovering more and more to uncover.

He found Antonius seated in an exedra, looking up at the height of the semi-dome above him.

"Is this not amazing?" he began, following his sight-line to the heavens.

"Sic transit gloria mundi," Antonius waxed philosophically.

"What do you mean?"

"When a conquering general returns to Rome, they throw him a parade. Thousands upon thousands of people turn out to laud him and sing his praises. But he always has a slave in the chariot with him, whispering in his ear, *sic transit gloria mundi* – thus passes the glory of the world."

Pancras did not comprehend – some moral lesson, perhaps? But there was too much beauty and wonder for him to worry about the parable.

Antonius stood and came up to Pancras, gazing at the gilded dome above them. "Where is Hadrian now?"

Pancras looked at him quizzically, but Antonius just smiled and walked away.

~~~

The golden sheen on the villa began to fade as the sun dipped beyond the horizon to take its repose. The three boys had been sitting against the wall, drinking in the last of the beauty to the dregs.

"We had better find a place to camp for the night," Antonius suggested, looking to the heavens where a couple stars had begun to blink.

They returned to the main road. A short walk upstream, through the thickets and away from the villa, produced a tranquil site, a wooded copse surrounded by umbrella pines and palmettos. They were on the banks of the river, surrounded on two sides by crags and cliffs.

Decian strung a length of twine between two trees, upon which Pancras affixed his woolen blanket as a tent. They split up to search for firewood; a few minutes of searching produced enough armfuls to keep a fire burning through the night. Gathering a number of large river stones, they fashioned a crude fire pit, clearing it of pine needles which would be used for kindling. Decian's flint and iron quickly produced a few sparks which were blown into a robust fire in moments. Their work done, they reclined beside the fire and partook of a simple meal.

"I wish I had brought my traps," Antonius commented, enjoying a crust of days-old bread.

"You trap animals?" This was the first he had ever mentioned it.

"Yes, it is not difficult. I put them out in the marsh around Vaticanus Hill. Sometimes I find a rabbit or groundhog. They are quite delicious. Even my sister likes them, cooked over the hearth."

"Really?" Decian verified. "I have never tasted groundhog. Rabbit, we always buy in the market."

"We could not afford that. We have had some hard years, in my family," Antonius replied wistfully. "There were many nights, a few years back, that we would go to bed hungry. My father's mill has not always had enough wheat to grind. The public dole was not sufficient for two growing children."

"Things are better now, I hope?" Pancras asked. He had never known of his family's hardships.

He shrugged. "Better, yes. But we are all one day away from poverty, are we not?"

112

"I certainly hope not," Pancras replied quickly. "My uncle has worked hard to bring us to where we are today."

"'In prosperity, let me remember adversity,'" Antonius quoted. "'In adversity, let me remember the days of prosperity.'"

"Where is that from?"

Antonius grew quiet. After a long pause he whispered, "I read it once."

Even Decian looked thoughtful on this night, as the dusk began to fall in earnest. The food had been consumed, the water drunk, and the fire alone remained, casting shadows upon the forest.

"I wonder about the fates of men," Decian said at last, breaking a meditative silence. "Why are some men princes, while others are paupers?"

"Yet both prince and pauper are the same beneath the skin," Antonius replied.

"I do not know," Pancras added, thinking of the beast-men that he had seen in the Forum. "For some men live such base lives. They act more like animals than men."

"Sometimes the most bestial men are those who live in palaces," Antonius pointed out.

A barely perceptible tension entered Decian's voice. "Is that a political comment?"

"Merely an observation."

He shrugged. "Fair enough."

"All of us have the capacity to be gods or animals," Pancras concluded. "Even in poverty we can keep our dignity."

"This is what we tried to do during those difficult years," Antonius explained. "There were days that we were tempted to stand outside the Temple of Jupiter to beg, as so many do. But to me, hunger was preferable to shame."

"I never knew all this about you, Antonius," Decian said seriously.

"There are many things you do not know about me," he replied cryptically.

"What other secrets are you holding within that curly head of yours?" he joked. "Hidden talents? Private loves?"

"Just a thousand ways to make fun of my friends, that is all!"

They laughed.

The evening wore on, darkness now becoming absolute. Through the canopy, the sky shone brightly with the lanterns of the gods. Pancras leaned back on his log and stared at the constellations, mesmerized. The Roman haze had always obscured them, but out here, far from the bustle of the city, they shined like diamonds upon the black velvet sky.

The time grew nigh to turn in, as all three boys settled under the tent for a night of sleep, in the wilds of the countryside. A constant drone of cicadas and the periodic buzz of mosquitos provided a fitting background noise as they tried to drift off.

But there were other sounds too, amplified in the darkness. The snapping of a stick, the far-off howl of a wolf. Accustomed only to the sounds of the city, Pancras found these unnerving and would bolt wide-awake when one would echo across the valley.

A low, guttural snuffing from somewhere behind the tent caused him to jump.

"What was that?" he whispered into the darkness.

"Oh, probably just a wild boar," Decian replied drowsily. "They roam these hills at night."

"Do we need to worry about them eating us?"

Muffled chuckles from both friends.

"No, usually not – unless you smell like raw meat!"

Pancras immediately regretted the dried pork he consumed for *cena*. He sat upright, bowing his head.

"What are you doing?"

Pancras looked over to see Decian propped on one arm, an exasperated look on his face.

"I am praying to the gods for protection."

"The gods!" he scoffed, laying back down. "You need to abandon that superstition, Pancras. The gods are not real – just statues. Antonius, you don't believe in the gods, do you?"

The question seemed to hang in silence interminably. At length he murmured, "No, I don't believe in the gods."

"See, Pancras? Mere superstition."

"But my father believed in them!" Pancras defended.

"People will believe anything to make themselves feel better. Rome is awash with cults, from those who worship Mithras to the Jews to those who worship that Christus. Those last are the worst cult of them all. I have heard stories of them…"

"What sort of stories?" Antonius asked, suddenly interested.

"Well, there are rumors of cannibalism. They claim to eat the body of their god and drink his blood in their rituals. How awful! They make believe that they will rise again after death – ludicrous! And they want to bring an end to the Empire. They hate the Emperor, the games, the celebrations – they will not burn incense to him or offer sacrifices like the rest of the good citizens of Rome."

"Have you ever met a Christian?" Antonius inquired.

"No, I have not," he declared proudly. "And with Diocletian's help, I will never meet one. He seems intent on putting them all to death."

"I have met a few," he replied quietly. "And I can tell you..."

Decian interrupted, "I hope you reported them all to the authorities. This cult is dangerous, I tell you."

"And I am telling you that this is completely false. They are peaceful people, who preach love of the brethren."

"The way you are defending them, I wonder if you are not a secret follower of Christus yourself!"

Antonius took a deep breath. "Calm down, Decian. You are getting yourself worked up. We must let everyone live in peace – Jew, Mithraist, Christian, Roman. The Empire is large enough for all."

Pancras was listening intently to the repartee, unsure of where he fell on this question. Only rumors of these Christ-followers had met his ears, having never met one in the flesh. He had no desire to enter the debate.

"All right, Antonius," Decian concluded, his temper deflating. "I am sorry. You know me and my fiery temperament."

"I admire your passion, Decian. Thank you for speaking your mind. But allow me to speak *my* mind: it is late, and I want to sleep!"

Mirthless laughter. "Good night, Antonius."

"Good night."

Desperately Pancras desired to think through the conversation, but sleep overtook him and he began to sail away into the land of dreams.

He was startled, then, when he was shaken awake by Antonius.

"Pancras! Decian is asleep and I need to talk to you."

The jolt of adrenaline caused by the unexpected awakening brought his senses alert. "What is it? Is something wrong?"

"Can we walk? I am troubled."

Reluctantly – for he was growing comfortable under the blanket – Pancras arose and walked with Antonius toward the river, a few paces away. The dying embers lingered red among the wood, wafting a charred smoke into the air. The chill of night quickly cut through their tunics, causing Pancras to shiver, his bulla trembling on his chest. They found two large rocks at the edge of the river and sat themselves upon them.

With a deep breath, Antonius began. "Pancras, my life may be drawing to a close very soon."

He was shocked further awake by his friend's sobriety. This young man before him looked down at the passing water with ages of grief in his eyes.

"What do you mean?"

"I must share with you a burden that grows heavy on my heart. Decian guessed correctly tonight."

"In what way?"

"I am a follower of the Christus."

Like a lens revolving into focus, Pancras saw with surprising clarity their friendship of the past three years.

"Caesar is persecuting us, and it is growing daily more intense," he continued. "I fear that, like so many of my fellow Christians, I too will end up as their sport in the barbaric games."

How could Pancras have been ignorant of this revelation? He had known his friend like a brother. So many questions arose in his mind, but he had to offer voice to the most pressing one.

"But why, Antonius? Why do they hate you? Those things that Decian was saying – is there truth to such accusations?"

"He misunderstands us completely, as does the Emperor. We follow the Lord Jesus, who was the Son of God. He was a man of peace, who loved us so much that He died to cleanse us of our sins. We who follow Him seek to live in peace, loving our brothers and sisters."

"Why would they be opposed to love?"

"You have seen this world, have you not? It is a world corrupted by lusts and hatred. Men find entertainment in watching each other suffer. The Christ offers us a better way to live – a Way that stands in judgment of the world."

This was an overwhelming revelation. They shared a silence, each dwelling on their own thoughts.

At length Pancras tore his gaze away from the water and looked at his friend. "And what must you think of me? I worship the gods of my fathers."

Pure kindness emanated from Antonius' smile. "You are my brother, Pancras. I knew you were trustworthy and good when I first met you."

He was humbled by the praise, but still troubled by the conversation. "But why must you cling to this religion if it will lead to death?"

"We believe that the dead will rise again," he replied. "I long to be with the Lord Jesus, Whom I love."

It had been years since the death-fear had overwhelmed him, and Pancras willed once again to stave it off, but its threatening tentacles began to creep back into his soul. "Antonius, how can you be sure? I have lost everyone I love in this world – I could not bear to lose my closest friend! You would die for a superstition?"

"It is not a superstition," he replied. "It is the truth. This man, the Lord Jesus, really walked this earth. He really died. And our forefathers really saw Him rise from the dead."

"Nonsense!" he blurted. The anxiety was arising – he could feel the telltale pressure in his chest. "This is nonsense. There are hundreds of legends of resurrection among the pantheon – yet for none of these would I be willing to die."

"Those legends bear witness to the truth. Our nature rebels against death. We know we were made to live forever. And in the Christ, we can do so."

"Have you stared death in the face? I have. One glance at my father's ashen face was enough to convince me that death has an awful finality. It is the end. There is nothing more."

"And yet why does your heart desire everlasting life?"

"I desire many things I cannot have. I cannot live in Hadrian's Villa, as much as I desire it. I desire to be the son of an Emperor, yet that will never happen."

Antonius looked down. The water flowed on and on, yet the sea was never filled. The stars continued their trek across the heavens, only to repeat the journey every night hence.

Finally he spoke, with an odd admixture of confidence and grief. "I would rather die with hope than live without it."

The brief argument over, Pancras' heart felt wrung out, grieving a death that hadn't yet happened.

"I do not want to lose you," he whispered meekly, his words washed away by the passing water.

Even in the darkness, Pancras could feel the kindness emanating from his friend. "Maybe you will not. I am not certain of the future. But please, I beg you, keep this conversation between us."

They rose and returned to the tent in silence.

Dawn could not arise with enough haste, he thought. For the day's joys had just been obliterated by this anguish. Why must his friend cling to this cult? Antonius had never tasted death like he had; and upon finding it repulsive, he would do anything to preserve his life. No conviction could be stronger than death.

He stared into the darkness, feeling it seep into his soul.

~~~

The morning came with no more word of the prior night's conversations. Decian was in his usual chipper mood, but Antonius and Pancras merely acted the part, occasionally slipping each other a sober glance. Their secret was safe with each other. But it weighed heavily on Pancras' heart.

They broke camp easily and quickly, heading down the mountain past the villa, which now glowed from the opposite side.

The first few stadia were covered in silence. A thousand questions were boiling within him, but he dared not ask them of Antonius in the presence of their unreliable companion.

How did you learn about the Christus? he wanted to ask. Why do you think it is the truth? Is this why you live so differently than us – refusing to wear a bulla, avoiding the games, scorning the *Parentalia* traditions? Do you really think you will die?

Yet he kept them inside. Especially the last one – he did not want to know the answer.

Decian must have sensed that the silence was not that of happy companions. He could not tolerate quiet for more than a few minutes without injecting his empty commentary.

"So! We have several days remaining on holiday. How do you plan to spend it?"

A long pause, as each sought for an answer that was appropriately lively.

"There are rumors of a foot race among the youth of my insula," Antonius reluctantly responded. "Perhaps I shall join them."

"Foot race? Blah!" Decian responded, pantomiming a disgusted face. "This little jaunt is quite enough physical fitness for me, I daresay."

Try as he might, Pancras could not remain depressed with his friend's ebullience. "Decian, it seems that you and Antonius are the antitheses of one another. Complete opposites. How is it that you became friends?"

"I saved his life," Antonius quickly interjected before Decian could answer.

"Saved my life?" he scoffed. "Hardly. 'Twas nothing more than a puppy."

Pancras smiled, grateful for another one of his stories. "Do tell!"

"It was like this," Decian began. "There I was, a young seven-year-old lad, fresh-faced and excited to see the world. We were there in the Gardens of Sallust, taking a walk – my mother, my three siblings, and myself. It was a fine autumn day, one of those days where the air is crisp and alive. We had just finished our picnic, and I had to run! As you may have noticed, I am not exactly the most tranquil of people."

Antonius snorted, smiling.

"I ran far ahead of my mother, delighting in the freedom. In fact, despite her frantic calls, I went around the corner, out of sight. It was then that I saw the monster."

"I thought it was a puppy?" Antonius clarified.

"Well, in hindsight it was no more than a few hands tall. But at the time, the dog looked like Cerberus! I feared for my life. I tried to turn around and run back, but I tripped on my fat little legs and fell to the path, shouting."

"Which is where I came in," Antonius added. "I heard his shouting and saw the dog bounding toward him – it was no small thing, by the way – and I jumped in between Decian and the dog. The dog took a bite out of me before its master came and hauled it away."

Decian picked up the thread. "My mother – and his mother - came running when they heard the commotion, and they saw Antonius bleeding and crying…"

"I was *not* crying," he clarified, offended.

"Oh, yes, you were. Blood was going everywhere, staining his tunic, dripping on the ground. We were both blubbering idiots, so our mothers brought us all back to the fountain at the center of the park where Antonius got cleaned up and consoled. And we've been friends ever since."

"And I have a scar to remember the occasion!" He rolled up his sleeve proudly to display the teeth marks, clearly visible on his shoulder.

Greatly amused, Pancras said, "Well, my friends, that is quite a story. And how did you bring Daphne into your friendship?"

"Oh, her mother was friends with mine," Decian replied. "I have known her since we were babes."

"A far less interesting story," Antonius added sardonically.

They exchanged laughter, allowing the mirth of their rich friendship to overcome their worries.

~~~

The day passed with surprising haste. Although sore from the exertion the day prior, this road was downhill, following the path of the river as it flowed into Rome. They made excellent time as they passed through the outlying towns in reverse order: Settecamini…Tor Cervara…Colli Aniene…

Decian was eloquently mocking various public figures as they passed beyond the town walls of Colli Aniene. His satirical impersonations kept the mood light. The milestone they passed encouraged them to continue, for Rome was but a couple dozen stadia ahead!

The road led through a particularly secluded stretch of farmland. No other living soul could be seen in any direction. The birds alone provided the company.

A small culvert lay up ahead, passing over a small stream which flowed north to join the mighty Tiberis.

As they strolled across the culvert, a rustle alerted them to a creature beneath the culvert.

"What was that?" Pancras froze, senses alert.

Peering into the ditch, they could see a man lying beside the rivulet, moaning in some sort of pain.

"Oh!" Pancras exclaimed. "What should we do?"

But no words of encouragement were necessary for Antonius, who had already begun to clamber down the steep bank.

"Antonius!" Decian called. "Have caution."

Pancras laughed interiorly – Decian was the one urging caution? This was a first!

His older friend spared nary a glance before he arrived at the injured man. "Sir! Sir! Are you all right?" He knelt beside the man and gently shook his shoulder.

The injured man quickly drew his knife and, pulling Antonius to the ground with him, held it to his throat. "Give me your money!"

Antonius, shaken, began to unfasten his knapsack. "Yes…yes of course."

Another man came out of the culvert, holding a sharpened pike. "Should we let this one live?"

The man on the ground, his arm a vise-grip on Antonius' neck, motioned with his head. "There are two more, on the road. Fetch them."

Pancras was a statue, immobile, too shocked to breathe.

The wild-eyed brigand quickly scaled the culvert and flashed the spear at them. "Come down with your friend."

It was as if he was watching this from some detached place. Pancras felt his body move, obeying orders, but his mind was only thinking – *this is the end of me.*

The one on the ground had sat up and found the paltry sum in Antonius' satchel. Unwashed and unkempt, the man looked over them with demon-eyes.

"Search their bags," he ordered the taller man, who smelled of death.

Pancras searched Antonius' stony face for some reassurance. As the oldest of the three, he would certainly know what to do, would he not?

Their bags were roughly torn from their shoulders, and given a cursory search. The few coins and knives they brought were quickly confiscated. The robbers pondered longer over the blankets, turning them over in their hands, folding and unfolding them. Finally deciding the items met their standards, they handed back the knapsacks.

Was this to be their death? Pancras wondered numbly. He was a mere observer of these events, beyond the point of terror to the place of unfeeling.

"You should know better, my boys, than to wander these roads unarmed," the smaller one said, a cruel smile playing on his lips. "Next time, we kill you."

They gathered up their new belongings and began to head east on the highway, laughing a mocking laugh all the way until they were out of sight.

The three boys were made of wood, trees planted into the ground, unable to move. Anxiously they cast furtive glances at one another, waiting until the brigands could no longer be heard.

At length Antonius broke the silence.

"Let us hasten home," he breathed.

And the curse was broken, they were able move freely. As fast as their legs could take them, they fled east, toward Rome.

~~~

The screaming was buried deep within, translated into speed as they ticked off the stadia in record time. One, two, three, four. Finally, with their lungs clamoring for rest, they slowed their pace, satisfied that they had put a distance between them and the robbers.

Panting from both exhaustion and fear, they could only gasp desperately at air, grateful that they were still on the breathing-side of the grave.

Decian broke the silence. "You should never have gone down there," he accused.

"Looking back, that was not the wisest decision I have ever made," Antonius dryly responded, but no one laughed.

"We could have died!" Pancras said to no one.

"The world is not safe and innocent," Decian continued, pushing.

"Yes, I know," Antonius replied. "I just thought..."

"I fear that you do not know," he shot back. "You are far too naïve for your own good."

"I was trying to help him!"

"And we almost died."

"You would rather that I ignored him?"

"I would rather that you do not assume the best in everyone."

"I do not assume the best..."

"You think everyone is good, like you. But open your eyes – there is so much hatred and evil in this world, we must be careful."

They walked together in silence. Gradually their heartbeat returned to its normal rate. Pancras looked over to his friend and saw that, for the first time he had ever seen, he was weeping.

"Antonius!"

Decian noticed it as well, and came up and put his arm on his shoulder. "I am sorry, Antonius. I am just shaken. I almost lost you!"

Antonius shook his head, not looking up. "No, I am sorry. I truly am."

"Never mind, it is not your fault. But I now know what I am doing tomorrow. I shall gather a small arsenal and find those men, and bring them to a just punishment!"

"Try to forgive them, Decian."

Decian sighed, irritated. "You can forgive them. One of us needs to bring about justice."

"Now who's being foolish? I don't want to lose *my* friend, either!"

But Pancras was taken silent by this conversation. Try to forgive them? Now that Pancras knew the clandestine life of the mop-haired boy walking beside him, he could only interpret Antonius' oddities in light of this secret. It is no wonder there are rumors and legends growing up around this cult. Their manner of life is so unlike that of other men! Forgive them? Utterly impractical, even impossible.

Yet these rumors about the Christ-followers - was that enough reason enough to kill them?

The question caught traction in his mind, and became a thought that refused to abandon him. He had almost lost his friend back there, beneath the culvert – would he lose him for good because of this Christian legend?

Although the conversation continued among the boys, the anxiety refused to be abated. It carried him all the way home until the Aurelian walls were in view. Never had he been so glad to see the dirty, ugly city of his exile!

~~~

He hoped that perhaps the servants would have saved him some *cena*. Led by a solitary light shining through the atrium, he left the dusk-soaked streets – along with their anxieties and cares – to enter the sanctuary of his domus.

His calls for his uncle went unanswered. Perhaps he was out late on business. The long hours he worked often resulted in an empty house.

Pancras wandered into the *triclinium* to see if remnants of the evening meal were left out, and was startled to see his uncle sprawled out on the floor in front of him. A river of drool connected the heavy balding man with the ground, and a jug of cheap wine lay upturned on the *mensa* table, its contents poured out in a puddle thereupon.

Drunk again.

He sighed, wishing once more that his uncle would cease this vice. How humiliating. He was never a violent drunk, merely one who would slosh around, blubbering and bumbling and drinking until he collapsed. It disgusted Pancras to no end. For a man who fancied himself a critical cog in the vital supply chain that kept the Empire fed, he certainly made a fool out of himself regularly.

A voice from behind him made him jump a bit.

"Will Master Pancras be needing food this night?"

The boy nodded to the servant. "Yes, thank you. You can bring it to my room. And, if you will, clean up this disgusting wretch."

~~~

Two weeks hence. Pancras and Dionysius traced out the labyrinth with their steps, wandering the alleyways of Rome to reach Subura. It was a section of the city that Pancras studiously avoided, except when necessity drove him into it. For it was filled with unsavory characters, the type that would just as soon shank you of your purse as pass you by with nothing but a surly glower. Like fish straining in a too-small net, the people here lived in insulae built one atop another. And it was here that Decian lived.

Oh, he had been here before, to visit his friend's dwelling. He would always be sure to leave before dark, though. It was harrowing to walk those streets where evil lurked around every hidden corner.

But here in the sunlight, beside his uncle, there was nothing to fear.

Why could life not be like this – safe and happy? Why must there be evil around every turn? he thought with a strange and wistful nostalgia. There was a desire in his heart to always be as it was today: safe, secure, surrounded by family and friends. Was this desire just wishful thinking, or did it point to a deeper truth?

He knew it was not that way. They were all one step from danger…Antonius, himself, everyone he loved. This thing called "life" – it is a fragile thing!

They walked in uncomfortable silence and soon arrived at the monstrosity that was Decian's insula. Hastening along the mud-and-filth caked hallways, offended by the smells of rotten offal and urine, they quickly found and entered the two-room apartment.

There was barely room to stand, as it was overflowing with family and friends. Pancras quickly caught Antonius' eye and gave him a smile, returned with a wave. Daphne was there, as was her whole family. The others must have been the extended family of Decian's parents.

But the young man of the hour was nowhere to be seen. A quiet murmur filled the room, eager anticipation of this important ceremony.

A couple minutes later, the curtain separating this room from its adjacent one was drawn back, and out stepped Decian and his father, processing to the front of the room together.

Decian stood somehow taller than yesterday, a proud radiance in his countenance. He must have just come from the baths, for he looked cleaner than the little ragamuffin had ever seemed. Somewhere they must have obtained an ivory-toothed comb, his wavy brown hair now slicked down and combed. An aura of perfume surrounded him, and he

129

was even wearing his *toga praetexta,* which was saved for the noblest occasions.

He strode forward, every eye upon him. With great ceremony, he removed his bulla from his neck, and gently laid it upon the Lares who occupied a small wooden shelf near the door.

His father intoned the prayer. "May the gods protect you, bring you good fortune, and watch over you all your days."

Decian laid before the altar an offering of honey cakes and a bushel of grapes, a small sacrifice to the gods who had protected him thus far.

Slowly, liturgically, he removed his toga and handed it to his mother, who draped it over her arms. Standing before the congregation in his tunic alone, he addressed them: "From my father's loins and my mother's womb have I come forth. Nursed by their sacrifice, I give them honor and lauds – and not to them alone, but to all my ancestors, who have prepared the pathway for me."

His father then took from a table the *toga recta* – the toga of good fortune – and began swaddling him in it. It was smaller than the final toga, and took a moment only to drape over his thin frame.

Atop this was placed the *toga virilis* – the toga of manhood. It was a complicated maneuver which took a while, but when they had finally wrapped Decian in the brilliant white of an expensive new linen toga, he looked the part of a true Roman citizen.

"Receive the toga of manhood," his father intoned solemnly. "Beneath the auspices of the gods, you will grow into the full rank of the men who have gone before you."

The gathered throng smiled appreciatively, proud of the lad – no, the man!

Dressed now in his toga of manhood, Decian led the throng out of his insula, and together in silence they processed down the narrow streets, heading toward the Forum. Each lost in his own private meditation, Pancras wondered what it would be like when he took his own *toga virilis*.

The streets spilled out into the broad Roman Forum, where Decian would enter for the first time as a man. His father led him, followed by the crowd, to the steps of the Temple of Saturn, where a small goat was tethered to a post, waiting for them.

Ascending the temple stairs, Decian's father turned to face the Forum and the gathering. "*Senatus Populusque Romanus*, I present to you my son, Decian Marcellus Romulus, a freeborn citizen of the Roman Empire. This day he has assumed all the rights and dignities of manhood."

The people cheered, and Pancras noted that the crowd had subsumed a goodly number of onlookers who watched the festivities with interest.

The father led his son and the goat into the temple to sacrifice. Much of the multitude, Pancras included, ascended the stairs to add their prayers to the offering. Passing through the threshold, he noted that Antonius was not among them.

Decian wielded the knife, placing his hands on the animal's head, with a deep breath of gathering courage. The bleating – pleading – of the goat was unheeded, and its throat was slashed. Blood flowed freely upon the ground. The young man scooped some in his hands and held it up to the heavens, an offering for his life. One life exchanged for another. One death suffered so another may live.

Prayers were offered, by the priests and his father. Decian added his own, his voice seemingly deeper and more solemn. Pancras watched in silence, wondering if his friend had begun to believe in the gods, or if this were merely a ceremony he performed. In any case, his friend had put aside his frivolity for the day. He carried himself as a nobleman throughout the rite.

The *haruspex* drew forth the innards of the animal, laying them out on the altar. Poking and prodding, sliding his hand along the slippery-smooth liver, he divined the fortunes and future of the boy. He proclaimed aloud to all assembled that Decian would live a long life, and would conquer every trial that came to him.

The ritual slaughter completed, Decian bathed his hands in a basin of water, and the assembly parted to allow him to exit the temple, amid great cheers and celebration.

The throng reassembled at Decian's house for a celebratory meal. And great was the rejoicing! Roast lamb, covered in the rarest *garum* sauce. Pickled eggs. Figs stuffed with the sweetest cheese he had ever tasted. Pastries topped with an assortment of woodland fruits. Even in his own home, Pancras had not tasted such luxury. Decian's family was not wealthy by any means – this must have been an incredible sacrifice!

But the party was made even more enjoyable by the company. Decian came and sat by his friends, positively aglow. There was a new maturity in him, as if this ritual actually caused what it symbolized. Antonius, who had rejoined his friends at the banquet, was feasting himself like never before.

As happy as Daphne was to be there, she paid relatively little attention to the feted boy – rather, there was a generous portion of glances being cast in Pancras' direction. He returned the favor, his heart growing warmer with each one. One of these days, he must summon the courage to speak to her of this hidden love! Surely she would understand – those lingering stares were not those of a sister!

During the few times he looked about the room, he noticed that even his uncle was enjoying himself in vivacious conversation with Decian's father. It brought a cascade of joy into Pancras' heart to see this – his uncle needed to enjoy himself more!

Antonius made a joke, which caused them to laugh. The robust conversation quieted a bit, and Pancras wished that he could cease the passage of time. Stay put!, he would tell the world. This is the way life should be! Joy, peace, laughter, friendship. No fear, no death. Let the world stop at this moment, and let us live here forever!

But alas, time went on. The time drew nigh for the conclusion of the party, and greetings and thanks were exchanged on every side. Pancras said his goodbyes to his hosts, with a hearty embrace for his celebrated friend.

"Do not let this change you, Decian," Pancras said. "Do not think yourself too mature for our games."

"Never!" he declared, returning the embrace. "We will be sixty years old and still playing on Vaticanus Hill!"

Dionysius and his nephew departed, beginning the long walk back home, across the city, towards the setting sun.

"I declare, what a fine celebration!" Dionysius exclaimed, with uncharacteristic enthusiasm.

"Yes, I enjoyed myself," Pancras replied. Secretly he wished it would never end.

"Do you realize that you will celebrate your *dies natale* in two months' time? You will be fourteen years old."

Pancras was surprised that he remembered. "Yes, I know it."

"Good. This year we must celebrate you. I wish to host a feast for you – a feast that will outdo even the grand celebration that Decian's family hosted."

"Truly?" Never before had they celebrated his birthday.

"Yes, truly."

"I would be most thankful."

"Wonderful! Let us, then, make it a day of celebration. Before the banquet, I shall take you to the games for the first time."

"I am grateful, but…"

"But nothing! It is time that you experienced the great joys of being a citizen of the greatest city on earth. These games are unlike any spectacle you have ever seen! In fact, I am surprised you have never asked to see them before – all the boys desire the games in the Colosseum."

His oath, spoken under duress, echoed in his mind. "I…I cannot. I am sorry. That is kind of you, but I do not wish to see the games."

"Come now! Do not be stubborn! You must see the grandeur of Rome's power!"

Pancras could sense his uncle's barely-concealed temper being stoked.

"Uncle, I made a promise to a friend that I would never…"

His response was laden with sarcasm. "Fine. I try to do something kind, and this is how I am repaid. I understand – and will respect your foolish oaths."

The words bit into him, small blades piercing the heart.

They walked on further before Dionysius took up the conversation again, more subdued this time.

"Pancras, I must confess to you. I know I have not been as Cleonius to you."

The mention of his father's name put a dart into this joyful day.

"I do not know how to be a father," he continued. "But I do love you. All the long hours I work, the villa that we purchased, the servants – it is all for you."

The afterglow of the party had put Dionysius in an introspective mood, Pancras thought, touched by his unexpected words.

"I thank you, Uncle."

"You are welcome. But I also seek your forgiveness. At times I have been gruff, distant. How am I to relate to my brother's son? I do not know. Should I be as a friend to you? Should I push you to stand on your own? Please forgive me for my excesses. I have tried…and I have failed."

The boy did not know how to respond. He wanted to reassure him that all was forgiven. But the arrows of his words and his silences were lodged deep within. He was not sure if he could – or wanted to – forgive him.

"Thank you for your apology, Uncle," he muttered. It was all he could say in truth.

The domus was there, atop the hill. Almost home.

"After your *dies natale* we must discuss your own *toga virilis* ceremony," Dionysius continued. "Surely at fourteen you must be ready to celebrate your manhood!"

Pancras did not respond. Give up his bulla? This he would never do. Subtly, without drawing attention, Pancras caressed it, feeling acutely the pain of loss. No, his uncle was no Cleonius. Cleonius was gone – and this bulla was his last remembrance of his father's love.

~~~

Even the walls seemed to perspire in the sweltering temperatures. It was a relief to enter into the shadowed halls of his villa at midday, a respite from the oppressive humidity that made even the finest foot-racers lethargic.

School dismissed early due to heat, and Pancras arrived home ready to eat. He was alone in the house save two servants whose presence could only be heard in a distant room. Hungry, he headed immediately to the triclinium, hoping to find something in the larder to eat.

Extracting a crusty loaf of bread, the remnants of a smoked sausage, a block of cheese that was quickly melting in the heat, and some grapes that had begun to wither, he placed them on a platter and reclined at table. He had enjoyed a couple of bites before a servant, anticipating his needs, delivered to him a cupful of wine mingled with copious water.

He closed his eyes, resting. Very few people would be stirring at this hour and in this weather, he knew. Strength was sapped on such a scorching day, and it was a comfort to lie on the cushions, relaxing.

A creak and a thud alerted him to someone entering the villa. Must be a servant, or his uncle, returning home for *prandium*.

Footsteps squeaked across the floor, leather on marble.

"Salve, Pancras," the boy heard.

Opening his eyes, he saw Decian enter and make himself comfortable on a couch opposite of his.

"Ah, Decian," he murmured, still feeling languid. "What brings you to my humble villa today?"

136

He helped himself to a chunk of bread. "I was suffering from boredom. You're my cure."

Pancras chuckled. "Looks like you are also suffering from hunger, judging by how you helped yourself to my *prandium*."

His mouth full, Decian shrugged. "You have more than enough to share."

"Indeed. Have as much as you wish."

"Well, if you insist..." He tore off a large lump of cheese and proceeded to shove it into his already-stuffed mouth.

Pancras lay back down, dropping grapes into his mouth one by one. "I have no energy today. This heat has sapped my strength."

His mouth spewed breadcrumbs as he spoke. "I as well. No desire to do anything."

"Except eat, apparently!"

"Alas, this *gives* me energy. Perhaps with some sausage I will have enough strength to go swimming this afternoon."

Pancras cut off a portion and handed it to him. "I should like to join you. In the Tiberis?"

"Where else? Not like Ostia is around the corner!"

"I don't know...perhaps the public fountains?"

Decian laughed. "I am not sure the populous is ready to see me without my toga."

"Yes, that is true. Many of them might die of horror on the spot."

A crust of bread was tossed in Pancras' direction, followed by a friendly cackle.

Speaking was too much of an exertion on such a day. It was as if the *caldarium* from the baths was covering the entire city, with no escape. The idea of swimming became a delightful thought – the only avenue of relief for such a summer's heat.

They were silent for a bit, each enjoying their meal in peace.

Decian picked up the thread again. "Was Antonius in school today?"

"No, he was not. Why do you ask?"

He shrugged. "I don't know; it was something strange. I happened upon a friend from across town as I made my way to school today. He said that last night he had seen legionaries come with torches into his insula and remove a few families in shackles. He said that one of the families included Antonius – this friend knows that Antonius and I are chums. But it was dark, and I'm sure he didn't have clear sight."

Sitting bolt-upright, Pancras' eyes were wide. "Antonius was arrested?"

"Let us not be hasty! Perhaps he was sick, and that is why he was absent. Have you heard of the mysterious plague infecting Rome? I hear it strikes with strange symptoms: nausea, seizures, headaches…"

Yes, yes, he had heard of this illness spreading among the common horde. But the more urgent concern was for his friend, whose beliefs ran afoul of the state religion.

"Decian, I beg you to tell me – did your friend truly see Antonius taken away in chains?"

With a nonchalant wave of his hand, Decian dismissed the idea. "I am sure my friend was mistaken. He probably saw another youth who looked similar. What could Antonius do wrong? He is the most virtuous of us all."

"Where would they take him?"

"Why are you so alarmed? Do you know something that I do not?"

Pancras stared into the face of his friend, still so imperturbable. Could he trust this face, which for years had been the source of nothing but jovial merriment? He was always one minute away from a snarky response or satirical jest. No, that smirk playing upon his lips, those brown eyes perennially squinted in laughter, could not be trusted.

"Decian, listen to me. Antonius might very well be in trouble."

His friend began to object, confused, but Pancras cut him short. "I know things that you do not. Antonius is no criminal, but he may have done things that are not approved by the state. Where would they take him?"

"Likely the Tullianum prison. It isn't far; on the Capitoline Hill." Confusion still played upon his features.

Surely Decian thought him mad, but Pancras was unconcerned. He rose to his feet immediately. "We need to go and find him."

"I still do not understand."

"If our friendship means anything, you must trust me. I cannot find Antonius alone – you must come with me, and he will explain everything."

Panicked, Pancras turned and began to hasten toward the street. Decian followed, asking, "Is he a political prisoner? For years he has been critical of the Emperor."

"His kingdom is not Rome," Pancras replied, spilling out of his villa onto the sun-baked street. "He claims his kingdom is not of this world."

"You are not making sense."

"No, the things Antonius believes do not make sense. But he believes them. And he may be in prison because of these things."

Just short of a trot, they dashed through the streets. The alleys were surprisingly vacant – the usual merchants and foot-traffic had escaped to cooler refuge. Their sweat beginning to pour off their brows, matting their hair, stifling their breath – Pancras could not shake the sense of doom.

The gleaming white of the Temple of Jupiter came into view, and beyond it stretched the Forum. But they took no notice of it, hastening around the temple to a side street that housed the underground prison.

A pair of legionaries stood at attention, guarding the cut-stone stairway that led to the jail. Their leather breastplates were soaked with sweat.

"Excuse me," Pancras began boldly, his heart racing. What was he doing here? This was madness! A nightmare, from which he would soon awake!

One of the legionaries barely nodded his head in acknowledgment.

"I need to visit a friend here."

"In the prison? What business do you have with them?"

"Please, sir." He reached into his toga, a desperate determination filling his mind. A small pouch with some coins rested on his chest; he extracted it and held it out.

The legionary took it and dumped out its contents into his upturned palm. Satisfied with the amount, he withdrew a large iron ring of keys, and unlocked the heavy iron gate.

"You are on your own," he said as they stepped aside and allowed the boys to enter the darkness.

A mere sliver of light shone upon the dozens of desperate faces, all covered with dirt and despair. They were tightly packed, with barely enough room for each to lie down. Pancras and Decian descended the stairs, conscious of the numerous eyes staring at them, fearing them, wondering if the boys were a harbinger of death.

"This is foolish!" Decian whispered, his voice trembling with fear. "Antonius is not here!"

But Pancras descended further, hearing only the clinking of chains and examining every face to see if they belonged to his friend. A stench invaded his nostrils. It was more than unwashed bodies and feces – it was the utter desolation of the condemned. Those more dead than alive.

There was a reshuffling as the crowd gave the boys a respectful berth. Standing in the middle of the silent crowd, Pancras declared, "I search for Antonius. He lived on the Via of the Aqueducts. Do you know of his whereabouts?"

"Search below, in the lower chamber," came a disembodied voice from the corner.

They became aware of a small circular hole in the center of the floor, covered in a thick iron grate. Quickly hastening to their knees over it, Pancras called out his friend's name into the darkness below.

There was a clinking of chains beneath, the groaning of bodies being forced to shift. The trickle of the underground spring flowing steadily beneath the lower chamber.

"Who calls my name?" came a deathly croak from directly beneath the grate.

Tears sprang unbidden to Pancras' eyes – tears mingling fear and relief. "Antonius! Is that you?"

A coughing, a rattling in the lungs.

"Yes, Pancras. It is I." The voice that came forth was sickening, coming through a swollen lips and a distended face. A small sliver of light shone down onto Antonius' countenance, and Pancras could see severe bruises and missing teeth.

"*Di Omnes*! What has happened to you? Is it as you feared?"

"Yes, Pancras. It is as I feared – and what I have long desired. Tomorrow is my day of glory."

Decian swallowed hard, utterly stunned that this most unlikely imprisonment has occurred. "Antonius!" he rasped. "You must tell me what is happening! Why are you here?"

"Decian, as I approach the day when I must sleep with the angels, I will speak the honest truth to you. I am a Christian."

"Insanity!" he declared loudly, uncaring of the eavesdroppers. "This is insanity!"

"What do we need to do to purchase your freedom?" Pancras offered desperately. This darkness was oppressing him; he felt short of breath and faint. A sense of unreality hung upon the scene. He was falling deeper, deeper into this nightmare.

A long pause ensued. Finally, from some distant shore, Antonius answered, "I do not wish to be free."

"A few grains of incense burnt to the Emperor – is that not all required?" Pancras suggested.

"I will not deny my God," he slurred. "He offers me eternal life."

"Your religion is nothing but a cesspool of myths!" Decian exclaimed, looking around at the crowd of bodies surrounding him, awaiting execution. "What sort of god would abandon you to this prison?"

"I am not abandoned. He is here with me."

"I do not see him!"

"Our God cannot be seen with human eyes. He is pure love."

"Love does not do this!" Decian shouted, panicking, looking around at the blackened stone walls.

"No, love does not do this. The evil in man has done this."

The full implications of this faith struck Decian as a heavy weight upon the breast. He began to gasp desperately.

"Antonius, come home," he pleaded, his tears falling through the grate upon his friend below. "Come home with us."

Pancras put a calming hand on Decian's shoulder, as his friend seemed to be growing unhinged.

"Please, Antonius," Pancras tried to reason, his voice wavering. "A little sacrifice, a simple oath to the Caesar. Do it for me. For our friendship."

"Deny my God for our friendship? Can you offer me salvation?"

Pancras was beyond tears, unheeding of the pain in his knees as stone protruded into flesh. Words failed to form on his lips; his mind had become a linen sheet, empty and white.

"What will happen to you?" Decian cried.

He spoke the words that filled them both with dread.

"There will be games tomorrow."

"Oh no," Pancras exclaimed. "Oh, no, no, no. Please, no."

"Fear not. We will see each other again."

Was this goodbye?

Pancras could detect a trace of fear in his friend's voice. Oh Antonius! Why must you hold to this superstition? It will end in death – and Pancras had tasted enough death to be sickened forever!

Chains rattled behind them, and the gates squeaked. A rough voice called out, "Boys, your time is up."

"Antonius, I beg you…"

"Go in peace, my friends. I shall pray for you before the Lord."

Reluctantly, they left the darkness and ascended into the light.

It was like a living dream, the walk back to his villa. He barely noticed where his feet led him. The sun shone black, the clear day was as an impenetrable fog.

Numb.

Nothing they could do. He was lost, forever.

And worse – willingly so.

"He is an idiot," Decian spat as they mounted the hill on which the villa was perched. "An absolute idiot. He deserves to die."

"No, he does not…"

Reaching the marble stairs, Decian grabbed his friend's shoulders with uncharacteristic roughness, until they faced each other. An unholy fury filled his eyes.

"Did I not tell you of the utter madness in this superstition? He is fifteen years old, and he wants to die. These are the lies that have captured his mind. He will not listen to reason!"

Pancras shook off his grip. "I will go to the games tomorrow. He needn't die alone. Will you come?"

A look of disgust crossed his face. "Never. I shall be at home, mourning the loss of my stupid friend." With that, he stormed away.

Pancras turned and went into his *domus*, wondering why he could not yet weep over this. He was too stunned, as one who falls from a horse feels no pain immediately for the shock that overtakes him.

A servant paused his sweeping to gaze thoughtfully at the boy.

"You there!" Pancras addressed him. "Where is my uncle? Do you know?"

"I believe he is inspecting the latest shipment in the *Horrea Galbae*," he replied with a respectful bow of the head.

With haste, Pancras departed to find his uncle.

Turning his feet south, he strode through the city, on his mission. He could think of little else. Find his uncle – receive permission to attend the games tomorrow – where…no, no, we will not think of this. Just the games are enough. A chance to see the inside of the Colosseum. Yes! That is a delightful thought. He has always wanted to see the inner workings of the grandest monument in Rome. It will be a beautiful day, perhaps they will have a naval battle or some fine gladiatorial games, or wild beasts…

No! This will not be thought of. Where is his uncle? The warehouse of Galbae was the largest in Rome. Impossible to miss. Just up ahead, not far – but first, must cross the Forum. There it is!

Must not look to the left, around the corner of the Temple, no. Nothing there to see. Forget about what he had seen down those stairs – it does not exist. What prison? Only going to see his uncle, ask him a simple question. As the sun crossed the sky, the merchants were coming out bit by bit – good distractions. Wool and wood, iron and olives. The stuff of life.

Life! Oh life! How precious, how short!

He found the street running alongside the Tiberis and made a left, turning south. The river flowed, flowed, flowed. A little dry this time of year, but still the breast at which the city nursed. Life springing forth. Yes, life. Think of these things.

Up ahead was the long brick warehouse sheltering the many imports that sailed up the Tiberis, including his uncle's grain silage. The *horrea* radiated heat like an oven, baking in the hot sun. As Pancras walked alongside it to the entrance, he could feel the heat searing him.

The two guards did not recognize him as they sat at their post in front of the entrance.

"Please…I am looking for Dionysius of Phrygia," Pancras pleaded breathlessly.

They nodded, recognizing the name of the greatest importer in the city. Stepping back wordlessly, they allowed him to pass.

If the humidity outside was oppressive, the atmosphere inside the horrea was even more severe. It left him gasping for air, his eyes watering. The odors of millions of goods made it difficult to breathe. Everything combined to overwhelm – wheat, leather, meat, wine, wax, flax, wool, olive oil. A few windows at the top of the tall walls cast a hazy beam upon the interior.

"Uncle!" he began to cry out, examining every open door for a sign of his kin.

Up ahead, his uncle and another man stepped out of a storeroom, both stained with sweat all over. Pancras rushed over.

"Well, Pancras, this is a surprise!" Dionysius exclaimed, befuddled. "Welcome to the hub of my industry. You have never been down here, no? Let me show you around."

"Yes, thank you. But before you do so, please answer me this – will you take me to the games tomorrow?"

"The games?" he exclaimed, surprised. "I thought you had given your word…"

"It is important that I attend," he said, trying – but failing – to keep the urgency from his voice. "I must meet a friend there tomorrow."

Dionysius threw his head back and laughed. "Of course! I am pleased to see the games with you. At last! You will finally be a true citizen of the world. You will enjoy them, I promise. To feast your eyes on the battles, the bloodshed – it makes one come alive!"

A sickening feeling settled upon him. Yes, he needed to do this. But he wanted nothing more than to flee to the farthest corners of the world and never hear of death again.

"Come, Pancras. Let me show you around my granary and introduce you to my associates."

The rest of the afternoon, Pancras played the part, putting on a mask as he spent the time with his uncle and those who trade with him. But his thoughts were cloaked in darkness, dwelling in a dungeon, awaiting death.

~~~

The cool of night did little to abate the humidity that caused one's tunic to cling to flesh like a second skin. Even the birds and insects were too heat-drugged to sing. The curtains hung limply upon the open window. And Pancras lay limply upon the bed, staring at the ceiling. His stomach ached; not for hunger or illness, he knew, but for the spectacle he would face the following day.

Breathe in, breathe out. Repeat a thousand times. Enjoy it while it lasts.

He wished the gods would listen to his fervent prayers. He had lifted them up faithfully for the past few hours. Could not Jupiter intervene? Could not Mercury perform a miracle?

Perhaps Decian was right – these gods were no more alive than the stone idols before which they bowed.

He clutched his bulla tight and sighed. No one would come to save Antonius – this he knew in his heart.

And the hours dragged him along, dreading the daylight.

~~~

An image of goats led to slaughter passed through his mind as they approached the Colosseum. Much like the sacrifices that poured blood upon the temple floor, he would be witnessing the innocent killed because of the guilty.

Oh, Antonius! The most innocent of us all! No lies upon his lips, no hatred in his heart, nothing but kindness and peace in his deeds. Why must he be killed at the hands of evil men?

The murder of the innocents did not absolve the guilty – the thought dawned upon him with stunning clarity. Not in the arena; not in the temples. Sacrificing an innocent lamb on an altar does nothing to reconcile us to the gods. Likewise this sacrifice will be useless, a wasteful shedding of blood.

Dionysius said little, but it was evident that his mood was light. He was proud to show his nephew the finest spectacle on earth.

They passed beneath the arches into the inner bowels of the structure, appearing to Pancras to be in the mouth of a great sea creature, or perhaps in an elaborate mausoleum. Up to the second level they climbed, ascending a series of ramps. These spilled out the patrons onto a terrace of stone seats, stratified according to social class. As wealthy citizens, Dionysius and Pancras were granted seats close to the action. They quickly found an unoccupied bench and sat.

The portly man took out a carpetbag of food, and offered it to his nephew, but he refused.

"Pancras, I am so glad to be here with you. This is good for you to experience," Dionysius began, tearing a piece of bread with his teeth.

His nephew merely looked around. The sun beat mercilessly on the patrons, who continued to fill the seating bowl. A light and cheerful spirit pervaded the air, despite the heat.

Here were people – men and women – whom he had passed in the streets. Merchants and laborers, senators and slaves, all gathered for this…this travesty. Pancras hung his head, ashamed to be counted among the debased.

Dionysius took note of it. "You seem to be unhappy," he commented, a note of severity entering his voice. "Why did you ask to come if you do not wish to be here?"

A statue was he, a gargoyle. Unspeaking. Ashamed of being here in the temple to Morta, goddess of death.

"You said you were meeting a friend here today," Dionysius recalled, unsmiling. "Where is he? Should we search among the crowd?"

Pancras shook his head, staring at the arena. He could not explain, would not explain, lest he be thought mad.

"I do not understand you, Pancras," he growled.

That makes two of them.

He pressed on. "I sacrifice, but never does a word of gratitude comfort me."

What are a few hurt feelings when death is coming – for Antonius, for all of them?

Frozen in his place, he awaited the tragedy.

Gradually the seating basin filled to capacity, the din of the crowd growing in anticipation of the events. Every grain of sand that fell in the hourglass of life only increased Pancras' terror.

He remained frozen beside his corpulent uncle, whose cheerful countenance had clouded over. When would this torture begin? The wait was interminable.

A roar and a cheer erupted from the distant part of the stadium, spreading around like an epidemic. Soon everyone was on their feet, cheering, as the Augustus Maximian stepped forth to take his seat in his reserved box. The Caesar graciously acknowledged the crowds, quieting them with his hands as he reclined to watch the festivities.

And then, without fanfare, the games began.

The gladiators took the stage, fighting mock battles, their swords flashing in their daring moves. Pancras had to squint to see if, perhaps, Antonius had been drafted to play a role in this fanciful war, but none of these men resembled him beneath their tin helmets and leather armor.

The assembled throng cheered when one of the gladiators drove his sword through the other's throat, flooding the arena with a torrent of blood.

Pancras could only gasp and swallow down a scream of horror.

The battle went on, the sand soaking up more red rivers. Some men fell and continued to fight. Other men fell and were pounced upon by their opponents, swords removing heads from their owners. Slashes given and slashes received, coating the swords and the armor with a crimson paint.

The horde of spectators cried out in delight when a gladiator landed a particularly deft strike, or deflected such a one. The raucous noise sounded as a preview of Tartarus, with the deafening screeching of titans and demons on all sides.

What was it like to be the only one of fifty-thousand strong who despised the exhibition? Pancras had never felt more alone, more oppressed. It was to drown in a sea of asps.

At long last, the gladiatorial battle had killed off all of its participants save one, who was properly feted with an olive-leaf crown and allowed to live another day. The attendants dragged the carcasses off the arena, leaving streaks of scarlet across the sand. Evidence of a needless war.

He was left breathless, panting, trying mightily not to vomit. It was now clear why Antonius hated these games!

A short intermission followed, before chariots made their way to the showground. Pancras exhaled peacefully upon seeing them, for this was, at least, an event that would not result in death.

The flag waved, and they were off! Sturdy war-horses raced at breakneck speed around the track, sending a spray of sand to cloud the air. Round and round the amphitheater they galloped, their riders barely holding on to the reigns. One chariot stood out as the clear favorite – that red one, down there – and established a significant lead in the race.

With reckless abandon the drivers navigated the harrowing turns, as the chariots had a tendency to become unstable, to drift, and even to lift onto one wheel. Yet they all successfully managed the maneuver, as the field of eight racers never slowed for a moment.

And then, on the fourteenth lap, one of the chariots hit a bump and the spokes on the wheel crumbled like kindling. The charioteer was sent flying, into the path of an oncoming chariot. Without hesitation, the other horse continued its course, trampling the man and dragging the chariot over his now-limp body.

As soon as the other chariots passed, a team of slaves raced onto the course and dragged the man by the arms to the underground tunnel where the dead would rest until their bodies were disposed of as so much garbage.

The bloodlust of the crowd was stoked once again. They cried out in delight at this unexpected turn of events, cheering on the remaining seven, and secretly hoping for another accidental demise.

Dionysius was among them, laughing and clapping his hands together. He slapped Pancras' back raucously, letting out a whoop of joy as he swigged again from his wineskin.

Pancras could only grit his teeth harder and will his eyes to stay attached to the arena. Where was Antonius? Was there more to come?

Indeed, there was. After fifty endless rounds, the red chariot passed the finish line to secure the victory. The driver, exultantly raising his sweat-caked arms in triumph, was given a bouquet of roses and a bag of coins, much to the satisfaction of the mob of spectators.

Another pause ensued as the assistants prepared the amphitheater for the climax of the day's games.

A small gate, shorter than Pancras, was raised on the side of the arena. Two legionaries stepped out and watched ominously as a group of simply-dressed people came forth. It was men and women, children and the elderly, all stripped down to their bare tunics and unshod, forced to march in procession to the center of the arena.

One legionary, unhappy with the haste of an elder, gave him a shove that caused him to tumble to the ground. The others in the group assisted him up.

They marched with heads high, unafraid and unashamed of their fate. Around twenty-five in total, they stayed close as a unified body, standing tall against whatever may befall them.

Pancras' heart hammered as he squinted to see the faces. Yes, there was Antonius' younger sister, and his mother as well. He was sure of it, even from this distance. His spirit fell to see them standing there, so stripped of dignity. But he could not make out any of the others, who faced away from him. There was none who sported the black, curly hair of his friend, though – that feature would stand out in any crowd, at any distance. Where was Antonius? Was he saved for a later torture? Or perhaps – by some miracle of the gods – spared?

Once the group was comfortably stationed in the center of the sandpit, the legionaries hastened back into the tunnel from whence they came, closing the gate behind them.

From across the arena squeaked open an awful sound, and the crowd grew silent in anticipation.

A gate was being swung wide, a gate from which the guttural growls of wild beasts could be heard. Yelping, snarling, and howling – all fifty thousand knew what was to come.

"Damnatio ad bestias," Dionysius murmured eagerly in the tense silence, such as foreshadows a terrible thunderstorm. "The best of it all! Feast your eyes upon this!"

Pancras could not remove his eyes for all the utter horror he felt.

And suddenly, in a flash, the beasts were upon them. Large creatures, such as Pancras had never seen – and never wanted to see. There was a cat the size of a horse, with fangs dripping saliva. Another feline with a shaggy mane around its neck tore into the flesh of an innocent girl. Two wild boars went on a goring rampage, shoving their tusks into human flesh. A bear came ambling forth, roaring and striking with knife-like claw.

The human beings – flesh and blood like himself! – put up no resistance, and one by one fell to the beasts. The blood-trickle turned into a creek, then a river, and before long a lake had formed beneath them. Some of them could be seen with hands raised, crying out to their deaf-god who was no use, no help. Innards were ripped apart, strewn about, as if they were the stuffing of a girl's play-doll. Faces were trampled beyond recognition. The beasts began to eat and devour the still-warm flesh.

Finally, finally, Pancras summoned every last shred of his will and was able to shut his eyes. He retched once, feeling nothing come out – because the blood was now inside him, in his mind, its awful blood-fingers grasping and choking his soul. This memory would never be erased. This blood could be cleaned from the arena floor, but not from his mind.

An offering to no god.

A sacrifice that forgave nothing.

Bloodshed for a few cheers.

Pancras felt a mortal stab in the inner core of his being. His eyes shut tight, he wished he could disappear. He longed for his own death, yet feared its coming. Oh, if he had died instead of Antonius' family! So this is hatred! So this is mankind!

The animals were finally recaptured after some hard work, and the unrecognizable body parts hauled away in a cart like manure.

When the Emperor descended from his throne to walk through the arena, surrounded by his majestic retinue, Pancras could take no more. He rose and fled, leaving his uncle behind with mouth agape.

Is this what it means to be a citizen of the world?
Inhuman!
But where...oh where was Antonius?

~~~

They reclined, the three of them, in the inner courtyard of Pancras' villa. It was quiet there, with few birds playing in the palmetto trees. And they remained silent as well, for no one knew the fate of their friend.

Dusk had almost given way to darkness, and the insects were out in force, but no one noticed. Their minds were abuzz with other thoughts.

Imagination was no help at all, for it seized upon every terrifying prospect that passed through the mind. Was he at the bottom of the sea? Hanging from a gibbet outside the city? Locked deep within a dungeon from which no man has escaped? The torture of not-knowing would soon be replaced by the torture of knowledge, they were sure.

Wordlessly, Pancras' friends emanated the same anguish. Hanging heads, worry lining their face, an inability to make even the smallest conversation for fear that the silent topic would be either ignored or explored.

A frantic banging on the door echoed through the house, spilling out onto the courtyard. Knowing a servant would answer it, Pancras did not bother to move. He was part of the statuary in the garden.

Suddenly the domus vomited forth a young man into the courtyard, stumbling and staggering in a frantic frenzy.

Pancras rose, surprised. "Alcander!" he exclaimed, recognizing his old classmate. It had been years since they studied together. During the intervening time, they had not seen one another.

155

The Greek boy panted, tripping as if drunk on some mysterious intoxicant. He sprawled his tall, dark frame on a low concrete bench.

"Pancras," he gasped, his face contorted in agony, immense pain of the psychological kind.

He did not elaborate, but wrung his hands and pounded his forehead as if to wake himself from a living nightmare.

Seating himself again, Pancras dreaded the news he came to share. But – as much as he knew his friend was dead – there was a burning to know.

"Alcander," he urged, conscious of his friends' stares of trepidation. "You come to share news?"

"It is Antonius…I know you were friends…" He would say no more. His face crumpling, he had no words to speak of the horror.

"We know. He has passed on from us." Saying it aloud made it true. Oh but how it hurt!

Choking on his voice, Alcander managed to sputter, "I was there, Pancras. I was in the gardens behind Maximian's villa. He was entertaining tonight, a celebration for his courtiers and military officers. My father was busying himself with the preparation of the food – a lavish feast it was! I was giving him help, chopping vegetables and roasting them on a spit. But then the steward stepped in, ordering me to help light the torches in the garden.

"He handed me a torch and I stepped out into the dusk, turning the corner. That is where I saw them all. Young and old, they hung there, six on each side of the main path. I had seen them before, helping with other banquets at the imperial palace, but I had never been asked to light them alive. I trembled at the task and approached the first one, suspended a man's height from the ground. I looked at the face – why! Oh why did I look! – and above the pitch-covered tunic was the head of Antonius.

"He was hard to recognize. His face – disfigured. He had been beaten so severely that he no longer resembled a man, but a heap of mangled flesh. Yet that hair was so distinctive, and I knew it was him.

"I called to him, and he opened his eyes a slit. He recognized me! I know he did; we hadn't seen each other in two years but he knew who would be his murderer. Barely, barely he nodded, as if encouraging me to light the fire that would consume him alive.

"But I could not! My limbs lost all strength and the torch slipped from my hand. I continued to stare – in horror! – at this, my friend.

"The steward passed by and saw my reluctance. He grabbed the torch from the ground and went forward with the…the…"

And he could speak no more. Ugly cries of anguish sounded forth, as tears gushed to the pavement, his face lost in his hands.

~~~

How did he get here? He briefly pondered this before remembering that it did not matter. Nothing mattered.

~~~

The shadows drifted across the wall. Pancras watched them with an empty mind and vapid gaze. It indicated the passing of time, but he did not care.

~~~

How long did he lie there, motionless in his bed? Perhaps merely a few hours, perhaps days. Drifting in and out of consciousness, he merely endured.

Numb.

His friends – what was a friend?, he wondered – had long gone home. He was alone. Alone in his room, alone in this world.

There was none of the usual pain and grief and sorrow that he had long ago endured. No, this time there was nothing but a void, an emptiness within him.

The wall was white and blank. His mind was white and blank.

He closed his eyes, because there was no reason to keep them open.

~~~

Screams that he never heard echoed in his ears.
Fire that he never saw pirouetted behind his eyelids.
Death that he never endured settled upon his soul.

~~~

There seemed to be no difference between waking and sleep. It was a drowsiness, a place in-between, that he was content to dwell in.

His mouth felt dry and full of sand, but no matter. Was this a bad thing, or his usual state? He could not remember and did not care.

There was a sharp pain in his stomach, but not nearly as sharp as flames licking the skin.

He cared not whether he lived or died. Let him drift off beyond the sunset of consciousness, off the edge of the earth.

~~~

It was dark again.

Why was that? Is it because he was blind? Or because it was night?

How many darknesses had passed since he took to his bed? He could not remember.

~~~

This time was different.

The first time he faced death, it came as a part of nature. The way of all flesh.

This time, it was an unspeakable horror. There were no words to describe it. Evil was too mild of a word; "cruelty" did not approximate it.

It was a realization that darkness will always win. Goodness will always be defeated. Hatred conquers all.

And in this new paradigm, there was no point in living.

After all, was this not the city that drinks blood as sport? The city that crucifies its sons and daughters? The city that took the kindest, most virtuous young men and burns their flesh to satisfy their lusts. A life: merely collateral damage to make for a festive orgy.

If this is the way of the world, Pancras wished to be annihilated.

~~~

Voices.

"Thank you for coming," said a familiar voice. Pancras recognized it but could not remember who it belonged to.

"You are welcome," came an unfamiliar one. "You say he has not moved for two days?"

"I have called him for *cena* and tried to rouse him, but he lies there in some sort of stupor."

"What prompted such behavior?"

"I do not know. We went to the games…"

A low guttural groan escaped the boy's lips upon mention of that travesty.

"…but he was fine thereafter. It was that evening, when an old classmate of his stopped by. I did not hear their conversation, but something transpired out in our courtyard that precipitated such a reaction."

"And he has not eaten nor drank?"

"Not a bit. Will you examine him, doctor?"

"Of course. Lead me to him."

A curtain opened and Pancras became aware of a presence beside him. He did not bother to respond to any of the poking. His eyelids were forcibly raised but Pancras refused to register what his eyes were seeing. Strong hands pressed in upon his flesh, checking for pulse and for the humors.

Some mysterious force raised his head, and he was aware of a moistened cup placed upon his lips. He cared not if he drank or thirsted, and water was poured down his throat. Dropped back down as a sack of beans, he rolled over to face the wall.

The nothingness continued to grow within him, consuming him. He was plunging into the void, into the meaningless universe, past the threshold of sanity and into the realm of oblivion. Soon he would be past the point of no return.

~~~

He was a vacuum, an empty consciousness taking up space.

He was nonexistence.

He was nothing.

Thinking of nothing.

Feeling nothing.

If he did not exist, he would not have to face the meaninglessness of existence.

~~~

It was the blackness of despair.

If there was strength in his sinews, he would find the nearest precipice and throw himself headlong.

If he could find a way to the water, he would walk into the depths and never return.

For evil wins.

It always wins.

And this makes life nothing but a fool's game, played by idiots.

~~~

In the third day of his desolation, he could hear noises from outside of his room.

"Yes, please, come in," came the familiar voice again. A man's voice.

"Thank you. I want to visit him," sang a familiar woman's voice. There was something about that voice…it was like a distant lantern shining in the thickest fog.

"Please do. I fear for him."

The curtain ruffled and a stool was dragged across the floor. He could sense that the woman-creature sat beside him.

"My dear Pancras," she began, "My heart is grieved, too, for my friend Antonius."

The mention of the name was a sword to slay him! An excruciating pain shivered through his body.

She continued, her words as drops of rain on a desert. "But I need you to help me grieve. I cannot do it alone. But together, *together*, we must be there for one another."

A memory was triggered. It was a painful one, but one that brought life. Pancras felt a spark of energy within his soul.

"I have never told you this, Pancras," she continued, her voice soothing and melancholy. "But I have always thought of us as a *together*. Ever since that day in the catacombs, when you rescued me…"

A warm hand, soft and tender, was gently laid upon his shoulder. He could hear a profound sadness in her voice when she spoke again.

"Pancras, I love you, and I need you to rescue me again. I am drifting away in this sorrow over Antonius. I cannot lose you as well!"

As one coming back from the shores of the underworld, Pancras' consciousness began to awaken. It was Daphne – oh Daphne! – he could recognize that voice anywhere.

162

He rolled over and affixed his eyes on her beautiful face, awaiting more ambrosia that fell from her lips.

"I have prayed to the gods for you," she whispered affectionately.

"But life means nothing," he rasped.

"Not if we live it together."

She offered him her hand. Weakly, he took it and rose up.

~~~

It would accost him at unexpected times, the memories of his friend. But he had to move on; he knew that much.

School resumed. It was a mere few weeks until he would be free from this *grammaticus*, graduating with high honors. It was as yet undecided if he would continue to the rhetorical school or be apprenticed to his uncle. He preferred the former, but his uncle – facing a significant tuition increase – favored the latter.

These last days should have been a time of freedom and delight. The coveted prize of an education was within reach! But his teacher would frequently catch the boy lost to his melancholy thoughts, his gaze turned to the solitary window.

After school let out – usually early in the day, due to the still-oppressive temperature and mugginess – Pancras would wander to the usual trysting place. They tried to play their usual childhood games, climbing trees and playing knucklebones and dice. But the frivolity was forced, the jesting was flat, the silences threatening to burst the dams of inner emotion.

A week after the…the passing (Pancras still could not bring himself to put the words 'Antonius' and 'Death' together), Decian stopped coming around. Perhaps Antonius had been the adhesive that brought such disparate personalities together. No matter – Pancras was content to be with his beloved alone, wandering along the shores of the Tiberis in silence.

It was one such day that Daphne and Pancras found themselves strolling south along the river, stealing bits of shade as they followed a thin path.

The breeze was an oven, a furnace. Pancras' tunic showed dark stains of perspiration.

Yet there was the freshness of lavender and rosewater about his beloved. It seemed that the heat did not penetrate her sacred aura.

The scratching of their sandals on the dirt was the only sound for a stadia or two.

And then she spoke.

"You are thoughtful today," she observed.

"No more than usual."

"What occupies your thoughts?"

But they both knew. There was no need to reopen that wound.

Instead, Pancras began to obliquely wax philosophical. "Have you ever gazed at the horizon and felt a longing?"

"A longing for what?"

A round pebble became a projectile in his hands, launched into the depths of the river.

"How can I explain it? It is beyond words. I am incomplete, Daphne. And I do not know what will complete me."

They strode on: he brooding, she ponderous.

164

After a time, she replied. "I feel adrift as well. Antonius' death…"

"What I feel is deeper than Antonius. His death was the spark, but now I question everything. Life. Death. Suffering. Joy. Meaning. Love. What is it all about? My heart aches to find the answer."

A downed log became their seat. Beyond the river, the city rose proud and triumphant.

"I feel like a door is opening before me," he continued. "It is offering me a peek, but I cannot peer outside. Perhaps I am afraid that there is nothing on the other side, but a dark void into which I will tumble, and there will be no return."

She searched his eyes, trying to decipher the riddle, but said nothing.

His gaze falling, he murmured, "I fear I make no sense. Perhaps I am becoming insane."

"No, you are not," she quickly corrected. "The sages of old wrestled with the same questions. But…but I am not sure…I am not sure we will ever find the answers."

"Then I will search until I die!" he cried with a ferocity that shocked even him.

This outburst brought on an uncomfortable silence.

They rose and began to stroll further. The trail wound around a bend in the river and the new views revealed the necropolis on Vaticanus Hill. Dozens of mausoleums rose from the earth.

He was surrounded by meaninglessness – from the river on his left that flowed eternally without filling the sea, to the city across the flume that consumed an insatiable amount of mammon, to the tombs up ahead where men's lives were proven worthless.

Turning to face his friend, he put a hand on her shoulder. "I want you to search with me."

"For what?"

"For the truth about everything. For the meaning behind it all. Do you not feel it in your heart? That it *must* be there?"

Pity filled her eyes. "I…I do not know…"

Crestfallen, he turned away and walked back upstream, alone.

~~~

Several days later, they wandered through the Forum on the market day. The agora was surprisingly empty, with fewer booths and patrons alike.

"This is strange," he mused, walking beside Daphne through the unoccupied quad. "Perhaps the heat has kept people away?"

"I fear more than that," she commented offhandedly, entranced by a merchant displaying beaten gold jewelry. "Have you not heard reports of the disease spreading through the city?"

"A couple classmates have been absent, yes. But I thought nothing of it."

"I have heard more and more coming down with the illness."

"What illness is it?"

"I have heard that it is like a plague: convulsions, stomach ailments, gangrene. But no one is sure of the cause. Half of my insula has caught it. I pray to the gods that I will not be next."

"Hmm," he thought aloud, concern furrowing his brow. "Quite serious."

"Yes, quite. But as there is nothing we can do about it except avoid those infected, we ought not dwell on it overmuch."

"This is true," he concluded, distracted by a blacksmith's craft on display in the corner near the Temple.

It was a good diversion to come here, to the place of wood and iron and stone and olive. He had been living too much in his head; it was time to return to the real world! There was no better cure for overthinking than to get one's hands dirty, to smell the earthy odors and handle the raw materials of life.

"Come along, Daphne, I will buy you something," he declared spontaneously, breaking out into a smile. "What do you desire?"

She returned one, bashfully. "That is not necessary, Pancras!"

"I have a bag of coins begging to be spent." He held them up and gave them a shake, the tinkling of aureus and follis. He adopted a falsetto and made the coins speak: "Spend me! Spend me!"

She laughed, and Pancras thought he had never heard a more delightful sound in his life. He smiled foolishly.

"If you insist!" she replied. "Come, let us look at these fine scarves over here."

She took his hand, and suddenly his doubts about the meaning of life evaporated as dew in the morning sun.

~~~

The sun continued its relentless course across the heavens, crossing the earth three more times before the following encounter ensued.

167

It was a fine afternoon, two days before he would be released from his scholastic prison forever. The worst of the heat had past, and in the cool of the day, they lounged on a sandbar in the middle of the river, their tunics damp from splashing around.

Daphne was picking up pebbles and examining them. They glistened as jasper and tiger's eye. Though worth nothing in the marketplace, they delighted the eye for the moment.

For his part, Pancras could not take his eyes off of her. The auburn hair flowed as a forest streamlet down her back, shimmering in the late afternoon sun. The reflected glow from the river sparkled and flickered upon her face. She was a goddess in the flesh. She was an antidote to the tragedy that flanked him on every side.

Perhaps this was what his incompleteness was lacking? This union of souls?

An urgent desire arose within him, to reach out and stroke her face. But no! His natural modesty would not permit it. Rather, a fluttering in the stomach began to grow incessantly, and he dared voice his thoughts.

"Daphne?" he inquired, and thirsted for her response.

She looked at him and smiled, an encouragement to go on.

"Have you ever thought about...you and I?"

Giggling, she replied, "Of course. Have you?"

"Every day."

Immediately he looked away, mortified at his response. He had not meant to sound so obsessed.

"As do I," she said demurely.

Amazed, they locked eyes.

"At times, when things are darkest, I think of you."
He lay on his back and gazed up at the clouds. "I have had
much darkness in my life. You are my light."

"I cannot be all that to you. I have my own darkness."

"But together, we can make a world of light."

"This I hope too. For I see a light in you, Pancras,
despite all of your darkness."

"If so, it is because you have drawn it out."

She screwed her face in disagreement. "You have
always had it, my dear Pancras. You are compassionate and
kind – you have shown that to me in so many ways in our
friendship. I can trust you. And that is a rare find."

A silence stretched comfortably between them. The
gurgling of water washed their cares away.

"My father," he muttered. "He taught me about
kindness and trust."

"What do you remember of him?"

"He was always ready to give to anyone who was
hungry or in need. We had plenty, back in Synnada. I never
hungered or went without. But if we were out on a journey,
he would take an extra loaf of bread to distribute to the poor.

"I even saw him give his own cloak to a poor widow
during a fiercely snowy winter. He tried to be unseen, but I
watched him do it through our oilskin window. She had
been begging along the road, her feet swollen and frozen.
My father caught sight of her out the window and made
some excuse about needing to check the cows. I watched
him give the clothing to her on the road, and I will never
forget her face – it shone with an adoration usually reserved
for the gods. When he came back in without the cloak, I
asked him where he lost it. He just smiled and would not
respond. I miss him, I truly do."

She lay down, joining him on the warm sand. "But you are just like him. He would be proud."

No, he was nothing like his father. He was dark and brooding, a boy who cared for himself alone. This he knew – but let her believe his carefully-crafted pretense. He was unworthy of his father's legacy, and unworthy of her. But could he learn to be the light she believed him to be?

He summoned the courage to pose the proposition burning on his heart. "I do not wish to presume, but I desire for our *together* to be forever."

"As do I, Pancras. As do I."

~~~

He helped himself to another roasted drumstick.

Across the *mensa* came the slurping and smacking of a wild beast. His uncle was already well into his cups. Pancras kept silent, not wanting to upset the fragile equilibrium between them.

A significant belch drew the boy's attention to his caretaker's greased face.

"We need to talk," Dionysius began, staring him straight in the eye. Was his look stern, or merely serious?

"Of what, uncle?"

"Of your future. In two days' time we will celebrate your grand achievement. What does the future hold?"

Hesitating, Pancras knew that a forthright answer might draw his uncle's ire. Nevertheless, he spoke his mind: "I hope to continue to study rhetoric. My teacher says I have the ability."

"No doubt you do," he replied, swigging more unmixed wine. Dionysius liked it straight, a custom unheard-of among the genteel class.

"He is willing to offer me a recommendation. He knows of a man…"

"Let us not anticipate my answer, Pancras. You have many gifts and talents, which can be put to good use in my granary."

He dreaded this response. "I suppose so…"

"It is my fondest dream for you to inherit this business. You know the long hours that I have invested to build it from nothing, and I am confident it will continue to grow. The population of Rome continues to increase, and more mouths means more grain! There are yet untapped regions that can bring in ever greater stores of wheat, and I have every confidence that in a few years' time, I can entrust you with these new accounts and territories."

"I am honored by your esteem for me," he replied, at a loss for more.

But his hesitation did not go unnoticed. "Yet you are not thrilled by the prospect. Have you other desires?"

He shook his head. "No, uncle. I do not know what I am to do. I have prayed to the gods for direction, but…"

"Cease your praying and think for once!" Dionysius exclaimed with a sardonic smile. "My nephew, such employment is hard to come by. As long as you have no better offers, I will insist that you work for me. Besides, I have lost three of my finest men to this mysterious illness that is striking across Rome; I am in need of help from someone I can trust."

There was no way out. Without another concrete plan, he would certainly end up working for his uncle for the time being.

Humbly he nodded. "Yes, uncle. I understand."

"Good," Dionysius grunted, going to work on the chicken breast, smothered in rosemary and basted with vinegar and oil. With his mouth full, he continued, "It will be good to have you with me. There is much I wish to teach you."

But Pancras had no desire to learn from this man. Was this arrangement in the boy's best interest, or merely for the advantage of his uncle?

The meal continued with a second course of an egg pastry, filled with chives and a smooth and pungent cheese. As solitary hermits they ate, each encapsulated in their own thoughts and worlds.

Pancras was beginning to resign himself to his fate. He did not know for certain, but this graduation would likely mean the end of his afternoon trysts. His one joy, the salt that flavored his bitter life, would soon be taken away.

A loud rapping at the door drew their attention away. Dionysius waved it away, saying, "Ah, do they not know that we are having *cena*? They can come back later."

Yet they could hear the servants fulfilling their porter's duty. Their low conversation was unintelligible, but in a trice the servant stood at the threshold of the triclinium.

"My lord, Flavius Dominius wishes to have a word with you."

A dark look crossed his uncle's eyes. "At this hour? Tell him to return in the morning."

"He insists that it is urgent."

Impatiently waving his hand, Dionysius replied, "Yes, yes, it is always urgent with the *praefectus annonae*. See him in."

The servant departed, and momentarily the threshold was breached by the government official and Decian's father. Pancras arose, surprised to see his friend's *paterfamilias*.

172

Dionysius struggled to lift his hefty frame to its feet. "This is a most inconvenient time," he began gruffly, clearly not intending to be bullied into submission by his superior.

"Surely you will excuse the trouble when you hear the reason for our visit," the prefect answered, tensely.

A showdown of wills was taking place, Pancras realized. He would have been amused, but for the friction that was palpable in the air.

"Speak, then. We have a third course to attend to."

The prefect looked at his corpulence with disdain. Sternly, he began, "Dionysius, surely you have heard of the plague affecting the citizens of Rome. Close to half of the city has been afflicted."

"Yes, I have heard of it. Several of my finest employees have taken ill."

"As has my son," Decian's father intoned.

So this was the reason for his disappearance! Pancras' heart filled with dread. Losing one friend was bad enough – may the gods have mercy on this other one!

"Caesar has spared no expense to seek out the cause and the cure of this illness. Doctors have been working around-the-clock, for this is unlike the plagues that have historically struck the city."

"I, too, am concerned," Dionysius replied, his voice trembling a bit. "But what can be done? These things happen with regularity. All we can do is wait, and avoid those infected."

"I refuse to watch my son suffer helplessly!" Decian's father exclaimed with vehemence.

"Fair enough. So let us seek a cure. Have the doctors or philosophers made any progress?"

"They have not," explained the prefect. "Despite their work, no cure has presented itself."

"I am saddened to hear this."

"Yet they have developed a theory about the genesis of this illness."

"Oh?" Dionysius replied, but Pancras could tell that he was not surprised at all.

"We would like to examine your storehouse of grain. We suspect that perhaps the heat and humidity have caused it to spoil. Perhaps a fungus has grown upon it."

"What evidence would you have for such a suspicion?" The hostility was rising, a storm threatening to overawe the room.

"We have no evidence," the prefect admitted. "But we are seeking the common thread among all the sick. All have drunk from the same public fountains; all have engaged in commerce in the Forum; all have attended the games. We are investigating all of these. Perhaps it was an infection in the water, in the air? We do not know. But we do know that everyone has eaten of your grain. So we include this in our investigation."

"And you think my grain has caused the plague? Preposterous!"

"We accuse you of nothing, Dionysius. But we are seeking to examine every alleyway, no matter how dim."

"I do not give permission," he adamantly refused. "I am inspected regularly, according to the law. You have no right..."

"I have a mandate from Caesar. He has authorized this."

"I will not allow it."

"I do not come for permission, Dionysius," he coldly clamped down. "I merely come to inform you of what we shall do this night. We will make a full report when we are finished."

"Come now, Dionysius," Decian's father offered desperately, extending the olive branch. "If young Pancras was ill, you too would travel to the ends of the earth to find the cure. If you have seen what I have seen…my son is too sick to eat, he moans in pain, and I fear that his hands and feet are turning the color of death."

"Truly, this is most unfortunate," Dionysius tried to sound compassionate, but his hard edge prevented it. "But I assure you that you will find nothing in my storehouse."

"We shall be the judge of that," the prefect replied.

"Flavius, I worked closely with your predecessor…"

"Yes, I know you did."

"And we had such a mutual respect and trust. I am sorry that I do not enjoy such trust in your eyes."

"Please, Dionysius. This is not personal."

His uncle was reduced to a mute glare.

The prefect turned to go. "We shall provide you with a comprehensive report this very night." He and his compatriot departed with nary a word of good will.

The echo of the door slamming reverberated through the house, and Dionysius turned, stricken. Slumping down on his couch, he drained the contents of his chalice in a single toss before barking orders to his servants to bring him another jug.

The hostility in the room lingered, and Pancras found himself unable to move. Something dark had overshadowed his uncle, who opened the new jug and began to drink from its contents directly.

Here he was, the proud and rich importer! The finest businessman the city had ever produced! And yet he sat, defeated and humbled. Instead of bowing beneath the rod, he appeared ready to lash out at any moment. An incipient anger began to grow.

"All this, Pancras," he growled, wiping his mouth on his sleeve.

Pancras looked around, unsure of what he was referring.

"Take a good look. This will come crumbling this very night." Another lengthy swig. "All this could have been yours. But now – who knows?"

"Do you believe they will find anything?" he asked timidly.

"Of course they will!" he roared. "And I knew it, I knew it all along." Another draught, longer than the first.

Breathing heavily, his face aglow with the heat and wine, Dionysius cleared his throat and began. "The heat had taken a toll on all of us. The shipments kept coming, but we had already begun to lose too much. We could not find the men to unload fast enough; they wearied from the simplest tasks. It was inhuman to drive them further, faster…so the profits began to slip. Oh, the nights I stayed awake, poring over the receipts by the light of a dismal lantern! I feared we would not be able to pay our creditors.

"And yet, I could not throw out the wheat – it was millions of measures – lest we fall into debt. It would not be as the debt we find when we purchase a Grecian urn; no, this would be utter destitution.

"I first saw the black mold two weeks ago. I prayed and hoped it would not spread, for I knew this would be the end of me. But to throw out the grain would be a greater loss. So it grew in the heat and the moisture, growing and growing until it spoiled everything. Everything! And not only did it spoil the grain…it made our lives turn sour as well."

"Surely it cannot be that bad…"

"You know nothing!" he slurred. "My reputation, my business, my clientele…we shall all descend in a fiery blaze, and then be extinguished forever."

He sought consolation again from the jug. Frozen in fear, Pancras could not even twitch, lest his drunken uncle do something rash.

Dionysius continued drinking as dusk slipped into darkness, and the servants began to light the torches around the domus. Out of the corner of his eye he saw one of them in the courtyard, struggling to reach a hanging oil lamp. The sight brought back a sudden and vivid memory…

He longed to sip from the bottle of forgetfulness, but Dionysius did not offer him any, as its contents were quickly consumed.

The sands in the hourglass continued their mad rush to the earth, as they both were frozen in the triclinium. Pancras sat down as the minutes turned to an hour, then two. Even from their lofty home, the rickety carts thundered down the avenue, jostling and bustling and breaking up the otherwise uneasy silence.

At a certain point Dionysius finally retired the jug and stood up, pacing the room.

"Perhaps we can flee, Pancras," he muttered, verging on incoherence. "Perhaps the countryside may hide us as refugees."

"Uncle, we may lose the domus, but…"

"We shall lose more than the domus, Pancras!" he exclaimed with watery eyes. "We shall be put to shame, to slavery, to death – I know not what." A few more paces and he had crossed the room again. "Bring me a sword, and I shall fall upon it."

"Uncle!"

At that moment the door swung open without the dignity of alerting the residents. The prefect and the paterfamilias reentered, their faces set like marble.

The air was thick with expectation as they paused to regard each other.

"Dionysius, we have indeed found the suspected cause."

The portly man groped a wall to keep his balance.

"I am sorry to report that your horrea is full of spoilt wheat. We fear that this might be infecting the citizens of Rome."

"What shall be done?"

"We have already hired several laborers to begin dumping the tainted grain into the Tiberis."

"No..." he whispered, a disproportionate horror covering his countenance. "No...you have ruined me..."

"I am truly sorry, Dionysius. It is most unfortunate."

"You have ruined me!" he roared back, stumbling over to the mensa and taking in his hand a knife from the stale dishes still sitting out. "You have ruined me!"

"My friend," the prefect exclaimed, stepping back. "I urge you to do nothing hasty!"

"You will pay!" came the shout. Two swift strides closed the distance between them, and before the prefect could react, the trader plunged the knife deep into the man's flesh.

He cried out and sunk to his knees as the knife made a second plunge, crimsoning his toga.

"What have you done!" his friend's father frantically exclaimed, rushing upon the scene to wrestle the knife out of the drunken man's grasp.

A tussle ensued, but Dionysius' inebriation caused him to soon fall to the floor and relinquish the tool.

"*Pro di immortales!* You have killed him!" the father screamed, checking the pulse of the man whose blood formed a river reaching out to lap up the terrified boy on the shores of the underworld.

Surreal – the scene was out of some myth. Pancras knew that until the day he died, he would never forget this tableau: this repulsive drunk, prone on the tile; the corpse leaking essential fluid upon his own floor; the man attending him, an admixture of terror and hatred shooting forth from his eyes; and he, the bystander, the scarred one.

The paterfamilias arose, towering over Dionysius. "He is dead, you wretch." Rearing back, his spit upon the drunken man.

Pancras could only watch helplessly as the father departed, leaving the body sprawled against the doorjamb. The lad might as well have become part of the statuary. A mummy, Pancras must have died and been embalmed there on the spot. Clearly he had gazed upon the face of Medusa, for he was an unfeeling stone, observing all things but never interacting with the horror in his own home.

He heard the soft crying of the lump of sodden flesh. His uncle's hypocritical tears did nothing to raise the dead to life.

Everywhere he looked, there was death.

Fire consumes the innocent. Knives penetrate the blameless.

And the guilty keep on killing, murdering, slaughtering.

His catatonic state lasted – how long? His shock registered no steady passage of time. It may have been years for all he knew. The cadaver kept his silence, while the contrite man's tears mingled with the blood-puddle. And the world continued its incessant plunge into futility.

179

Vanity of vanity, all is vanity!

The spell was broken by the inrushing of heavily-armored men, the *cohortes urbanae*. They assessed the scene quickly and began to drag Dionysius to his feet, binding his hands behind his back with ropes and chains.

When he was well-secured and led away, to the shock of the unfeeling Pancras, two of the cohorts came to him and forced his hands behind his back, securing them as well.

"What...?" he whispered, too numb to fear. "Why?"

"Your uncle will have quite some debt to pay," one of them responded with a grim smile, forcing Pancras forward with a shove. "You will fetch a tidy sum at auction."

Unable to resist, the boy stepped over the corpse, blood staining his sandals. He left bloody footprints behind as he stepped across the threshold and into the night.

PART THREE: *House of Redemption*

So here he was. Chained to the ground, in the deepest dungeon of Rome. The moon cast a silver shaft into the prison, as life continued upon the surface of the earth. But he was no longer among the living. Cast into darkness, let the wailing and gnashing of teeth begin!

As the night wore on, Pancras began to get his wits about him, even as he shivered in the subterranean cavern. Though his flesh was chilled, his interior numbness began to thaw, and he assessed the situation.

Half of the city was dying. His uncle was a murderer. He would be sold as a slave.

It was that simple, and it was that complicated.

Slowly, slowly a fire began to build in his breast. But this was unlike the fire that he was accustomed to – no, not the fire of anxiety and fear at all. This was the fire of wrath.

How dare they! How dare his uncle commit a crime in cold blood! How dare they take him as collateral!

Still just a flicker, a mere candle-flame, but the wrath was stoked – and he knew he would not go quietly. This injustice must be repaired. For too long had the boy been a victim as things were stolen from him. No, this time he would fight back – fight back if it killed him.

His chains clinked as he drew his knees to his chest, trying to conserve precious heat. The surface of the earth baked in a sultry oven, while beneath the crust, in the depths of the underworld, there was only ice.

But within his breast, a fire grew. Candle flame turned to hearth-fire, and hearth-fire grew until it raged and burned like a pyre. Cast his dead on this interior fire, let them be consumed, and avenge…avenge all that has happened. The deaths of the innocent. The imprisonment of the guiltless. The slavery of the free man. The eternal conquering of evil. No, he will no longer go quietly. Somehow – some way – he will fight all this.

I will escape, he promised himself. I will not submit. I will rage and rage until I am free, or until they kill me – freedom from the shackles of mortality.

Leaning against the dew-dampened stone, he knew sleep would be elusive. Yet he closed his eyes and began to formulate his freedom-plan.

In that moment, he swore upon his life that he would seek freedom, no matter the cost. The furnace raged within him, consuming the old self with its fears and trepidation. No, that Pancras had been reduced to ashes. The new Pancras, standing like a phoenix in the fire, would not be a slave. He was born a free man, and, galvanizing his will, he would remain free, no matter the cost.

He had suffered much, but would suffer no more.

And then he heard the voice.

It came from beyond the waterfall of moonlight, in the opposite darkness. Singing. Singing in a place like this! Pancras was initially disgusted to hear music in the underworld, but the words were haunting somehow, a glimpse of another world that existed only in dreams.

"He emptied himself, and took the form of a slave
Being born in the likeness of men
And it was thus that he humbled himself,
Accepting even death…"

The low baritone faltered here, reduced to coughing and wheezing.

Amazed that another person dwelt unnoticed in this jail cell, Pancras paused his freedom-plans for a moment.

"That was beautiful, sir," he encouraged. "Please continue."

There was a shuffling, the scraping of metal on stone, as the man dragged himself to catch a corner of the light. Pancras could see that the man seemed ancient, withered. His beard hung down to the center of his threadbare robe. With unseeing eyes, he allowed his gaze to rest on Pancras.

"Oh, my son, my son," he intoned solemnly.

"I am sorry, but you are mistaken. I am not…"

"Oh but you are," he replied, and his voice brought peace. It began to calm the raging bonfire within the boy.

"Do you know me?"

"I see you with the spirit. You are one of the Lord's anointed, yes. Oh, he has fine plans for you, son!"

"What *Lord* are you speaking of?"

"His hand is upon you, my boy. Be not afraid. You will go far and suffer much, but all this will be redeemed."

Peace like a balm began to fill his soul, even as confusion filled his mind.

The sage cast his gaze heavenward, allowing the light to shower his face, radiant even in the darkness. "I see the Lord God bringing you through fire and tempest, out of the underworld and to the very shores of Heaven."

"But I do not believe in the gods." They were as mute as the stone from which they were carved, and equally as useless in time of need.

"The idols you have worshiped are made by human hands. But the God who formed heaven and earth, who is the Living and True…in him we live and move and have our being. Oh, how good he is! How good he is!"

His voice echoed off the stone, as the man withdrew into obscurity again.

"Who…who are you?" Pancras whispered, but the man said no more.

His words lingered on, assuaging the boy's troubled spirit. The ramblings of a lunatic could not produce such peace. No, perhaps he had been visited by a prophet.

Stillness descended upon him, and he was able to rest for a while.

~~~

His repose was interrupted by the heavy rattling of keys, followed by the creak of rusty iron hinges. A soldier descended the stairs, glowing in the moonlight.

"Boy! I have brought food," he declared plainly, without malice or kindness. He placed a loaf of something edible on the ground, with a clay cup of water. "Eat well. No one wants to purchase a starving slave."

Pancras eyed the food with hunger. He had lost track of which watch of the night it was, but he must have spent several hours underground.

In the dim shaft of light he saw the legionary's cloak flutter as he gave a kick to the old man across the cell. "And none for you, old man. We don't waste food on the dead." Turning crisply on his heel, the soldier ascended the stairs and secured the lock.

Pancras' gaze alternated between the food – for he was truly hungry – and the man lying silently on his side, his chest rasping and heaving in pain.

And in his mind's eye, he was suddenly transported back to Synnada, at his father's side as they wandered through town, searching out the poor beneath the temple awning and the alleyways. Their arms full of bread, they unloaded their gifts on these unworthy recipients, their gratitude the only repayment accepted.

Pancras shuffled across the floor, taking his repast and placing it in the center of the illuminated circle.

"Please, you may have it."

The clanking preceded the man's sorry frame crawling across the floor to the simple meal.

"May God bless you, son."

Pancras watched him consume the bread with vigor. It had been days since he had tasted food, apparently.

The meal consumed, they retreated to their corners of Hades. Pancras wished he could continue the conversation, for the peace he had received was abating somewhat, but perhaps the man did not wish the same. Instead, he lay in silence, beginning to float in and out of sleep.

Time passed. How much time, he could not say, for the shadows and light played upon the floor in disorienting patterns. At a certain point he noticed that the moonlight had begun to give way to the dawn.

Just as the morning sun peeked its head over the horizon, the gate was opened once again and another terrestrial being descended.

It was another man, dressed with the uniform of a Praetorian Guard. His spear at the ready, he hastened down and addressed the elderly prisoner.

"My deepest apologies. I arrived as soon as I could – I have had three days of service without a pause." He unloaded a leather satchel, placing it on the ground. "I was told you have not received rations. I have brought bread and cheese and wine…"

"Many thanks, Nereus," the older man replied, his voice wavering with the weakness of old age. "But fear not – this young lad has provided for my needs."

"Who?" asked the guard, turning to face Pancras.

"He is one of the anointed ones," the prophet affirmed.

The soldier named Nereus peered at him curiously, coming closer until he towered over the huddled boy.

"What is your name?" he demanded gruffly.

All of those daft dreams of rebellion against his slavery melted away in the presence of a pike.

"P...Pancras," he stuttered, seeing only the silhouette of the well-decorated veteran.

"Where are you from?"

"Synnada."

"Synnada? Where is that?"

"In Phrygia, sir."

"I see," he growled. "What is your crime?"

"I have committed no crime, sir. I am being sold to pay my uncle's debts."

"Sold to pay debts!" he echoed mockingly. "Why did you help this prisoner? Do you not know he will suffer *damnatio ad bestias* this very day?"

"I...I am sorry, sir. My father taught me to look to those less fortunate. I am sorry if I have broken a law..."

"You have broken no law. It is merely unexpected."

Pancras did not know how to respond.

"For your kindness, I invite you to partake of the food as well. But eat quickly – they will come shortly to escort you to the auction."

Nodding gratefully, he watched as the guardsman returned to the elderly man, giving him an embrace and exchanging greetings.

Pancras could only hear the final phrase: "Pray for me at the banquet feast of the lamb."

The older man nodded before the soldier ascended the stairs and was seen no more. Crawling forth, he motioned for Pancras to draw near to the feast. Gratefully they ate together in silence.

Who was this prophet from another world? he wanted to ask. What was his crime? For surely he too was the victim of injustice. No criminal could exude this kindness, or speak words that bring such peace.

But he feared to ask, for perhaps this mysterious specter was only a hallucination. Or perhaps he did not wish to discuss the intimate details of his case with a mere boy, given to bouts of depression and anger.

The meal was shared until the guards came and took Pancras away.

As he ascended on unsteady legs, his ankles and wrists bound tightly in shackles, he could hear the man call out, "Courage! The Lord God is your refuge! I will pray for you!"

And he returned to the land of the living, blinded by the heat and the sunshine.

~~~

A modest but motley crowd surrounded the scaffolding. He felt like so much livestock. At least a bull was not conscious of his lack of dignity. As the dozens of pairs of eyes appraised his flesh and health and strength, Pancras felt a bolt of shame, and wished he could hide somewhere, anywhere.

O earth, open up and swallow me! he pleaded interiorly. O sky, fall upon me and cover me!

There were two others with him – a swarthy man of African origins, lanky and heavily scarred with tribal tattoos, and a woman whose better days were behind her, with missing teeth and stringy hair testifying to a life of dissipation. Briefly Pancras wondered where Dionysius was; he had been taken to his own prison the prior night and was not present at the auction.

The man went first. In the prime of his life, he commanded a precious price. The bidding was fierce, as the auctioneer called out the rising denarii. Is a man's life worth five hundred? Six hundred? What was the price of life? Is all reduced to commerce?

Finally, at seven hundred and fifty denarii, the man was awarded to a senator's steward, who came to collect him. The man was led off, still in chains, through the crowd until he could be seen no more, lost in the pandemonium that was the Forum.

The woman did not fetch such a fine sum. People seemed reluctant to risk their money for this wench. The auctioneer, an oily man with graying temples and a smarmy attitude, wheedled the crowd incessantly, urging them to consider her advantages and overlook her flaws.

"Look at her!" he directed the crowd. "She is sturdy, accustomed to hard work! She will make a fine household servant!"

Despite her dissipation, she was a pillar of ignominy. She dared not look into the crowd for their humiliating lechery. Pancras was stung, her own disgrace covering him like a filthy cloak. She is more than a piece of flesh! he wanted to cry out.

Finally, almost reluctantly, a patron offered seventy-five denarii. Reluctantly the auctioneer released her to the older man, disappointed that she would not fetch a higher price.

Pancras was simultaneously pushed and dragged to the center of the raised platform. The glare of the crowd was tangible. He was being judged, seen as merely another faceless slave in a city swarming with them.

Quickly Pancras scanned the Forum, grateful that Daphne was nowhere to be seen.

"And this young man, of almost fourteen years, well-educated and in good health. He will be a fine catch for whatever you need – for your household, or for your personal use."

The crowd murmured its appreciation for such a fine specimen before them. Pancras could not remove his eyes from the wooden stage, a silent rage seething within him at this indignity.

"Four hundred denarii!" came a call from somewhere.

A quick rebuttal echoed forth. "Five hundred!"

The auctioneer glowed with pleasure, knowing this youth would bring in a fortune, and his commission would be fortunate indeed.

"Six hundred!"

"Seven!"

Pancras briefly glanced up to see the identity of these two competitors. One, an older man, likely a noble with his purple stripe accenting his toga, stood imperiously off to the side of the ordinary rabble, as if his station in life made him rise above the lowborn and the common.

"Eight hundred denarii!" he barked vigorously.

"Nine hundred!" came the response. Pancras was surprised to see the respondent as none other than the praetorian Nereus in full regalia, who had so generously fed him the night before.

"One thousand!" the other man reechoed, his frustration mounting at having to bid so high.

His offer echoed above the din of the crowd, who always appreciated a lively auction, even if most had no means to join in the contest.

Nereus stood across the assembled throng, scratching his chin, deep in thought. But he spoke not, and the bid stood at the exorbitant price of one thousand denarii.

"Alas, we have one thousand," crowed the auctioneer. "Do I hear any more? No? All right, then he is…"

"Fifteen hundred," Nereus exclaimed with intensity.

"By the gods, man, why do you want him so?" the nobleman declared, offended. "I did not think the Praetorians had the salary to waste on a mere youth. I fear that this is the reason our taxes are so high!"

Appreciative laugher bubbled from the crowd. Nereus' face was frozen in a stern glare.

"Do you wish to top this bid?" the auctioneer offered. "No? You are allowing this soldier to steal this prize from the tetrarch? What would Maximian think of this?"

The nobleman threw up his hands in disbelief. "He has forbidden me from breaching a thousand!" With that he wandered away, shaking his head.

Nereus navigated through the crowd, who, upon seeing the end of the auction, wandered away with disinterest. Pancras was led down the stairs to stand before his new master.

Nereus looked him over, up and down, studying with particular interest the bulla draped about his neck. Nodding to the soldier standing guard, he ordered him, "Unbind him. He is coming with me."

"Unbind him? But sir, he is liable to…"

"I trust him. Unbind him."

190

The shackles were removed, and Pancras rubbed his wrists to regain feeling.

"Come with me," his master ordered.

Pancras followed, fearful.

They quickly crossed the Forum and began ascending the Avetine Hill, to the south of the agora. Pancras was too overwhelmed to plan any escape. A mere day ago, he was living in a villa and preparing for his valediction, and now he was enslaved and destitute!

When they had left the bustle of the crowds behind and entered the relative silence of the streets, Nereus muttered, "I saved your life. Do not forget this."

"Why? Who was the other man who..."

"You are not to ask questions," Nereus commanded softly, keeping his eyes downcast. "We live in a harsh world, Pancras of Phrygia."

"This I know..." he replied, but did not elaborate.

They walked on, turning a corner and reaching a deserted alleyway. Nereus motioned for him to stop. Taking a rock from the ground, he drew an arc in the dust of the street.

Pancras gazed at it, unsure of its meaning.

Straightening up, Nereus asked gruffly, "Do you understand?"

Shaking his head, the slave-boy was uncomprehending.

"Never mind. Let us continue."

On the far side of the hill was a modest domus, off the street a bit and surrounded by a garden oasis of blooming poppies and bottle palms. It exuded peace and order, a refuge from the madness of the city. If it were not for the reality of the situation, this would be a fine place to stop for an afternoon chat, Pancras thought.

Into the house they went, stepping forth into the cooler vestibule. The closing of the door alerted the residents to the incoming personages.

"My love!" called out a female voice, followed by her appearance at the door. "I had been anxious for your safety – you had not returned as you said."

"My apologies," Nereus replied, exchanging a kiss. "I was waylaid."

"I have no doubt. And who is this young man with you?"

"Pancras of Phrygia. I will see him to his room, and then we must speak."

She rested her kind and curious eyes on him as the master and servant departed down a hallway.

Nereus drew back a curtain to reveal a small windowless alcove, barely large enough for a reed bed and a small table. "Here you shall stay. I know that you must be tired from your ordeal. Rest here a while, and when you are refreshed, you may begin your service."

Pancras nodded solemnly, and lay down gratefully on the mattress, a thin pad of hay covered in wool. Pulling a blanket over his weary body, he tried to rest, but his mind had just awoken. Like a bird that is temporarily stunned upon a collision with a window, but soon recovers its senses, Pancras was beginning to regain his wits about him. The nightmarish sequence of events that led him to this villa coalesced into a cohesive timeline.

And the fire began to resurface. He would right this wrong, to be certain. Treated like cattle! An outrage! Did they not know that he was the son of Cleonius, who answered to no one?

How? When? The escape must be planned. Where would he go? No matter – he would run until he was beyond their leviathan tentacles. Freedom sang its siren song, and he must answer or be destroyed in the process.

Humiliation burned his ears, the bonfire growing in his breast. He would not tolerate this for long. He was a freeman, not a slave. To seek after liberty was only to claim his birthright. Justice would not be denied him, for he was innocent. Yes, take Dionysius – he had taken a life, and the scales of justice would not be balanced until his uncle paid his due. But he, Pancras...what had he done to deserve this?

He refused to be cowed by the circumstances. No, he was a bird, free in his mind if not in body.

The outrage would simmer, he knew. Let it seethe, fester, smolder. Whether tomorrow or next month, it would burst into an inferno, and nothing could stop him. A mad dash for freedom was beckoning. He was unafraid to answer, come what may.

I *will* be free, he resolved. I will not be a slave forever.

But how? That will be determined once he had examined the landscape. Give it time, he told himself. The opportunity will come.

He closed his eyes, and wished that he could pray for divine assistance. But he could not be a slave to those worthless idols of wood and stone, either. They could not save his friend; they would not save him. He was alone in the world. Alone, but not helpless.

The anger roiling beneath his tranquil exterior made it impossible to find sleep. That, and the stifling humidity. Cheekily, he imagined running somewhere north, where the air had a perpetual chill and he needn't suffer any more indignity.

Voices floated down the hallway, hanging on the thick and stagnant air.

"I don't know what we're going to do with him," came the woman's voice.

The response was muffled.

"I see. Perhaps you are right. But how much did you…?"

"Fifteen hundred."

The woman's voice turned into a conspiratorial whisper. "Fifteen hundred! We cannot afford that!"

"I have some property outside the city I am prepared to sell to answer the debt," Nereus responded. "We can use him around here."

"But what do you really know about him? Can you trust him? You deal with matters of the highest sensitivity."

Silence, then indistinguishable muttering. Although he wished he didn't care, Pancras hoped that his master was giving a positive testimony of his character.

The woman began to respond, but Pancras only caught a few words. "…urchin…seen it before. He…liability we cannot afford…whole community at risk."

"Perhaps," came the response. Nereus must have been facing a different direction, as his words were clearer. "But I have a distinct feeling this is from the spirit."

"We must test every spirit," she replied. "Not all hunches are inspirations."

"Yes, but I feel that God has placed him…"

"Lower your voice! We must guard our words now."

The remainder of the conversation was uttered sotto voce, unintelligible to the boy who lay awake, wondering about the misfortunes of fate.

~~~

"Well, well! They...they told me there was another one, but I didn't know it would be a lad!"

Pancras must've dozed off, for he opened his eyes to see a strange creature peering at him from the doorway. This large man, with a cheerfully rounded face and short-cropped thinning black hair, stared at him with mirth. He wore the simple tunic of the poor, but was corpulent enough to show that he was not starving. His large ears protruded humorously, and his enlarged proboscis gave him the air of a comedic actor.

The boy rubbed his eyes wearily and rose. The air had cooled, as the day drifted into the late afternoon. He sat upon his mat, awaiting introductions.

"Name's Achilleus," said the jolly giant, in a voice unnaturally high for a man his size. "Named after the tragic hero, you know of him? Homer?"

Pancras looked at him sleepily and murmured, "Yes, I know the Iliad and Odyssey. I have read them both."

"Well, mighty fine! Mighty fine indeed! Not too many slaves know their classics! You will be of great service here!"

The boy began to chafe at the reminder of his servitude. "And may I ask you of your relations with this family?" he demanded somewhat tartly.

"I am their steward," he replied cheerfully, despite the sobriety of the topic. "I have served them happily for nine years. A fine couple, these two!"

"And you are happy about this?" Pancras verified, incredulous.

"They saved my life," he replied. "In more ways than one. I owe them everything, yes, my entire life!"

Pancras just stared. He made up his mind quickly: this man – if you could call such a creature a "man", for he looked more like a pantomime meant for children's play – was one of those poor souls, simple of mind, who needed the constant care of a patron. No one thinking aright would be happy about such a lot in life.

"Come, Pancras," he instructed, proffering his hand and helping him rise. "I will show you around. We will be working together to keep this homestead operating smoothly!"

Reluctantly, Pancras rose and followed him through the villa.

It was not a large domus; perhaps a third of the size of his own. His own? He had forgotten for a moment that those blood-stained floors now belonged to someone else…his uncle's creditors or the state, he knew not which.

They wandered the halls and peered into the rooms. Achilleus offered commentary on their various duties: dusting and cleaning, cooking and serving. Running errands. Keeping the larder well-stocked. At times, accompanying Nereus on his journeys. Patching torn tunics, fetching water from the public fountain. Carrying the accoutrements for the daily visit to the baths. Sharpening and shining the weaponry. Tending the garden, which was laden with midsummer vegetables.

"And as you are literate," Achilleus concluded, showing the way into the small library stocked with scrolls, "You will serve as Nereus' secretary."

"He needs a secretary?" Pancras asked.

"Nereus? Yes of course! There is a whole garrison under his command! Yes, our master is well-respected! A fine man!"

"*You* seem to respect him."

"Respect him? I love him. He is a brother to me."

Pancras was taken aback. He would never have considered the four men who served at his old domus to be anything but the underlings they were. No, he did not approve of the cruelty with which Dionysius treated them, but neither would he treat them as equals. They were slaves – nothing more, nothing less.

"How did you arrive at this position?"

Suddenly his open face began to darken. "That, my friend, is for another day. Let us speak only of the present, not of the past."

Yes, agreed – Pancras had no desire to repeat his own harrowing journey to this point.

They wandered into the kitchen, where they began to prepare a simple dinner for the couple. Bread and wine, cheese and sausage. Achilleus sent the boy out to the garden to pick some cabbages and cucumbers for the evening meal.

From the garden behind the domus, Pancras surveyed his environment at leisure. It would be difficult to scale the fence, as tall as two men. There seemed to be no means of escape from the yard. Although it would be easy enough to walk out the front door of the house, Achilleus had been sure to show him the considerable arsenal of swords and halberds, pikes and battle-axes that stood at the ready. How could he escape, then?

He bent down to pluck a couple cucumbers from their vines. When he straightened up, he could see through the open window his fellow slave, humming a cheerful tune, a smile on his face.

How could anyone rejoice in servitude? Clearly this Achilleus fellow was a simpleton, or just plain crazy. Pancras recalled seeing the insane drifting along the corners of the Forum. Sometimes they ranted and raved, sometimes there was a quiet moroseness about them, but at times they laughed and smiled an empty grin. Pity was the only way to deal with such fools, who had no wits between their ears.

But Achilleus seemed different; he did not seem to be among the witless. His joy seemed more than even a quiet resignation to his state; no, there was something profound about his happiness.

Pancras shook his head in disbelief, and headed inside.

The meal preparation completed, Achilleus rang a bell inside the triclinium and the family came from their various locations to eat. Nereus and his wife reclined upon the couches as Achilleus and Pancras brought out the dishes, spreading them on a low oaken table.

"Thank you," Nereus said, presenting a grudging smile. Once the dishes had been served, Pancras returned to the kitchen to await their further command.

"Where are you going?" called out his wife.

He froze. Was there an unwritten rule that he transgressed?

"Come, recline with us."

Turning, he saw that Nereus' wife was gesturing to an unoccupied couch flanking the table. Achilleus himself had sprawled upon another one, and was freely helping himself to the repast.

"But...but I am your slave..."

"Come, Pancras. You are welcome here."

With some reluctance, he came back to recline at table. He knew he should be grateful, but this was unprecedented! Slaves do not share the table with their master! The stratified society made that clear; everyone knew their place. This was a social convention shattered!

Suspicion nagged at him – for what purpose would they include him in this meal?

"I apologize that I have not formally introduced myself," she began. "I am Aquila."

"Yes, Domina," he replied, using the respectful form.

"You have come a long way."

This was true on so many levels! "I am from Phrygia, though I have lived in Rome for three years."

"Yes, I knew your uncle," Nereus added. "He kept my men well-fed. I owe him a debt of gratitude."

Although he did not want to peer into the mouth of Sheol, his curiosity prevailed, and he replied, "Do you have news of him?"

He shook his head. "No, sadly. I do not know where they have taken him."

Did he miss him? Pancras could not tell amongst the jumble of emotions intertwined in his heart.

Aquila brought the conversation to brighter topics. "You have been in Rome for three years – and yet you still have an accent! I suppose you cannot remove the provinces from the soul."

"I do miss Phrygia," he admitted. And he missed his father, but he needn't add that.

"Have you studied during your time in Rome?"

"Yes, with Master Ludinium. Tomorrow would have been the graduation ceremonies."

She penetrated him with a glance of compassion. "Ah, my sorrows for you. But we know of Master Ludinium's excellent reputation. It is providential, for Nereus was in need of someone to handle his correspondence."

"And his debts!" Achilleus jested, prompting a gruff laugh from his master.

What was this? The help is free to offer witticisms to their superiors? Unheard of! Pancras continued to sit immobile, unsure how to react. All of his presuppositions of slavery had been shattered and reshuffled.

Aquila noticed his discomfort. "Please, Pancras, eat. You will need your strength."

Mechanically he tore off a piece of bread. He did not even notice it as it entered his mouth and was masticated.

"My dear, tomorrow I need my tunics fulled," Nereus grumbled. "Perhaps you can give them to Pancras to take to the fuller?"

"Yes, of course."

Turning his attention to his slave – or was he a slave? Perhaps he was merely the surrogate son they never had – Nereus asked, "Tell me about your homeland. In all my assignments I have never made it that far east."

Guardedly, Pancras began to describe his homestead, the farm he had enjoyed, the games he played with his friends. There was no need to delve into personal details; a mere travelogue would suffice.

"Ah, how I long to see the near East!" he replied wistfully, his gravelly voice not losing its roughness. "I have been all over the north country on campaign, mostly in Gaul and Iberia. A certain charm, doubtless. But I long for the warmth and the open fields of Phrygia. I have heard the sun casts a sheen on that land unlike anywhere else in the Empire."

"But certainly my native Corinth gleams finer than any city of the East," Achilleus added.

"I have never been there, but you should have seen the vineyards of the south of Gaul!"

The conversation continued pleasantly, with every member free to add their own thoughts. Unlike the omnipresent tension during his meals with his volatile uncle, there was an ease here, as the evening flowed like a river lazily meandering through a field. Pancras did not speak unless he was directly questioned; no, he was occupied trying to discern the interpersonal dynamics hidden beneath their words.

Yes, he could see that Achilleus had a great fondness for his employer. Did Nereus feel the same bond of kinship for the steward? That was hard to determine, for the soldier had a perpetual scowl on his countenance, although his words were kind. Perhaps his eyes had seen things he wished he hadn't, and his troubled memory did not permit peaceful sleep. If so, then he would not be too unlike the lonely boy who, affixed to his seat, was no more than a statuary ornament in the middle of the pleasant conversation.

Aquila seemed the ideal of a matron. Her smile demure, her words a balm, she offered refuge from the harshness of the world. She reminded him of Daphne –

And a pang of loss pierced him straight through, sharper than any weapon in Nereus' arsenal.

He steeled his will once again to flee – for there was one waiting for him, sharing a mutual desire to be *together* forever.

"…used to bring me back tokens from that land," Aquila was saying, adding her part to the conversation. But she cut herself off quickly, and peered at Pancras.

No! Was his pain visible on his face? He quickly tried to flash a weak smile, picking at the boiled cabbage.

"Pancras, you are still reeling from everything that has happened today," she soothed. "It has been a great deal to absorb. But please know that you are welcome here."

He suddenly became aware of his utter exhaustion.

"You have lost much in your life," she continued, "but I believe that it will all work out for good."

Pancras could only stare at the floor, still aching from a pain unnamed.

By mutual consent, the meal was over.

~~~

He had just lain down when the dance of an oil-lamp flame approached.

Nereus drew back the curtain to behold the boy prone on his mat. With characteristic gruffness, he said, "Pancras, tomorrow we shall set about purchasing needed items for you – a second tunic, personal items. Rest well, now. You are safe here."

He began to turn away, but had an afterthought. "Also, if you would be so kind, please remove your bulla. We do not keep the old gods in this household."

Pancras' hand unthinkingly gripped the idol. He had been able to cling to his father's memory this long – would this be the final separation?

Tremulously, he stammered, "If...if you please, Dominum, I...I wish to keep it."

"No, it does not please me. Hand it over."

"But sir!" he exclaimed, a terror coming over him. "This is the only memento I have from my father! Please do not take it from me!" He knew it was childish, but he could barely contain himself.

They stared at one another for a tense moment. Nereus looked at him queerly, but silently withdrew his hand.

"As you wish. You have been through enough these past two days. Rest in peace this night."

The curtain flowed back, and Pancras was left alone in the dark. He clutched the amulet as the old anxieties crept back into his heart.

~~~

Dragged, unwillingly, into another day, he departed after a brief breakfast with his arms full of rank clothing, ready for the fuller's mill. They trusted him enough to perform this errand alone, and thus the fire of escape burned hotter than the sultry southern wind.

He knew the way; he had often passed by the shop, across the Forum and down one of the many urban veins that led away from the great heart of Rome. His eyes searched for a route that would take him anywhere that was not here. He would flee to Tivoli, perhaps – he knew the route – and live by gleaning the standing wheat along the way. No! He would go back to Ostia, for the water was beautiful and tranquil and no one would find him there. He would learn to fish! Yes, he could apprentice as a fisherman and make a fine living, then after a year or two come back and take Daphne, who will be waiting for him. Hard work did not scare him, nor the loneliness of exile. Freedom was the greater goal – to claim his birthright as a free man, to find his own justice from this absurd slavery. Whatever the cost.

His overflowing load, safely stored in a carpetbag, would first find its way to the cleaner's. Then – he would be gone, leaving the sorrows of this city in the past.

Finding the mill, he quickly deposited the tunics, promising the proprietor that Achilleus would return two days hence to retrieve the garments. Then back into the streets, where he wandered north, away from his prison.

Prison? Well, perhaps not *that*. They did show him remarkable kindness. For this he was grateful. His ache for freedom was not because of any personal animosity towards Nereus. A kind and generous master is still a master. And Pancras would be no slave!

He took the stroll leisurely, reasoning that haste would arouse suspicion from onlookers. It was as if he was seeing the city with new eyes – these streets he used to roam so carefree with Decian and Antonius – oh, Antonius! – those days seemed like a lifetime ago. So much water had passed beneath Milvian Bridge since then; so much sand had fallen in the hourglass of life, never to return.

The alleyway wound around a sharp bend stalked by angular insulae, blotting out the morning sun. As he made the turn, his eyes locked with a most unfortunate fellow.

Standing a few paces ahead was the auctioneer who had sold him yesterday. Although absorbed in a conversation with another man, the auctioneer by chance looked up immediately as Pancras rounded the corner. Their eyes met, and recognition dawned on both faces.

In a panic, Pancras turned and fled.

The man pursued him with surprising agility for his age. "Halt! Halt, lad!"

But Pancras paid no heed. His legs sought freedom, but his mind was terrified of the consequences. Would it be the gallows for him if he were caught? The games? In that case, he must run forever, that he would never be captured again.

The pursuit was evenly matched, however, and Pancras could gain no advantage as he fled through the narrow streets, packed with more and more people as he neared the Forum. He dodged and weaved, narrowly missing a cart overladen with wool.

Just as he whirled around another corner, his sandal caught on an upturned cobblestone and he heard a rip echo through the street. A quick glance down confirmed that the leather straps had indeed burst.

The pause allowed the auctioneer to close the distance and tackle him to the ground. A crowd had gathered to see the tumult, including a couple urban cohorts on duty, in full regalia with lances drawn.

"I know you!" the auctioneer declared as he struggled to his feet. "You were sold at auction yesterday, were you not? What are you doing on this side of town – and fleeing?"

Pancras coughed the dust from his lungs. "No, no!" he protested to the crowd. "I am not seeking escape. I am merely running an errand for my master."

"What errand?"

"I brought his tunics to the fuller's mill."

"The fuller's mill is a stadia south of here, and your master's house is southerly still."

"I know, but I...I...I was lost, seeking to return home," he lied.

"We shall see if Nereus accepts such an excuse," concluded the auctioneer. He bent down and lifted Pancras' sleeve, disgusted to see that he had not yet been tattooed. "He must keep better watch over his slaves. Letting them wander freely like this!" Addressing the cohort, he told them, "Take this ruffian to the home of Nereus – you know the way."

They nodded solemnly, dragging the boy to his feet and urging him onward with the prick of the lance.

~~~

The door swung open, and judgment day dawned.

"Dominum! Tribune Nereus!" they called out into the vacant aula.

From his study, Nereus appeared, approaching. "You summon me?"

"This is your slave?"

"Yes, purchased yesterday."

"We caught him fleeing, near the…"

"I was not fleeing!" Pancras shouted, panic-stricken. "I merely lost my way!"

"He claims to have been running an errand, but was approaching the Servian walls to the north. Shall we take care of the lout?"

"No, that will not be necessary," he answered brusquely, his face betraying no emotion. "I shall take him hence. I thank you for your service."

They nodded solemnly, and with a bow departed for the streets.

Nereus, the imposing Nereus, the decorated soldier, commander of legions, struck fear into Pancras' heart without a word. His even gaze, serious and solemn, seemed to read his soul.

"I…I completed your errand, and was seeking to return but was unfamiliar with that part of Rome," he stumbled, each word piercing his heart with its lies. "All of the lanes looked the same, and the alleyways…"

"You understand the penalty for a slave caught fleeing."

Yes, he knew. The Forum was the site of many a public flogging. One time he was visiting a tavern with his uncle, and was served by a crippled slave who bore an iron

206

collar about his neck with the name of his owner. At the time, young Pancras thought the man looked much like a mongrel dog, whipped into submission.

Pancras could barely stand and stare into those unsmiling eyes, towering over him by two hands' height. He was a liar, a fugitive, a wretch.

"I trusted you," Nereus growled.

"I didn't..." he started, but felt he was not being believed.

"I had thought you possessed an uncommon decency."

The shame was more painful than the slavery. Please, apply the stripes! But withhold the dishonor!

The silence stretched on, as Nereus appeared to be thinking over the consequences.

"Please, Dominum," Pancras pleaded, on the verge of tears. "I shall not disappoint you again."

Shaking his head sternly, the man muttered, "Mercy triumphs over judgment. I shall show you mercy this time, for your youth and indiscretion. But know what awaits such a transgression in the future."

Pancras dared not raise his head.

"Aquila," his master called, "summon Achilleus. Pancras' foot is injured."

The foot that lost the sandal had sustained bloody scrapes along the cobblestone.

Aquila came from the kitchen. "Achilleus is at the market." She looked at the contrite boy, seeing his injury. "Ah, Pancras. Come with me. I shall wash your feet."

Taking him by the shoulder, she led him out into the courtyard, seating him on a marble bench growing warm in the sun. Fetching a basin and pitcher and towel, she knelt at his feet and gently began the ritual cleansing. She made herself the slave of a slave – what indignity! Mud and blood flowed into the basin, along with his shame and corruption.

She only looked up when she felt the hot tears raining down upon her hands.

"Why? Why are you kind to me?" he choked out, overwhelmed with mercies undeserved.

A smile was his only answer.

"I *was* running away. I was seeking to flee."

"Yes, I know. And Nereus knows as well."

"Then why did he not punish me? I deserve it! You have shown me nothing but kindness, and in my ingratitude I betrayed your trust."

A breeze brushed the trees, whisking away the heat and the pride.

Aquila chose her words carefully. "Nereus…was once a slave as well. As was I. Not as we think of slavery, for it was no earthly master. But a slave nonetheless. And we were liberated by a mercy unearned."

"What kind of master?"

"Every man is a slave to his own humanity. His lusts, his greed, his pride make for a more cruel master than man could ever be."

"I do not understand."

"I do not expect you to, for every man thinks himself free. But allow me to ask – when you lied to Nereus there, were you acting in freedom?"

"Yes. No – well, I am not sure."

"You were a slave to fear. Fear of punishment. And every man is a slave to those elemental forces that carry us along this life. Fear of death, force of emotion, our animal desires. These things rule over us."

His uncle and the wine that was his master – and understanding began to dawn.

"Yes, I have seen such things," he replied, as she dried off his foot with the towel. "Men can act as animals, dependent on wine or pleasures to carry them through the day. But how did you find freedom?"

She did not respond as, dutifully, she wrapped his foot in strips of cloth to staunch the bleeding.

But Pancras would not accept a silent reply. He needed to know – he *ached* to know. His tears long dried, there was the emerging realization that he himself had been a slave to his fear of death. How could one overcome such slavery? Was freedom possible?

"Please, tell me," he urged quietly.

A smile greeted him as she searched his eyes, looking for – something. "If you prove yourself trustworthy, then I will share the secret knowledge."

"You wish to keep me a slave, then!"

"No, I wish for you to be free, interiorly, in the province of the soul," she gently whispered, placing a tranquil hand on his heart. "But not every man is ready to receive this freedom. It can do great damage to those who are unprepared."

"I am prepared!"

She rose, her tranquility never leaving her face. "Then show us."

He nodded, solemnly, knowing what he must do.

~~~

And so his captivity began in earnest. He was slowly, slowly making peace with it. The days merged into one another as an artist blends colors on a palette, until they were all a blur. With each passing day, the fire within his chest quieted a bit more, replaced by a subtle peace. This was not how he would have written the script of his life, but somehow it was working out all right.

The kindly overtures helped to assuage the shame of being a slave. Slave – that word did not describe his servitude. No, he was treated as a member of a family. One with an excessive amount of chores, perhaps – including the unpleasant ones such as emptying the chamber pots, which he abhorred – but with the privileges of a friend. The hidden smiles they offered him; the encouraging words, the invitations to eat together, the polite questions about his health and background – these genuine touches of humanity lessened the humiliation of his station.

Duty called Nereus away frequently. Galerius the tetrarch was coming shortly, after brokering an uneasy peace in his campaigns of Nisibis and Persia. Pancras could not understand the full workings of Roman politics and military might, but the shrapnel he could gather from Nereus' straightforward conversations with Achilleus informed him of tension in the Empire. Oh well, the war-machine marches onward.

But in a city as diverse as Rome, a significant faction would oppose the tetrarch's presence – and Nereus was often called upon to organize security for the entourage. He would arrive home late at night, or at times as the dawn was breaking, after a long shift. His sweat-soaked leather breastplate would be drawn off and deposited by the entryway, for Pancras to come and clean it. At times, his sword would be unhitched and left there as well. The boy hated this – for it meant that the sword was covered in blood, spilt from an enemy of Rome. Could he find it in his patriotic heart to hate these enemies, killed by the blade he held in his hands?

Nevertheless, at home, Nereus was the paragon of virtue. He brought nothing of his personal tragedies and memories to his wife and servants. But his eyes were always hard, and his face was carved from granite. At times, Pancras would wonder what these eyes had seen.

While going about his routine, Pancras' mind would frequently wander to his friends, a world away from this quiet villa. Was Decian recovering from his illness? Did Daphne ever wonder where he was? It was in these quiet moments, sweeping the cobblestones or pruning the shrubbery, that wave after wave of sorrow would wash over him, threatening to drag him away to the shores of the underworld. But then he would hear a stitch of song from Aquila, echoing from the far reaches of the house, or would see a lark soaring above the parapet, and the desperate homesickness would abate a bit.

It was one such day as this, a bright and cloudless day that mingled the warmth of late summer with the crisp breezes of autumn, that he was sent out to draw water from the public fountain. For all of their moderate luxury, Nereus had never tapped into the public water supply, and it fell to the servants to fetch their daily usage, much to the boy's dismay.

He came sloshing back with the water in twin wooden buckets, suspended by rope handles. It was an exhausting task, done twice daily, and his forearms screamed for mercy. But the water slapping up his thighs called him back to earlier days…

It was a similar day, clear and warm. The fields of Synnada glowed gold in the afternoon sun. It must have been the year before his father passed, for he stood on the banks of the Kali in the glory of manhood. They were

211

driving the cattle through the stream, bringing them to market.

But Pancras had not been paying much attention. The little stream was insignificant to men, but to a boy it was an ocean, a vast playground. He saw a section where the bank receded into a pool, and without hesitating, leapt into it, plunging to the depths.

He resurfaced to see his father splashing water at him. Ducking and laughing, Pancras exchanged the gesture. A few more splashes completed the battle. Thoroughly soaked and laughing, Cleonius turned his attention back to his heifers.

But Pancras was taken in by the beauty. He tossed a handful of water into the air, noting that they separated into a thousand diamonds upon their return to earth. A thousand reflections of the sun.

Laughing, Cleonius asked, "What are you doing, my son?"

"See, Father! See how it is beautiful!"

"It is like you have never seen water before!"

"Never like this!"

Cleonius cupped his hands and dipped them in the river. It was clear as crystal that day, unlike those days when the water was colored as the earth.

"Let this water cleanse your soul," he intoned, pouring the water on the crown of his son's head.

Pancras felt a strange regeneration within. It was as if his words had effected what they symbolized. "Can water do that?"

"Water can cleanse all things," his father responded cryptically.

"It can cleanse my face!" the boy declared, being silly. He splashed handful after handful over his face, his hair, his shoulders.

"You do not remember it, but I recall clearly your *lustratio*. We washed you in water then to cleanse more than your body."

"Tell me about it!" he said with eager dancing eyes.

"You were nine days old. Your grandfather brought you to the temple priests, who offered sacrifice on your behalf. You were as yet unnamed, but we could not resist naming you Pancras, for you were alert and grabbed on to everything! You would grip at the collar of my robes, holding on as your lifeline. But if anything else came into your sight – a shiny trinket, a cup, a housefly – you would reach out and grab it.

"But that day in the Temple, after the sacrifices, we ritually washed you in water before clothing you in the bulla. That *lustratio* absolved you from all wrongdoing." The father looked impishly at his son as they climbed the riverbank, trailing their herd. "Looks like it is time to do it again!"

"Why! What wrong have I done?"

His father laughed. "Oh, Pancras. All of mankind is stained; there has never been a perfect man."

"But what about you? You never do wrong."

He thought for a moment. "I try to avoid it, but I am not perfect. At times, I am too harsh with you or with our employees. In my interior life, my thoughts are sometimes filled with judgment or anger."

Interior life? Pancras did not understand the concept at the time, trudging across the plains – although the lad trudging back to the Roman villa was beginning to grasp it.

213

They had walked along in silence for a moment. Pancras the boy, the innocent one, before the tragedies that stole his life from him, was ponderous.

"So can we still be cleaned?" he asked his father. "After we do wrong?" For he had many things to be cleaned from.

Dusty scratches from their sandals filled the empty air.

"Yes, I have hope that one day all things will be restored."

At this point the memory faded to black. But Pancras took solace from those words. Years later, they still rang with hope. A hope, he earnestly believed, that would not disappoint.

The intense longing began arising again, the incompleteness that he felt that day along another river, with his *together*.

And he let it rise over him, wreathe him in its obscure depths. Someday he would find that which his heart called out to. It was more than missing his friends or his father. Rather, he was lacking a part of himself.

~~~

"I fear that Galerius is on the march again."

The wine on his lips had loosened them. He looked troubled.

"Will not Diocletian rein him in? He has no use for such bloodshed," Achilleus rebounded.

"Most certainly *he* has no use for it," Nereus replied. "But Galerius has acquired the taste for blood. He will not rest until the earth has soaked up every last drop of every enemy of Rome."

"These are dark times, Nereus."

"Damn this quadrumvirate. Damn it to the very pits of Sheol. I long for the days of yore."

"One tyrant or four?"

"No matter. It is all the same for common man."

The other man took a draught, noting Aquila's perceptive silence. "And worse for men like us. Will you campaign with him again?"

"I doubt I will have a choice."

Pancras took longer than necessary to light the oil lamps. Dusk settled earlier these days, necessitating the artificial light. The conversation offered a fascinating window into the cesspool of Roman politics, and Pancras was riveted but wished to appear to be ignoring it.

"What is his purpose for this visit?" Achilleus asked.

"To stir up trouble, no doubt. The official documents from Milan state that it is to investigate Nummius. There have been rumors, you know."

"Yes, but the *praefectus* did not misappropriate those funds."

"Of this we are both certain, but Galerius needs an excuse to throw the city into chaos."

"I doubt there will be rebellions this time."

"Perhaps not. But Rome is full of factions. The very air grows more tumultuous by the day."

"You see things that most men would tremble before."

"It is not the seeing that troubles me. It is where my sword must land that causes me anxiety. For he who lives by the sword will die by the sword."

"If that is the case, better to cast down your sword..."

"If my sword is cast down, it shall be my neck that receives it."

"Is it better to receive blows than to give them?"

"The time is coming when we will *all* receive blows."

"Then let us be found faultless on that day. No man will be spared in this quagmire of Roman intrigue."

Nereus stared at the floor in response.

"Whatever comes, you are not alone," Aquila added, resting her hand on his clasped palm.

He nodded, setting his jaw. "This I know. But you have heard what they did in Nicomedia."

"We walk in the footsteps of the *hagioi*."

The holy ones? Pancras paused for a moment to ponder this. The mention of Nicomedia triggered his heart to pound – it was not far from his home in Phrygia. What happened in that city?

"Bloody footsteps they are."

"Nevertheless, they lead to the banquet."

Nereus readjusted himself on the seat. They drank their libations in silence.

Finally the soldier spoke. "I hear they are bringing the whole retinue. This means cloth from the East!"

Aquila laughed and gently slapped him. "I have enough cloth, thank you!"

Achilleus added with a smile, "But if you find a hairpiece, please save it for me!"

Not even Pancras could resist a laugh, in secret with his back turned as he pretended to fiddle with a wick.

"I shall not go looking for such things!" Nereus declared, a rare smile breaking forth. It faded as quickly as it shone. "In fact, I shall seek to avoid the pomp entirely. The deadly breath of contagion arises from such splendor."

"But surely you are stronger than that."

Nereus, the man whose sword had slain its thousands, gazed soberly at his wife. "Who among us can withstand the flaming arrows of the enemy? There will be more than cloth and ivory in such a procession."

Achilleus murmured his agreement, and Pancras was left to wonder.

Suddenly, Nereus addressed him. "Enough of this talk. You! Boy! Come here."

The startled lad obeyed.

"We must not speak of such darkness. Come, you must know some poetry. Recite some for us, amuse us."

Their smiles were encouraging, but this was unexpected! His mind emptied all of its contents, their whereabouts unknown.

"Come now, Nereus," his wife reproached. "We have made him nervous. Pancras, recline with us. We shall *all* share poetry. Achilleus, surely you have committed your namesake to memory?"

"But of course, dear." And he began:

Sing, O goddess, the anger of Achilles,
That brought countless ills upon the world.
Many a brave soul did it send hurrying down to Hades,
Many a hero did it yield a prey to dogs.

How familiar did this sound to Pancras! Once again he was a boy, lying on the goatskin rug beside the hearth, as his father echoed these same words.

Now here, in an obscure villa in a fading city, he heard them again with new ears. The cadences, the rhythms, the undulating Greek words brought an unexpected comfort.

A few more verses passed his ears, and Pancras began to sail away to Troy with the great hero. A minor jealousy arose in his heart for this fictional man. To play the hero in a grand epic – was this not the dream of every boy? And man, for that matter.

The light patter of applause brought him back to Rome.

"Ah, I never tire of it," Nereus murmured contentedly. "Brings me back to boyhood."

In the silence that followed, Pancras summoned the courage to speak.

"I recall a poem."

"Please, proceed!" Nereus encouraged.

The boy stood, noting their expectant eyes. His heart thundered, at once a performer on a stage and a member of the family. With a heavy breath he began:

They fashioned a tomb for you, holy and high one,
Cretans, always liars, evil beasts, idle bellies.
But you are not dead: you live and abide forever,
For in you we live and move and have our being.
For even a tomb, King, of you
They made, who never died, but ever shall be.

The silence following the recitation was unnerving. Why was this not well-received?

"Epimenides. *Cretica*. Eight centuries ago," he explained.

Furtive glances danced between the three, inexplicable.

Crumpling on the seat, he wondered what offence he committed.

"That was very...powerful," Aquila offered, a nervous smile that was clearly pasted upon with effort.

"Surely you have heard it before," he replied. "It was one of my father's favorite..."

"Yes, a line or two sounds familiar," came the brusque interruption from the paterfamilias. "Who is this Epimenides?"

Pancras squeezed his mind for the hidden dew of memory. "I believe...I believe he was from Crete. A philosopher. There were many legends about him, but not much history."

"And of whom does he speak in this poem?"

"I think it was of Zeus, who..."

"I see," he concluded sharply. "Very interesting, indeed. I should like to study this philosopher-poet further. It sounds as if he has much to say to our time."

"Did I speak wrongly? I only meant to..."

Abruptly rising, Nereus concluded the evening. "I believe the hour is late, and we ought to retire. Thank you for the amusement, Pancras. I shall see you all on the morrow."

Bewildered, Pancras did not initially rise but waited until the other three had departed. Aquila offered him another thin smile behind her husband's back before she extinguished the lamps, and the house echoed in the vacant darkness.

~~~

Tension subtly slipped into their peaceful household. Nereus' countenance was lined with an unspoken anxiety. Doubtless the impending visit of the tetrarch weighed upon him, and such unease spilled out from his taciturn mind into the very stones of the house.

Pancras busied himself as best as he was able, trying to stay out of the way to ease the burden.

It was on one such day that he found himself with a cloth rag, wiping down the library. It was not very extensive – perhaps twelve or fifteen scrolls, residing in sturdy wooden racks. A desk bordered the distant wall, strewn with quills and inkwells. A series of blank papyri stood upright in an urn. Two clay oil lamps hung suspended from the ceiling, swaying gently in the breeze that wafted from the open window.

From disuse, the office had gathered a significant coating of dust. He wiped the desk, and then planned to extract each scroll separately and give it a thorough cleansing.

The first one extracted, he sat upon the stool at the desk to dust it. But holding such a prized artifact in his hand excited a curiosity long dormant within him...

How long had it been since he had nourished his mind! He never thought he would miss the days of old, when his daily task involved the Pythagorean theorem and the recitation of Ovid! School had been such a burden when he was a pupil; but now he longed to know what sort of knowledge-treasures were contained in this parchment.

A quick glance to the door confirmed his suspicions – he was alone. Was this permitted? He did not know; they had never discussed it.

But his heart beat hard, knowing that he possessed in his hands a portal to another world. For some reason beyond comprehension, he felt that there was a power in these words, a power that would be unleashed if he read on.

With trembling fingers he undid the twine, ears like a mouse for its predator. Hearing nothing, he unrolled it and peered at the first words.

KATA MARKOS

According to Mark.

A strange opening, he thought, but not unknown in the ancient world. So this was an account of some event according to a man named Mark. His Greek was rusty from disuse; he would have to focus hard to interpret these words.

The scroll was lowered a bit more until the first line became visible.

The beginning of the good news of Jesus the Christ, the son of God.

Footsteps drew near.

With haste he wrapped up the scroll and began to tie it, his hands fumbling badly as his eyes locked on the doorway, fearful.

Suddenly Achilleus appeared in the entrance. His face betrayed shock and fear.

"Pancras! What have you seen?"

The lad sought for a convincing alibi. "I was…I was trying to help…clean up the scrolls. I took this one out for dusting, and the wrapping fell off, and…"

Achilleus crossed the room in two long strides, his knobby knees stretching out beneath the toga. With a quick swipe, he appropriated the scroll, deftly securing it and giving it a fierce shove into the rack.

"Danger here, boy!" he cried out. It was not in anger, no – it was something more primal, more raw.

"I'm…I'm sorry, I didn't know."

Achilleus wiped his hand across his brow and heaved a heavy sigh. "No, no, it's all right. We are all on edge."

"I have perceived it, too. Why is Nereus so concerned? Is it Galerius' visit?"

The man nodded reluctantly. "Yes, yes it is."

"Why?"

A shake of the head was his only response. Clearly it was something he did not wish to discuss.

But Pancras was not content with such a response. He rose and followed the steward out of the room. "And why is there danger in those scrolls? What sort of *gnosis* is contained within?"

"I cannot tell you. The less you know, the less you will have to deny."

"Come now," he replied, impetuously. He would no longer live in these shadows of ignorance! "Knowledge cannot cause such harm."

Achilleus wheeled around, a rare frown upon his face. His ridiculous features were made more ridiculous still by his attempt at sternness, and Pancras had to stifle a laugh.

"Let me tell you a parable, Pancras. Once there was a man and a woman who lived in paradise. They had everything they ever needed, and were perfectly happy. They only had one requirement for everything to stay perfect: not to eat a cursed apple which hung from a tree. But a serpent entered their garden, telling pretty lies that kindled their curiosity. Oh, the serpent told them that they would not die, no, they would become like gods if they ate that fruit! The thirst for knowledge was too great, and they reached out their hands to that wicked tree."

"Then what happened?"

"And the ancient curse descended upon the human race."

"Hah! A fable. Nothing more than a myth."

"Truer than you or I could ever know. Have you ever seen something you wish you could unsee?"

An image of crucifixes, rows of condemned men, blood and pus and befoulment disfiguring their dignity.

Achilleus read him astutely. "And the scrolls in that room would inflict those sufferings upon us – you and me alike."

"But they spoke of good news."

"Surely you know by now that men hate the light."

This idea – this concept – this thought…it called to mind a certain curly-haired friend, and wounds reopened that would bleed interminably.

As he watched Achilleus turn away, understanding slowly dawned upon the slave-boy. Dread washed over him. Dread…and a sort of peace that he could not yet articulate.

~~~

The following day, the lad and his steward were busying themselves by shining the considerable collection of weaponry. Out in the pleasant courtyard, they used a paste of wood ash and water to scrub the metal faces until they shone and reflected their own faces.

"Achilleus, you have never told me how you came to be in the service of Nereus," the boy began. "You promised me the story!"

Achilleus was totally absorbed in a particularly difficult corner of the halberd. Or at least pretended to be.

Pancras allowed the silence to stretch on before urging, "Please?"

With a sigh, Achilleus replied, "Your persistence drives me mad, you know?"

The boy grinned at him, and Achilleus returned it.

"As you wish, boy. I have known Nereus for many, many years. We served together in the campaign against Gaul. A pair of brothers-at-arms, were we."

"You were in the Praetorian Guard?"

"No, my boy. Not exactly. I was a legionary, as was he. He rose quickly in the ranks, but not I. No, we have taken different paths. But in Gaul we were equals. I had joined the legion to rise above my station – my father was a poor tenant farmer. A very few potatoes and chickens to call his own, on a rocky crag of land. We had very little, and I wanted a better life. So I joined the military.

"But he! No, he was from better stock. His father was a senator in the old Rome – back before..." – he glanced around to make sure no interlopers could take his treasonous words – "before that bastard Diocletian took the throne. He joined because, as the second son, he would not inherit the homestead. Oh, he would gather a tidy sum for his inheritance, but the farm would not be his. His brother still lives there, a fine plot of land outside the city walls, the ancestral heritage.

"We met in Gaul, as part of the Eighth Legion of Augusta, keeping the *pax Romana*. And it was quite a challenge! For those Gauls were a feisty lot! They were more Gallican than Roman; almost once each moon we would be called in to subdue a riot here, a rebellion there. Never an end to the action. When we were not fighting, we were mobilizing for yet another campaign.

"But there came a time when I was sickened by all the bloodshed. What was I doing? These hands slew a hundred men. My fellows took pride in the crimson stains on their tunics; I was disgusted by it. It is an unnerving thing to look into the eyes of your fellow man as your sword disembowels him. Perhaps my fellow legionaries treated them as subhuman, but I knew these men had wives and children and homes.

"I cast down my sword at the foot of my centurion one day, declaring that I would no longer fight. Now, understand, this is usually a death sentence. I had sworn my *sacramentum* – I still owed the Empire another two years of service. But I had a fine centurion, yes! A finer man I have never worked beneath. He had an uncommon compassion, and he offered to allow me to serve as a medic. I gratefully accepted.

"It was in the battle outside of Argentoratum – I shall never forget that city – that I was captured by the Gauls. What a miserable time! Seeing as I was unarmed, they took me prisoner instead of running the sword through me immediately. I was made sport of for several days, scourged, starved – I know, hard to believe, with this belly! – and I was fearful for my life.

"One night I was chained to a tree, outside of the camp. I could see small fires dotting the landscape, as the conversation of men floated at a distance. But in the flickering firelight, I saw a man dressed in the standard of the Eighth Legion, gesturing wildly. I could not hear his words, but some sort of exchange was taking place. One of the Gauls came over to me after a while and, loosening the chains, and led me to the man.

"It was Nereus. He had paid for my freedom out of his own inheritance."

Pancras became aware that he had not moved in several minutes, enraptured by the story. Hastily returning his attention to the sword in his hand, he continued the scrubbing, amazed at what he heard.

Achilleus, for his part, laid down his polearm and retrieved a spear to clean.

A bustle in the house signaled the return of Aquila, who absented herself most mornings to fulfill some unknown task. The master of the house was himself out among his guardsmen, readying them for the imperial visit.

Pancras picked up the theme again.

"Why did he do such a thing?"

There was a long, working pause.

"He is a good man, Pancras. He appears stern, but he would sacrifice his life for you."

"And thus you have served him ever since?"

"No, not exactly. He purchased my freedom – not my servitude. He told me to return home, to find a way to make an honest life for myself."

"Did you do so?"

"There was nothing for me in Corinth. Nay, I came to Rome and began to work as a laborer, a beast of burden. Odd jobs, here and there."

"Then how did you become Nereus' steward?"

"In two years' time, he returned to Rome, and with his connections he quickly acquired a prestigious position in the Praetorian Guard. When I had heard that my liberator had returned to Rome, I came to offer my life to him in thanksgiving."

This was beyond reason! This man is the servant of the master, not because of any compulsion, but as a free gift?

"You are not a slave, then?"

"I am forever indebted to him."

"But you are free to leave at any time."

"He has no legal claim on me, yes. But in my soul I know that I owe him my life."

"So the slavery is self-imposed?"

"I do not consider it slavery. It is a freedom unlike any other to give oneself away to one you love."

"I do not understand!"

"Do you consider marriage to be slavery?"

"Of course not! It is a contract between two persons so they can begin a family."

"But if it is done properly – and how rarely it is done well! – it is a type of mutual servitude. But they serve one another out of love. A free gift of self to the other. And in

226

giving themselves, they find a deeper happiness than if they had withheld the gift."

Pancras realized that his initial impression of Achilleus – the bumbling, ludicrous clown – had been completely obliterated by this insight. His ears still protruded, his teeth still jutted out at odd angles, but his mind contained an ocean of wisdom that was profound in its depths, perceptive in its insights.

They worked aside each other for a while. The sword began to shimmer, reflecting the light of the sun – and the boy's own face. He looked at his reflection for a long time, gazing deeply into his own eyes. Did he have the capacity to love in such measure?

Probably not. Those eyes were always turned in upon themselves, seeking only his own pride, his own freedom. He still chafed at the thought of being enslaved, as much as he was used to the routine. Pancras hated to admit it to himself – he did not have the ability to love, not like Achilleus, not like Aquila or Nereus.

After a very long pause studying his reflection, during which time Achilleus thought he had lost interest in the topic, Pancras asked pointedly:

"That day you decided to drop your sword – was that the day you became a Christian?"

The spear clattered to the ground.

"How did you..."

Pancras turned his sober attention directly to the steward. "Answer me this, I beg you."

"We must never speak of this again. For my sake – and for yours."

"But you do not deny it."

"Do you understand what you are saying? This is sedition. You are yet a boy. You do not know the penalty..."

"I know it with full certainty," he replied firmly. "My best friend became a lantern at a garden party. His family was consumed by lions as I watched on. Do not think me naïve."

"The fire will not leave you untouched," the man said sharply. Straightening up, he commanded, "Finish your work. This conversation never happened." He threw down his rag on Pancras' lap and left.

Pancras tossed the rags on the floor in frustration, tempted to curse behind the man's back. This misplaced desire to protect him – he was no mere youth, ignorant of life and death. He needed to know; he *deserved* to know. For if death were to come for him, he did not want to cower like a child. He wanted to face it like a man.

~~~

He awoke to a strange unease. What day was it? How long had he been there? Had it been two moons, or less?

Stumbling out into the dismal dawn, shafts of light barely illuminating the domus, it seemed more like a tomb than a dwelling. There was something unsettling about today. In clouded thinking, he wondered if this was the day Galerius arrived, but no, that event was still two days hence.

"With haste!" he heard Achilleus call to him. "You have slept late."

He knew that the family would be awaiting their repast, so he hurried into the *culina* and began to pour warm milk into pottery.

"Achilleus, what day is it?" he grogged.

"I believe it is the third day before the ides of September. Why do you ask?"

Ah. His *dies natale*. He had completely forgotten.

"No reason."

Masking his sadness, he went about the motions. A cup here, a plate there. Fetch the figs, pour the porridge into the cauldron.

He brought out a bowl of the steaming cereal to Aquila, who was already reclining. Nereus was no doubt still at the garrison, spending long hours readying his troops.

"Thank you, Pancras," she murmured.

He nodded his assent.

And then she pierced him with her brown eyes of benevolence. "You look unwell."

No response was necessary. He would return to his cell until this passed, yes. He needn't burden the family during this difficult time.

Hastening away from her penetrating concern, he returned to the kitchen and collapsed upon a stool. This was to be the day he took his *toga virilis*. The celebration had been anticipated for months. His uncle would have slaughtered the finest young calf, brought in entertainers – oh, now he missed him! And he reproached himself for only missing his uncle for the party he would bankroll.

And his friends would be in attendance, all of them, yes even Antonius if he had not believed that deadly myth. Pancras would have invited them to his villa for a day of laughter and mirth. That is where he should have been today. Instead of drowning in regret.

As a mirage, Aquila appeared in the kitchen. He had not heard her enter.

"Please, Domina," he pleaded, "Give me a task. Anything. I need to put my hands to something…"

"Your task is to tell me what bothers you."

Plaintively, he shook his head. He wished to rush to an unlit room, to draw the shades and nurse his grief in private.

But she seemed disinclined to move. The shadows crossed the floor with greater speed than she whose compassionate persistence seemed content to while away the day.

At last he broke. "Forgive me, Domina. I mean no harm. But today is my *dies natale*, the day I should have had taken the *toga virilis*. I was just reminiscing…"

She nodded, sharing the grief.

"I miss them, truly I do. My uncle, my friends, my father most of all. This would have been a fine day for him! He would have lifted the bulla from my shoulders and dedicated it to the Lares and we would have celebrated with a feast." His voice choked. "I hope that I have made him proud. But I will never know."

"Oh, Pancras," she murmured, as if she was vicariously feeling the pain.

Heaving a heavy sigh, he concluded, "But there is no use lamenting what might have been. I am with you and Dominum Nereus, and for that, I am most grateful."

"If you could do anything today, what would it be?"

Such a question! The possibilities – or rather, the impossibilities – loomed large. "I do not know. I would love to visit my friends, but I know that is not allowed."

Aquila was silent for a moment, her eyes cast down in thought. Pancras observed her silently, noticing for the first time the grey in her hair, the wrinkles lining her brow. She has endured her own griefs, he realized. Had she lost a child? Or never been able to bear?

"It is not impossible," she replied.

Was that a pinprick of hope she offered?

"I do not wish to burden you," he answered, sliding off the stool, preparing to busy his hands with something, anything. "You have been kind to me."

"You have earned my trust, Pancras. Your faithfulness has not been unnoticed."

He cast a weary glance at her, as he continued to straighten up the pots and pans. They needed no tidying, but he did it anyway, a distraction.

"Would you care to visit a friend this night?"

"Yes, I would be grateful."

"Consider it done. I will send Achilleus with you to visit whomever you choose."

"Achilleus? Why? You expressed your trust in me. I shall not seek to escape again."

"It is not you I distrust. No, it is merely human nature."

"You think a man is not as good as his word?" He knew himself impertinent to challenge her, but her goodness invited honest words.

"There are forces stronger than a man's word at work in the world."

"Ah yes, the ancient curse and all that."

She did not immediately respond. Instead, she took up a sponge to scrub down the dishes she had used from breakfast. Such parallel work allowed Pancras to avoid eye contact as he wrestled within himself.

Finally he spoke, uncaring whether his impetuous questions would bring down a severe reaction. "Why did Nereus purchase me? I have served you poorly."

"Nonsense. Nereus sees in you a destiny that you yourself are ignorant of."

"A destiny? I am destined to die a slave. My life has ever been a tragedy that the most cynical poets could not have foreseen."

"And yet you define yourself by such sorrows?"

"What else is there?"

"Nereus sees a hope for your future."

"Then why did he enslave me? He could have released me as he released Achilleus."

"He did so to protect you. The world is dangerous…"

"Yes, he warned me of this. But I have seen the world. I am confident I can survive without the protection of patrons. My father died when I was ten. I had to take on the mantle of responsibility since then." He bit off the last phrase; he was unable to avoid the bitterness that entered his voice.

"I do not wish to argue," she calmly stated, inching imperceptibly closer to the boy. "But freedom without character is mere license. The thieves in their dens, the prostitutes at the Temple gates, the money-changers who cheat the poor from their last penny – they are free as well, but they have no virtue."

"Am I without virtue?"

He felt a damp hand rest gently upon his shoulder. After a search for the proper words, she replied, "You have yet to learn how to sacrifice."

Although her words were gentle, his shoulders sagged. Such words were disturbingly accurate.

"But do not fear," she continued, encouragingly. "For you will learn it. The lessons will be painful, but they will make you into a man your father would be proud of."

He nodded, at a loss for words.

"Go," she urged with a smile, "You have water to fetch."

~~~

The air bit and nipped at their flesh as they crossed the city's vacant streets. Anticipation fluttered his heart; he was trembling as they approached the insula of his beloved. Even with the hastening dusk, his feet knew the way.

They were quickly admitted but gravely disappointed to find that the apartment was empty. The occupants were out for the night, explained the neighbors. No, they did not know when they would return.

"I will wait, then!" Pancras declared, and Achilleus looked amused, perhaps remembering sweethearts of his own.

Seated on the alleyway steps, her face was ever before his mind's eye. Oh, where was she? Would this meeting only remind him of everything he could never possess?

And two figures were seen approaching, their silhouettes backlit by the glow of a hundred window-lamps. He could recognize her unmistakable gait, the way her braided hair cascaded in a single river down her back.

"Daphne!" he cried, racing toward her.

It took a moment, but when she recognized the voice, her footsteps also broke into a run.

The embrace that ensued was the sweetest reunion in history. It was an entwining of limbs and flesh, twirling, mingling tears and shouts of joy. Their cries were inarticulate, as if words failed to express their longing for each other. For a moment, they forgot their mutual exile.

They tried to speak, but their voices choked on the myriad of roiling emotions. Instead they contented themselves with the encirclement, periodically drawing back to drink from the sight of the other's face.

At length, they collapsed on the stoop, oblivious to Achilleus and Daphne's father watching from some distance, in amazement.

"I had given you up for dead," she began, her tears rivers on which fire burned.

"So much has happened! So much!" he replied. And he began to tell her of the saga from the night of the murder to the present day.

Her eyes wide in wonder, she remained planted on the stoop, immobile until the recounting was complete.

"My dear, dear Pancras!" she exclaimed, encompassing him again in a union of arms and hearts. "I am grateful you are alive. Rumors had swirled, that you were to be executed for your uncle's crimes, or at least banished from the city. I sought information everywhere – inquiring every legionary, magistrate, anyone. I could find nothing but gossip, many who were glad your uncle received his comeuppance. But I knew that you were innocent, and so I prayed that you would receive the justice your innocence deserved. Desperately, every day, in the Temple and at home, I sought the gods for your favor. My life had become a living prayer, a sacrifice consuming me from the inside. And my prayer has been answered in a way quite unexpected!"

"I do not know if it was your prayer," he replied, remaining agnostic on the question. "But it was certainly your love – the memory of it – which sustained me in darkest times."

"Your master – does he treat you well?"

"More than well. They have been gracious beyond what I could expect. In fact, I am more a part of their family than a mere slave."

"Thanks to the gods! They have not beaten you too severely?"

"Never."

"And they allowed you out this night?"

"Today is my *dies natale*."

"Ah yes, felicitations!"

And the exchange of news continued, the minutes rushing by before the darkness was complete. When the conversation was reduced to embers, they sat beside one another in quiet, their hands interlocked and unbreakable.

At length, the steward and the father gestured that the hour was late, and this reunion must conclude.

The *together* stood and once more embraced.

"Wait for me, Daphne," he whispered into her ear. "I will be free, and I will find you. Wait for me."

"I will, Pancras," she replied. "I will wait until eternity for you."

He felt a stern hand on his shoulder, and the embrace was torn apart. Equally rent asunder was his heart, as he watched her enter the insula beyond his sight. This last parting was agonizing. It was as if his heart went with her, torn out of his own chest and left in this decrepit brick building.

The pain was throbbing, aching, but oh was he grateful for it!

~~~

The family made ready the following morn. Every seven days, they abandoned the homestead at dawn, leaving Pancras alone. They were perpetually oblique about their whereabouts. The lad only knew that he was not to come, not to disturb their morning trysts.

Nereus gave him the instructions before departure: "Remain here. We shall return by midday. While we are gone, you are to wash the curtains, for everything must be in order by the time Galerius comes, on the morrow. We may be conscripted to quarter some of his retinue; sometimes he requests that if he brings a particularly large number of attendants. This poor villa must shine with an uncommon luster."

Pancras nodded solemnly. He would make his master proud.

Soon, the door echoed shut and he was alone.

The task was not difficult, but Pancras found it unpleasant. Dragging a stool around to the windows, he unfastened the curtains one-by-one and piled them in the center of the atrium. When the dozen sets of thin linen draperies had been removed, he went forth to draw water from the local fountain. The courtyard had a designated wooden tub for washing, into which he poured the fresh water. Mingled in would be a concentrated solution of ammonia and water – stored from the collective urine of the family, who would use the designated jug as a chamber pot in the middle of the night.

This was disgusting! But it did bleach the fabrics a brilliant white, he was noticing, as his hands worked the curtains vigorously up and down a washboard.

And then he heard the crash.

His heart leapt to his throat, as he jumped to his feet. Who had invaded the home? Hadn't Nereus locked the door upon his departure?

Senses alert, he rinsed his hands in clean water, and began to creep towards the kitchen.

Another crash shook him further. Clay on stone. Who was ransacking the kitchen? And why were they destroying everything?

His heart racing, he slinked into the house, edging to the kitchen in silence, lest this intruder be armed.

More crashes. This would be a mess! But more pressingly, how would Pancras subdue this creature? He had no weapons – the arsenal was across the house. Oh well – he had to put a stop to this before more was destroyed!

With a fierce cry, he rushed into the room, hoping to startle the burglar.

But it was he who leapt back, startled, upon seeing the cat, perched on a shelf, breakfasting on the dried fish that were stacked up high. The cat seemed unconcerned – he had found what he desired.

Shaking his head with dismay, he stifled a laugh. What a foolish creature! Stepping forward, he heard the pots crunch beneath his feet – what a mess! Expensive garum spilled across the floor. Over there was a pile of flour, becoming sullied with dirt.

Growling and shouting, flailing his arms, he tried to scare the creature. The cat jumped, knocking over a jar of oil, which splashed on his feet as it tumbled to the ground.

"You foolish cat!" he screamed, giving chase as it ran a circle around the kitchen, knocking over dishes and cups. The piles of detritus continued to grow around the room.

The tawny striped creature hissed at him, looking offended. Who are you to interrupt my meal?, it asked with a frown.

It was soon trapped in a corner, mewing and hissing and bearing its teeth.

"You do not frighten me!" Pancras declared, excitement running through his veins. He went in for the catch, but the feline gave him a swipe with claws flailing, before darting between his legs and escaping the trap.

"No! You fiend!" he cried out, wheeling around to catch a whisk of a tail flying down the hallway. He followed on winged feet, chasing the cat into his master's bedroom.

A deft leap put the cat firmly within the open trunk containing the many fine silken tunics that Aquila would wear for an evening gala. He could hear the tearing of fabrics as this nest of silk was torn asunder by the beast's claws.

"Get out of there!" he ordered, but once again the cat was too quick for the boy's slow grasp. The animal quickly dodged him and bounded out, stringing a couple shawls behind him, still attached to his claws.

The pursuit continued throughout the whole house, leading back to the atrium, around the vestibule and the triclinium, across the kitchen again, into Achilleus' room (where the cat deposited a gift upon his pillow), and back into the main bedroom.

Finally hurdling upon the heights of the scroll rack in the library, the cat perched atop the structure, glowering at the boy. Challenging him – come and get me!

Panting and frantic, Pancras reluctantly looked back at the trail of destruction that the tomcat had wreaked. It was strewn all across the house – the trail of flour and sheets, the shattered earthen vessels, the ever-expanding lake of olive oil. How was he going to clean this up? And perhaps more pressingly – how would he ever chase this cat out of the house? All of the windows were already open, and he had thrown wide the door leading to the courtyard, but this beast seemed disinclined to depart. Like a daemon, this poltergeist was continuing to haunt the house – what magic would dispel him? Glaring from the tower of scrolls, the cat made a mockery of him.

Achilleus. He would know how to rid the house of this beast. He would also help him clean up the mess, that good-hearted soul.

Without a second thought, Pancras bolted out the front door, intent on finding the help he needed to exorcize the house of this evil creature.

The streets were starting to bustle at this time of day. The hubbub of city life began to creak and groan, preparing to roar to life. A few hardy souls were already upon the street: some heading to labor for their daily bread, the young to their school, the elderly to their wisdom-seat at the Forum, where they would pass judgment all the day long.

A familiar face bobbed up and down ahead: a lawyer, who had come by the domus in the past to consult with Nereus on some obscure governmental matter. Pancras stopped him in the street. "Please, sir. Do you know the whereabouts of my master Nereus? There is an urgent matter at home he must attend to."

"Nereus? Yes, I believe I saw him, not long ago, on the street of Crispus. He and Aquila seemed to be visiting the large villa close to Porta Caperna."

"Which villa?"

"I do not know who owns it, but it was the one with the wall surrounding it, with the tall cypress trees. You cannot miss it."

"Thank you, sir! Thank you!" he called out, as he hastened away.

There was no difficulty in finding the street, nor the elegant villa to which he referred. The wall towered higher than his head, so that the house could be completely concealed behind it.

Entrance was forbidden behind a heavy wrought-iron gate.

He gripped the bars in frustration, giving them a shake but to no avail. It was securely locked, and no one was in sight.

"I need help! Please! Someone!"

But his voice echoed across the empty courtyard, returning to him without summoning a soul.

With visions of the havoc the cat could be wreaking filling his mind with vivid and horrifying detail, he kept shaking, desperate.

"Please! Please, open for me! I mean you no harm! I need help!"

Silence was the only response.

Stepping back, he realized that there was only one way to gain access: the wall must be scaled. He took three steps back, trying to find a place where he could grip upon a protrusion or a crack. But seeing none, he raced forward, hoping to leap like that dastardly cat.

With his outstretched arms reaching frantically to the heights, his fingertips managed to wrap themselves over the top of the wall. With great struggle and flailing, he gasped and panted, his sweat leaving a smear up the wall as he dragged his leg over, then the other.

"Alas! Boy!"

A quick glance to the road showed a furious passer-by, concerned that this lad was engaged in some sort of thievery or other illicit pursuit.

Pancras had to jump – but the other side of the wall featured an army of cypresses, tall and thick. There was no place to descend except through the gauntlet of unforgiving branches. He looked around for another way, but none presented itself.

The man had fetched a large stone and was winding up to throw it directly at Pancras.

So down he went! Branch upon branch swiped his face, his arms, his legs. He could feel the tiny scourges drawing blood, before he hit the ground with a thud.

He quickly scrambled through the lower branches before making a mad dash to the domus. The entryway was clear – large paving stones marked the way to the three steps, leading up to one of the finest homes he had ever seen. But no time to admire the craftsmanship, lest his own home become a ransacked shanty!

His furious pounding on the door produced a servant.

"Yes?"

"Please," he panted. "Please, I need to see Nereus and Achilleus. Are they in there?"

"How did you get past the gate?"

"Forgive my trespass, but this is urgent. May I see them?"

"I apologize, but I cannot let you in."

"Are they inside?"

"This is a private home. Only guests are welcome to enter." He was unfailingly polite, even apologetic, but his words were firm.

"This is an emergency of the first order. Would you ask them to see me immediately? I am their servant."

"Again, I would ask that you depart. Wait for them at home. They will return at midday." With that, the door closed and he could hear the finality of a key turning in the lock.

Discouraged, bloodied and filthy, he knew he could not come this far to fail in his mission! Surely there must be an unlocked door, an open window, an underground cellar entrance?

He began to tread the manicured lawn interspersed with exotic imported plants – from the Indies, doubtless – circling the house for an alternate entrance. And there it was, on the side: an open window.

Another leap allowed him to grab hold, dragging his corpse up and in. Once inside, he could hear the odd sound of chanting echoing down the corridors. Following the source of the sound, he wandered down a hallway, marveling briefly at the impressive Doric columns reaching to the heavens.

The chanting was haunting and beautiful. Old men, young women, matrons and boys blended and harmonized, falling into unison and breaking apart in glorious polyphony. Still driven by haste – or drawn by the beauty, he was unsure - he crossed an interior courtyard and approached a large assembly room.

A muscled man stood blocking the entryway, facing into the gathering chamber, his arms folded but weaponless. Pancras considered how to get around him, but could see no way to do so without being apprehended. So, exhausted and bruised and lacking ideas, he slunk down against a column, to listen to the music and discern his next maneuver.

The back of his hand served as a towel to wipe his brow, as his racing heart gradually slowed. The tranquility of this chant was a welcome relief. Although he could tell it was in Greek, the words were muddled and hard to decipher. Fragments of texts floated through the air:

Let the rushing of winds, all the surging rivers cease
In the presence of him...
...let all the powers answer,

Amen, Amen, strength and praise…
…the giver of all good things…

What was taking place inside this chamber? He was filled with a strange sense of awe, as if he were on the cusp of something holy, some mystery inexplicable.

His eyes closed on their own, a river of peace sweeping him away. Never mind the dirt and the blood – he was afloat on a tranquil current, listening and sailing to a land beyond the sorrows of this world. The music ceased, replaced by a profound silence…

The irritation overcame him with such haste that he could not hold back his vicious sneeze, which echoed across the house with surprising volume.

His eyes flew open, in shock at his own outburst. The burly guard was glaring at him with an admixture of surprise and horror.

"Who are you?" he demanded, towering over him. "What business brings you here?"

"Pardon me, sir," he answered, shaken. "I seek Nereus and Achilleus. Are they here? There is an urgent matter at home…"

With some suspicion, the man nodded, quickly disappearing into the crowd assembled within the gathering space. Moments later, Nereus appeared, looking none too pleased at the interruption.

Pancras struggled to his feet. "Forgive me, Dominum…"

"Come," he ordered sternly, grabbing Pancras by the elbow and leading him away from the singing-room. As they walked away, they could hear the echoes of a man's voice, its timbre solemn.

"I instructed you not to interrupt us," he growled when they had arrived at a secluded corridor.

"Please, sir. We have had a problem at home…"

"Do you understand where you are?"

Pancras pondered the implications. Yes, he knew where he was.

"This is a sacred ritual, is it not?"

Nereus returned an impenetrable stare.

"I am aware that you are among the Christians," Pancras spilled out. "But please do not fear – I know that I must hold this with unbreakable secrecy."

"Your precocious curiosity has put you in mortal danger. We had a suspicion that you had known all along."

"But I do not share your belief."

"You know nothing!" Nereus exclaimed, spittle flying forth with vehemence. "You think you will be spared? You think you can convince the executioner of your innocence?"

"I will certainly burn a grain of incense to the Emperor."

"Not before you betray us – out of fear."

"You are my family. I will never reveal this secret."

"They would torture it out of you."

"Never!"

Nereus shook his head. "It is no longer safe for you to dwell with us."

A fearful thought took root. "What shall you do, then?"

"Come, follow me."

Nereus led him out of the house by a different entrance, which deposited them directly on the streets. Walking with a determined purpose, they trod through the streets with a vigor that frightened Pancras. What penalty would Nereus exact for this knowledge? Beatings? Exile? Imprisonment?

Through the city they walked, heading toward the Campus Agrippae. Pancras was trembling by the time they entered the main square. The bustle of life surrounded them – but once again, as it had been so often, his own life was in jeopardy.

Nereus, a man of few words, was taciturn on the journey, offering no glimmer of hope.

His master led him to the steps of the Temple to *Sol Invictus* – the Unconquerable Sun. Ascending quickly, he approached one of the magistrates who held court in the courtyard before the temple proper. Beneath the shade of the majestic columns, gleaming a brilliant white in the midmorning sun, the judges sat upon low couches, making declarations and issuing judgments to all who approached their august position.

"Hail, Caesar," greeted the magistrate, tossing his purple-and-red *trabea* over his shoulder, his rank clearly visible to all in the campus.

"Hail, friend," Nereus responded.

"Ah, Nereus," the magistrate responded, after formalities had concluded. "You are looking well. How is your health? And that of your most beautiful wife?"

"We are well, thank you. I have come on a matter of business this morning."

"Yes, of course."

"I wish to grant manumission to this slave-boy."

Ah, so this was the penalty – freedom? Was this a punishment, or a gift?

The official looked Pancras up and down, assessing his worth, judging his physical strength and character.

"He looks like a fine servant, Nereus. It would be a shame to lose him."

"Nevertheless I wish to set him free. And quickly, at that."

"But surely you paid quite a price for him! He must have fetched at least seven-fifty."

"Double that amount."

"Whew! And are you certain that you wish to release him?"

"Yes, please."

The magistrate shrugged. "As you wish."

Standing behind the boy, Nereus roughly gripped Pancras' shoulders. Then he performed the rite that had come down through the centuries, the rite of bestowing precious freedom.

"I do solemnly declare that I, Nereus, release Pancras of Phrygia from my service."

"For what reason do you release him?" asked the magistrate, following the script.

"He has earned his freedom through faithful service and good works. With my blessing he may join the ranks of the freedmen of this city."

The magistrate's secretary stepped forward and placed the judgment rod upon Pancras' head.

"By the power vested in me by the Emperor Diocletian and the Tetrarchs Galerius and Maximian, I hereby declare that you, Pancras of Phrygia, are to be freed from service to Nereus and to all other earthly masters. You are a free man."

Nereus turned him around, so that the expanse of the agora stretched before Pancras.

"Go forth, my son. Go forth and take your place among the citizens of Rome."

A slight shove forced Pancras to descend. Unsteadily and unsurely he stumbled down, bewildered. Pausing at the base of the stairs, he tried to grasp what had just occurred so quickly.

Without a word Nereus himself descended. The former master did not even grant him a glance as he passed by.

"Dominum!" Pancras cried out. "What am I to do now?"

Nereus turned, and his voice was hard. "You may do as you wish. But I beg you – if you have any goodness in your heart, please forget that you ever knew us."

Pancras watched until he had strode out of sight, melting into the faceless crowd.

~~~

Lost. Not that he had become disoriented in the city that he loathed to love. No, he knew where he was. The greater quandary was *who* he was.

His feet traced out the streets that had become a family heirloom. His sandals knew the way. But they wandered aimlessly, for he had nowhere to go.

The hours passed, but no answers dawned.

He was now homeless, yet another casualty of the brutally harsh world into which he was born. Thrust into the light against his will, victimized many times over, he cursed this recent twist of fate. From prosperous lad to servant to abandoned – the degradation was complete.

Who did he have left? He could not ask Decian for shelter, for his friend's father watched his uncle commit an unspeakable crime. Daphne would delight to offer her home, but her father would never allow the budding romance to take root beneath their roof.

And so his feet moved of their own accord, as if they would discover the solution on their own through constant motion. Perhaps he would not need a home if he were never to be still. A pilgrim passing through a transient world, aloof from the quotidian cares of the plebes.

Yet the needs of the body cried out – hunger and thirst and exhaustion. Sweat from his brow stained his collar, as his feet burned from their constant usage. Hour after hour he wandered, breathing but not alive.

Oh, would the gods render an accounting for this life! What had he done to deserve such treatment from those ruthless forces bent on inflicting suffering upon him at every turn? Must everything be stripped away, so that he knew not even who he was?

The sun had dipped far into the west, casting shadows across the Forum and shrouding the alleyways in dusk. Driven by some primal urge, his feet kept up their insistent march.

And it was thus that he came back again to the Forum. It looked different now in the setting sun, as the merchants were closing their shops. The nightlife began to stir, bringing out the undesirables.

Over there were the whores, sitting on the Temple steps and calling out prices to passers-by. The tavern on the south side vomited out two patrons who were involved in a vicious brawl, their shouts echoing across the quickly-emptying plain.

He would have kept going, but his feet pleaded for mercy. So there he sat, in the exact center of the Forum, the place where money and bodies and human lives were traded daily. The dust cried out – *vanity!* And the skies echoed back – *meaningless!*

Deeply weary, he put his head down on his knees and started to weep. There seemed no end to this suffering. Every good thing would be taken. Joy would be replaced by sorrow. Futility! His entire life was futility! And he wept at the frustration of it all.

His tears flowed until the lamps were lit and the stars began to emerge, one by one.

"Take me!" he whispered aloud to the elements. "Take my life! I have nothing, I am nothing, let me cease to exist."

And nothing heard, no one responded.

When there were no more tears, he looked up and realized he was alone and deserted. The merchants had gone home, the ne'er-do-wells were silent, and the square seemed a vast and empty desert.

His life was far more empty, however. His stomach was empty. His mind was empty. His soul – if he had one – was empty.

Go home.

Where was home? He knew not.

Go home.

He had no home!, he protested to the ether. His home was far, far across the sea, in a warm and fertile land.

Go home.

The thought would not abandon him. But where was this *home* which drew his heart in hope?

He rose, famished and weak, and began to walk anew. His feet knew the way.

It was his only hope. Could mercy be extended even to the outcast? Though he knew not what he had done wrong.

On and on he walked, the inky black night enveloping him.

It came upon him almost by surprise, the villa that had been his home for the past two months. Hoping against hope, he climbed the stairs and rapped on the door, his heart pounding in fear.

As soon as the door opened, Pancras fell prostrate upon his face, groveling. "Please, sir. I have no one and nowhere to go. I offer you my service, my strength, my very life. I will sacrifice all things to serve you. If you but pity your servant, I shall be faithful to you all of my days. I offer myself to you."

And, placing his request at the feet of his master, he waited, face down in the dust. For dust he was!

When the response was not forthcoming, he glanced up and was startled to see Nereus' face in a rare smile, his eyes brimming with mirth.

"Now I know of your loyalty, Pancras," he said, stooping to help him to his feet. "My son, let us begin."

PART FOUR: *The Night Watch*

"Come back to me safely, Nereus," Aquila cooed to the setting sun.

He hoisted the breastplate over his head, donning the uniform that threatened the ends of the earth into submission. "I will try, my love."

Fingering over the rack of weapons, he chose his broadsword, holding it up to watch his reflection in its gleam.

"You have done well, Pancras. This shines like it just arose from the swordsmith's table."

Pancras grinned and bowed, grateful for the praise.

With a shove, the sword was sheathed as the armor continued to mask the man beneath. Helmet with the colorful plumage on its crest, armband, shield decorated with eagle and standard. It featured the letters "SPQR" – a vestige from better days, when no tyrants ruled, when no persecutions threatened.

"Do you fear there will be riots?" Aquila questioned, her maternal anxieties evident.

"Of course there will be. There are enough Persians in this city to form their own army. They saved their own lives by fleeing Satala, but they have long memories."

"In addition to those unhappy about the taxes."

"Is that not the same in every age!"

A round of laughter lightened the mood.

The soldier adjusted his gear. "Achilleus, look after my wife."

His friend nodded somberly.

"I pray that I may return by tomorrow, for supper at the least."

"We pray so, as well," Aquila purred, embracing him in that desperate longing of a future widow.

"Fare thee well, then."

"Go with God."

And with that, the master of the house was gone.

The silence echoed an uneasy premonition. Achilleus sensed it and said, "My dear, let us beseech the Lord on behalf of our master."

Aquila nodded, and they strode down the corridor to the bedroom where the closed door obscured their prayers.

With no further instructions, Pancras was free to do as he pleased. A tickling thirst was slaked with a quick draught from the jug of warm milk. It was too early to retire, for the sun still hovered above the horizon. But what was there to do?

He took a crust of stale bread with him to the back garden. There, in the setting sun, he tossed crumbs into the air, delighted when they were snatched up by the sparrows who sat at his feet, little slaves to the giant master.

More! More!, they cried, chirping and bouncing about in a delightful freedom.

Ah, how he longed for such a carefree existence!

Nevertheless, he was grateful for the tranquility he enjoyed here. It was not what he would have envisioned for his life. But he could see more clearly now that the valley of suffering has been watered by the springs of life. Perhaps this valley may bear fruit after all?

The sky was a riot of color, a palette of orange and purple, bleeding reds merging and blending into the dusky blue. It was an evening of striking beauty, which was in short supply in the brutish city. But Pancras wondered curiously whether it was an omen – foretelling an event good or ill, who could tell?

Such contented musings could not last forever, and a loud rapping at the door brought him out of his reverie. He hastened to attend to it.

"Please, sir," greeted a breathless young man, a lad of twenty or so. He seemed to have dashed from his former location, frantic with the importance of his message. "I need to speak with Nereus. Is he here?"

"I am afraid not," Pancras replied. "May I inquire the nature of your business?"

"It is of the most sensitive matter, and urgent, at that."

"Allow me to summon his steward, please," the boy replied. Leaving the door open, he went to fetch Achilleus. He was found seated on a stool, hands raised in supplication, with Aquila seated calmly on the bed, her head bowed in prayer.

"Forgive the intrusion, Achilleus, but you are needed."

The man nodded and rose, hastening to the door.

Before Achilleus could speak, the story began to spill out. "Pardon, Achilleus, but there is a grave emergency at the palace. Domitilla has been outed."

"Outed? Is her life in danger?"

"Most certainly. I need to speak with Nereus."

"He is at the barracks." He ran his hand through his wispy hair in frustration. "This visit of Galerius has thrown the entire city into a frenzy, and Nereus is needed to keep the peace."

"Can you take me to him? If Domitilla becomes a victim, there will be greater riots than this city has ever seen."

Achilleus appeared to be thinking it over.

Abruptly, he turned to Pancras. "Do you know the way to the barracks?"

Surprised, Pancras nodded slowly.

"I should stay here with Aquila. But this message is truly urgent. Please accompany this man to find Nereus. A life is at stake."

Once again he nodded, realizing the gravity of the situation.

"But before you go…" Achilleus went into another room and quickly returned with a dagger in a leather scabbard. "You may meet unsavory characters on the way. Go with courage, and go with God."

Pancras was about to object, but thought better of it. Perhaps Achilleus' deity could be of some assistance.

The two of them set off into the darkening city. The usual bustle of the city was replaced by an eerie calm. No carts rattled the streets, and there was a pall over the normal human activity. Rather, off in the distance, shouts could be heard; bloodthirsty cries, more beastly than human. It sounded like a mob was gathering, ready to massacre anything that dared to cross its path.

They made haste across city streets, but Pancras' insatiable curiosity nagged at him until he burst with questions:

"Who is Domitilla, and why is she in danger? What has she been suspected of?"

The young man, for being unacquainted with Pancras, was surprisingly forthright with his answers. "She is Diocletian's niece – and a member of our community. She worships with the Equestrians in the north of the city; so I can understand why you have never encountered her. But her faith is deep and her love is strong, to this I can attest. I know that she is happy to spill her blood for the Name, but we are not prepared to lose her…"

"So she is a Christ-follower, then?"

"One of the holiest. And she had taken a vow of virginity, as a testament to her dedication. But Galerius saw her and desired to give her in marriage to his son. It would be an alliance most strong, you understand."

"Certainly. To unite Galerius and Diocletian would be of mutual benefit to them both."

"Rumor has it that Galerius wants Italia back, but Maximian is not the sort to give up such power."

"So with an alliance between Galerius and Diocletian, he could potentially break apart the tetrarchy."

"With bloodshed, if it came to that."

"From what little I know, it likely will."

"Indeed. What happened in Nicomedia was atrocious. Hard to fathom that a man could excise another man's tongue, torture him with fire, and then allow the rope to perform the dirty deed. He razed our churches, burnt our Scriptures, and hacked our children limb from limb."

Pancras was silent. This was the man who his master served?

"We in the northern church have considered resisting."

"With arms?"

"We do not know; we are divided."

"Is this why you need Nereus? To command your rebellion?"

"No, for he would not do such a thing. His sword is to defend the Empire, not destroy it."

"Then why do you seek him?"

"He will know how to rescue Domitilla."

Memories surfaced of Antonius, dwelling in the pit of darkness. They had offered him a rescue, but he seemed content to embrace his impending death.

"I thought you Christians welcomed death. Is it not a gateway to eternal life?"

The young man stopped abruptly. Even in the darkness, Pancras could see the shock that registered on his pale features.

"*You* Christians?" he exclaimed. "You are not one of us?"

And Pancras was suddenly aware of his unfortunate word choice. "I...I...uh..." he stumbled, unable to recover.

The young man grabbed the collar of his robe and drew him close, so that Pancras could feel the hot breath breathing on his face.

"Tell me the truth," he demanded through clenched teeth.

"I mean you no harm!" Pancras blurted. "I serve a Christian master, and would lay down my life for him!"

With a vicious throw, the young man slammed him against the brick wall they had been walking beside. "You may have the chance," he growled.

"Please. If you wish to find Nereus, you must trust me."

Black eyes bore into Pancras. "Lead the way," he was ordered.

They walked in silence the remaining half-stadium. Immediately before they began the approach up the Palatine Hill towards the Domus Flavia, which was aglow with lamplight and bustle, they turned off the main street and onto a small alleyway. Two doors further and they could hear the guttural conversations of men.

A brief knock on the door produced a soldier, a tall and imposing figure whose tremendous muscles rippled beneath the armor.

"What urgency brings you here at this hour?" he demanded, none too happy about being drawn away from the dice game that was occurring in the background.

"We seek Nereus. It is of utmost importance."

He stepped away, allowing entrance into the low stone-walled room. A boisterous game took up the bulk of the room, with perhaps a dozen soldiers hovering over a table. With every roll of the dice, cries of elation or dismay arose from the crowd. Other soldiers busied themselves with steins of strong *posca,* made with sour wine and raw eggs. Their jests brought forth raucous laughter, unsettling and strong. Another couple men sat in a corner, sharpening their swords with rhythmic passes of a whetting stone. They glanced up, surly and threatening.

There, by the far window, sat Nereus. He stared out into the night, listening and watching. The breeze would catch his face, ruffling the plumage on the helmet he held in his hands. His face was thoughtful, brooding – expectant for something.

Nereus' face registered surprise when the two young men came to him. "Lucius! Pancras! What brings you here?"

They sat upon a wooden crate before beginning. "I fear we bear urgent news. Domitilla has been outed this very night."

"How do you know this?"

"Nicolai of Antioch – you know him?"

"Yes, he works in the palace."

"He was privy to the conversation. Galerius was furious at Domitilla's refusal to marry his son. She has been condemned to the arena during tomorrow's games."

"This troubles me," he replied, gazing out the window, his face dark. It was clear that he was disturbed but not surprised, mulling over this latest travesty.

"She is in the Tullianum now, sir. We have had nary a moment to pay her a visit; I hastened to you when I found out."

"And you are certain that she is to be executed tomorrow? Publicly?"

"Yes, Nicolai told me that Galerius was rabidly angry. Frothing, eyes bulging...you know his temper. He decreed to all the palace that she would be making an appearance at the games."

Nereus rubbed his face in disbelief. "This would be a foolish move for Galerius. Think how it would upset Diocletian!"

"I agree, sir, but Galerius has forced Diocletian's hand in these troubles. He knows that the emperor is growing ill and does not have the courage to resist his iron will."

"This is true," Nereus replied, his voice lowering further, for the words he spoke were traitorous. "Galerius may be seeking to consolidate all power in himself."

"Then we must act!"

"Agreed. If Galerius is able to make a public spectacle of the Emperor's niece, his persecution will know no bounds."

"What shall we do?" Pancras asked, for the first time making his voice heard.

"We shall gather the elders. Lucius, do you know where to find the *episcopus* and the *presbuteroi*?"

The overseer and the elders – Pancras reasoned these were the leaders of the community of believers.

"I believe so," Lucius replied.

"Then let us meet at the beginning of the third watch of the night, in the home of the Chief Shepherd. This gives us very little time. Make haste!"

Lucius nodded, rising and fleeing with Mercurial feet.

Eagerly, trembling with fear and youthful excitement, Pancras asked, "And what shall I do?"

"Stay here with me. Much may be required of you this night."

"I am ready."

"You may need a weapon," Nereus added.

The boy silently drew his dagger from the folds of his cloak to show his master, before replacing it.

The old soldier, looking weary in the lamp-lit glow, nodded. "Pray, Pancras, that you will not have the occasion to draw it tonight."

~~~

The anticipation made the night drag on. Pancras had sunk into a pile of straw and dozed off as the games and drinking drew towards their conclusion.

In his drowsy stupor he noticed that the door opened and a squadron of four soldiers entered, returning from their night watch. Four more soldiers made ready to replace them.

"Now," Nereus whispered, gently shaking him awake. "The time has come."

The two of them hastened into the night, noting that the window-lamps had been extinguished. Bare moonlight was their torch, leading them along the way.

A damp chill hung upon the night, but Pancras could not be sure if that was why he was shivering. There was also a dew of anticipation that settled upon his goose-fleshed skin. Anticipation of what? There was a lethal gravity about Nereus' footsteps. Did he expect bloodshed this night?

The cries from the distant demonstration faded along with the torch-lit glow as they wandered north, into the heart of the seven hills.

Nary was a word exchanged between them during the passing hour. At length they found a small domus, in a decrepit part of Vaticanus, where the low murmuring of voices and the dim blush of candles signified the terminus of their journey.

The domus was already bursting with men, perhaps twenty or twenty-five, alternately standing or seated around a low table. All offered a nod of greeting to Nereus as he entered.

"...it was as I explained, Galerius was livid. His mouth foamed, he paced to and fro. He cursed us, cursed our God, and swore oaths to destroy every last follower of the Christus before he drew his final breath. I believe he is keen on fulfilling that vow."

A murmur of understanding rippled through the crowd.

"That threat which had been carried out fitfully will now be completed," the man continued. "I doubt we, or our children, will be spared."

"How will they find us, Nicolai?"

"Anyone with any position in society will be forced to burn incense. A few lapsi will reveal names, locations. The rack and the lash have a way of loosening the tongue of the most stalwart believers."

"Would he really...?" called out a doubter.

"Nicomedia is your answer," he replied.

Men nodded, having heard of the atrocities committed on their oriental brethren.

"We must fight, then!" Lucius offered. "Do not the Scriptures say that the Kingdom of Heaven suffers violence, and the violent bear it away?"

"Yet they also say that he who lives by the sword will die by the sword."

"We will likely die in either case. But for the sake of our families, our homes, our faith – would we not be willing to take up arms?"

"And become another victim in an endless line of squelched rebellions?"

"But this time, we have God on our side."

"A God who chose to die rather than fight back."

"But he does not forbid us."

"Nay, he does not. But will this not provoke the wrath of Rome further?"

"The fear must end!" Lucius adamantly declared. "We are not sheep to be…"

"Yet we are," came an even voice. "We are called to follow the shepherd – even to laying down our lives for him."

"Besides," said another man. "Our chances are slim. We must not risk utter extermination."

"More pressingly, how will we help Domitilla?" they were reminded by a sobering voice.

"Yes, her death would spark a watershed," replied a gnarled man, his long white hair affording him uncommon deference. "I fear that if her execution is public as planned, it will turn the tide of public opinion against us. The people of Rome are sheep; they will hate what the tetrarch hates, and love what he loves."

"Are they truly so gullible?" another man asked. "For we are held in esteem by many for our aid during the plague."

"They know whose hand feeds them," Nicolai responded with a cynical smirk.

This caused an eruption of discussion among the men. Pancras could only hear snippets clearly. Debates raged about the relative virtues of their pagan neighbors, while others offered various solutions to the current crisis. His eyes wide, he took it all in without a word, still in shock.

At the same time, there was a distinct discomfort of being an interloper. He did not belong here! He did not believe in this persecuted god! It was only a matter of time until they discovered his unbelief. Pancras had no doubt that he could be unreliable – would he betray them under duress? Or would they kill him when they realized he was a traitor in their midst?

Perhaps Nereus was correct – perhaps it would be a danger to him and to them to continue to serve this Christian master.

He glanced up at the weathered face of his patron, his sweat-caked hair clinging to his brow. Nereus had yet to speak, but his presence bespoke tranquility in the midst of the storm. As if reading the boy's questions, the old soldier placed a calming hand on his shoulder, in the ageless gesture of paternity.

Yes, it was right to return home.

Yes, Pancras was destined to be here, according to some unfathomable plan. And his self-doubt faded into the background.

A man in a purple-lined toga held his hand for silence. When attention had been given to him, he spoke along a thread that had likely been growing in silence in everyone's thoughts.

"When will we acknowledge the plain truth: Rome is no longer safe for us? For those with the means, we should consider fleeing to the countryside, or to the provinces. We will be able to worship in peace when we dwell beyond the reach of the Empire."

"Is there any place beyond their reach?" came a response.

"There will be peace in countryside," he replied.

Murmurs of agreement.

"Perhaps this is possible," Nereus agreed, his rich voice exercised for the first time. "Perhaps flight is the optimal solution for some of us. This is something we need to discern with the spirit, in time."

"Time is in short supply," Nicolai retorted.

"Indeed," Nereus replied. "And this is why I propose that I offer Galerius to take Domitilla away for a while."

"Upon what pretext?" he was challenged.

"Domitilla is the niece of the Emperor, is she not? How would his alliance look if he made a public spectacle of Diocletian's relative? I will tell him that I will perform the execution in private, away from the public eye. And I will shuttle her to safety instead."

"Galerius will not suspect an ulterior motive?"

"I believe I have his trust."

"You had better," grumbled the grizzled man. "If your betrayal becomes known, Galerius' rage will know no bounds."

"It is a risk, I admit," Nereus acknowledged. "But this is our sister – we cannot abandon her in her time of need."

By unspoken agreement, all eyes turned to an elderly man who sat in the corner. He was not the oldest man there, nor the strongest. But there was a mystical aura surrounding him that commanded respect. As a silent observer of the dialogue, he appeared to be weighing the arguments and passing a final judgment.

"Yes, Nereus. You have my blessing."

The commander of legions bowed his head. "Thank you, Papa."

Papa? Who is this man that all defer to with such an intimate name?

"I counsel all to consider their position," the Papa continued. "There is no cowardice in fleeing; rather, it is prudent for us all. May God deliver us from the trials to come."

An "Amen" of agreement arose full-throated.

Nereus begged their pardon, for he would hasten immediately to visit their imprisoned sister. The men wished him well, promising prayers and encouragement as he and Pancras slipped out the door.

By this time the night was far gone, and Pancras was growing weary. But he knew better than to complain of his aching feet, for he too felt the urgency of the task at hand.

Returning across town, they approached the Tullianum prison. Foul memories returned to Pancras, sullying his mood. It was here that he spent a restless night in anguish; it was here that he last conversed with his closest friend.

Oh, Antonius! It had been months since those memories afflicted him with sadness, but he felt accosted by them again, plagued by the grief that would never end.

This time it was intermingled with a sobering realization that he might suffer the same fate. An image of himself, hanging from a tree with fire climbing higher, licking his feet, settled in his mind. He shook his head to clear it, and tried to focus on the present.

He followed the tribune down the stairs yet again, forcing himself to cease imagining the tortures to come. No use wondering about the future! He had thrown in his lot with this family of Christians, come what may.

They reached the bottom, where a young woman huddled against the wall, her ankles bound with the familiar iron shackles. Most remarkably, she possessed no clothing but her long hair provided enough cover for modesty's sake. Despite the bruises causing her eye to swell and her lips to bleed, she radiated an uncommon beauty and poise, such that Pancras was enamored. It was not the corporeal flame that he felt with Daphne; no, this was an interior admiration for wonders wrought in the soul.

"My dear dove, what have they done to you?" Nereus exclaimed, kneeling down beside her. He stripped off his cloak and wrapped it around her shivering flesh.

She offered a weak smile. "I have no fear."

"Your spirit is unbroken, then?"

"The Lord is my strength and my song, whom shall I fear?"

Nereus smiled and chuckled, a disjointed reaction in such glum surroundings. "I am happy that he is sustaining you."

"And he will continue to do so, even to the lions."

Who was this *Lord* they speak of? Was he the same as the Christ, or a different god? Despite following the conversation closely, Pancras was mystified.

"Nevertheless, I have come with hope," Nereus offered. "The *ecclesia* met this evening with our Papa, and I will bring you to a place of safety."

She smiled demurely, the sweetness of innocence. An undefiled flower in a graveyard of bones. A song rising above the cacophony of noise.

"I go to speak to Galerius now. Please pray, Domitilla. Pray as you never have before. If this goes well, I will come for you two nights hence. If it does not, then I shall join you in the arena."

Pancras was shocked and studied his face for a trace of irony or humor, but found none.

"I am ready to do his will," Domitilla replied with an unearthly peace. And that was it – no trembling before fang and claw, no anger at the unjust fate that brought her to this place of torment. No, surrender alone would be her weapon – and Pancras took note of it. It reminded him of the resignation of his old friend, a resignation that seemed foolish at the time. Yet now, such acceptance seemed nothing less than an act of heroic courage.

"May God bless you, my sister," Nereus concluded, laying a chaste kiss on her mud-caked hand.

Nereus and Pancras rose and ascended, but for some reason unfathomable Pancras did so with reluctance. What was it about her presence that drew him? He would have been content to spend all night in the bowels of the earth with her, rather than return to the pedantic world of men.

But return they did, and with a firm heart, they began a journey that spanned yet another watch in a night that dragged interminably long.

~~~

"At this hour? You must be mad!" exclaimed the Praetorian Guard on the palace steps.

"All the same, I beg you to rouse him," Nereus replied evenly.

"He will have my head. His temper…"

"Yes, I know. It is a fearsome thing. Then allow me passage and I will rouse him myself."

"I am under strict orders…"

266

"And I am of higher rank."

"I will grant passage if you leave the sword with me."

Nereus unbuckled the leather straps and handed the sword and scabbard to the guardsman. "As you wish."

"So you are serious?"

"This matter is urgent and cannot wait until morning."

The guardsman stepped aside, allowing passage for Nereus and his young charge. The two began a rapid march through the marble hallways lined with brightly-colored linen banners, a testimony to the festive spirit that accompanied the visiting tetrarch. Under ordinary circumstances, Pancras would have loved to leisurely stroll the halls, wondering at the fine statuary and the intricate capitals that topped the towering columns. But these were not usual circumstances – and Pancras' stomach was tightening with each step. To meet the tetrarch, the co-Emperor, one of the four most powerful men in the Empire, and to do so while holding their lives in their hands!

Nereus was familiar with the layout, and he quickly found the room he had been searching for.

"Justus!" he called out to the sleeping figure, prone on the bed.

Startled, he looked up. "Who is there?" he demanded groggily.

"It is I, Nereus. I need you to wake Galerius and meet me in the atrium. There is an urgent matter I must discuss."

"He is likely to be piss-drunk," he coarsely responded, making no motion to move. "I doubt he will come."

"All the same. He needs to adjudicate an urgent case."

A heavy sigh, then a roll out of bed. "Meet us there in a bit."

Satisfied, Nereus took Pancras back out into the large atrium. It was covered in frescos, the likes of which Pancras had never seen. Tired as he was, he delighted to see such art. Nymphs played in fountains, satyrs pranced around ancient oaks. The gods had taken human form, throwing thunderbolts across the sky. Here and there were the virtues personified. The epic struggle of Romulus and Remus formed a border over the main entryway. Pancras was entranced, drinking it in as the hanging lanterns threw a sepia wash over the walls.

Nereus, exhausted and perhaps feeling more acutely the burden of his station, sat upon a low couch at the end of the room, watching young Pancras' wonder.

"Pancras," he said at length, his voice weary and aging quickly.

Pancras gave him a grateful smile.

"Do not speak in this meeting."

He nodded soberly, sensing the somberness of the moment.

At that time, the man named Justus came in, along with a balding, well-built man. Both were wearing togas of many colors, but the other man's was wreathed in a gold trim, and a coronet of golden olive leaves ringed his brow.

Nereus stood and bowed. "My lord."

"Nereus, my old friend," Galerius replied, drowsily. "I had wished to see you during this visit to Rome, but not at this hour!"

They laughed appreciatively, but it was forced.

"Please forgive the intrusion, sir. But I wish to make an intervention on a case that is most pressing."

In the dim light, Pancras became aware that the man named Justus was eyeing him oddly.

"Please, proceed. But first, who is this fine young man you have brought with you?"

"This is…"

"I know you!" Justus interrupted coldly. "You were at the auction. I had tried to purchase you for Maximian."

Dark memories resurfaced, swimming in shadows. Pancras was frozen to the floor.

"Ah, you have good taste, Justus," Galerius crooned, sickeningly sweet. He softly caressed Pancras' face, close enough that the boy's nostrils were offended by the lingering odor of sour wine on the junior emperor's breath. "He is beautiful, beautiful…"

"As I recall," Justus added, "You paid an exorbitant sum. He is educated, sturdy, upright…"

With a firm grip, Galerius grabbed the boy's shoulders. "Educated, you say? My boy, you were saved from Maximian, so that you might belong to me."

"Pancras is no longer a slave," Nereus interjected, alarmed at this intoxicated behavior. "He is a free man, a citizen of Rome."

"Ah! In that case, I am not able purchase him, am I? No? But I can still make him an offer. See, Pancras, this palace!" He stumbled back, still shaking off his drunken stupor, and swept his arms around the room, gesticulating grandly at the artwork. "See this grandeur! Do you not wish to be a part of this?"

Pancras looked desperately at Nereus, who commanded with his eyes – *be silent!*

"How would you, Pancras, like to be the son of an emperor?"

269

The boy did not respond. But the offer kindled a spark of desire in his heart. Who could pass up such an opportunity? Glory and wealth, honors and pleasures! Only the bizarre behavior of the emperor himself prevented Pancras from leaping at the offer.

"Galerius, I do not wish to keep you," Nereus hastily said. "Perhaps I may explain the reason for my visit..."

"No, no, not yet. I am not done with your young friend," Galerius replied, still prancing gaily around the room. "Now, Pancras, my house is empty. My son is grown, my wife is distant. The palace echoes with the voices of sycophants, but nary is there one whom I can love like a son."

His feet became unsteady, so he leaned up against the couch. "If you grow weary of this filthy soldier and his sniveling steward, I will welcome you here." He laughed at his own joke, oblivious to the stone-faced soldier he just insulted.

Once again Nereus tried to bring the topic back. "Your excellency, it has come to my attention that the niece of Diocletian is currently in prison, awaiting execution."

He snorted. "She spurned an offer of marriage. It is a dangerous thing to turn down an offer from an Emperor." His bemused smile was aimed directly at Pancras.

Was that a veiled threat?

"Be that as it may, I ask for your permission to take her and execute her myself, outside of the city walls," Nereus said. "I fear that a public spectacle would only serve to anger Diocletian and provoke a public reaction."

"But she broke the law. Surely you are aware of the Edict against such people."

"Yes, I am aware. But consider the political implications of executing a person of such stature. As the niece of the Emperor, her death would have ramifications across the Empire that might be for your downfall."

"Thank you for your concern," he droned sarcastically. "I want to feast my eyes upon her blood. She humiliated me!"

"I will bring back her head, that you may see with your own eyes that she has suffered the penalty."

Such words shocked the boy! How could his master promise such a gruesome thing? This was incongruous with the kind and gentle father he saw in the prison, who treated Domitilla with such tenderness.

"You promise me?" Galerius asked like an immature child hoping for a treat from his father. "You promise you will bring me her head?"

"Your excellency, I myself have a vested interest in this," Nereus replied soberly.

"Yes, yes I suppose you do. Have there been insurrections since my return to Rome?"

"They remember what you did in Nicomedia and Persia."

The Emperor looked solemnly at the floor. Was that repentance on his face, or resignation? He was inscrutable; or perhaps he was still drunk.

"You may do as you propose," he replied at last. "Justus, see to it that Domitilla is not led to the arena tomorrow."

The palace steward nodded his response.

"But as for you, young man," he continued, addressing Pancras with a smile that was profoundly unsettling, "Come here, sit by me."

Torn loyalties – should he obey his master, or this emperor? His heart hammering and his stomach turning, he slowly went over to the Emperor and sat beside him.

Galerius wrapped his arm around the boy, far too familiar for comfort. "Pancras, I am not the monster they make me out to be."

He looked up to the graying emperor, who was aging quickly. Had those lips truly ordered the death of the innocent? He looked like a harmless grandfather, on the cusp of dotage. Perhaps the Christians had been spreading propaganda about him, lies to besmirch his reputation among the populous.

"Truly, my son. I have always wanted what was best for the Empire. And I will always want what is best for you. Stay here with me. You must be tired – I will prepare a bed for you…"

The boy noticed that Nereus was barely concealing his loathing for this man.

"Thank you, but I must return home with Nereus," Pancras replied, rising and hastening to his master's side.

The emperor nodded sadly, and Pancras felt a pang of compassion for his loneliness. Despite the gold and silk, he was a man – no more, no less.

"I thank thee, Emperor. We will take our leave and allow you your rest. Hail, Caesar!" His arm shot out in the classical salute.

Galerius half-heartedly returned it.

With urgency, Nereus and Pancras hastened – no, *fled* would be more accurate – from the Emperor's presence.

"I was mistaken to bring you," Nereus muttered under his breath. "Now Galerius knows of your existence. He fancies himself a god – he speaks, and it is done."

"Yet he did not seem evil. Merely an old man who yearns to be loved."

"On this, you must trust me. I have seen things that would send you to the shores of the underworld."

Pancras was silent. It was a hard world.

But it was made harder by the ambiguity of man. How could Nereus promise to commit an atrocity? Where was this god of love he professed to follow?

He was about to give voice to such thoughts, when Nereus spoke first.

"Where is my sword? Where is the guardsman?"

The guardsman stationed at the palace door had vanished, and the threshold lay unattended.

"This is most unusual," he exclaimed, throwing wide the door to behold a scene out of the most deranged Greek tragedy.

The city appeared as on fire with an unearthly glow. A roar of men echoed across the streets, a pride of lions intent on destruction. From their perch atop the palace stairs, the violence had already become visible, as men marched with torches toward the villa. Swords gleamed in the torchlight, intent on bloodshed.

"They have arrived. Stay here, Pancras." Nereus quickly cascaded down the steps.

"Where are you going?" the boy cried out, acutely aware of his vulnerability.

"To fetch my legion," came the response.

But that was not necessary. The rhythmic tramping of boots swelled, signifying the approach of the Praetorian Guard and the *cohortes urbanae*.

Dozens of soldiers came forth from the barracks, lining the stairs of the palace. Nereus took his place among them and began to bark orders, sending some here, others there. The battle was fast approaching.

The rioting men were speaking an obscure tongue, for they were yet another tribe that called this city their home. Pouring into the street with weapons bared, they threatened and goaded the soldiers to make the first move. But the well-trained guardsmen would not be provoked. Their shields formed a wall, which proclaimed: this far shall you go, and no farther!

The tension was boiling, threatening to break the thin veneer of peace at any moment. This was no democratic demonstration; no, these men meant war. Whatever grievances they had against Galerius would be settled by the shedding of blood this night.

"Down with Galerius!" some cried in Latin. "His head on a pike!"

These were yet more of the people aggrieved by the bloodlust of Rome. How shall they solve such atrocities, except by murder and violence themselves?

And then, from the back of the crowd sailed a rock, then a small hailstorm of them. Some guardsmen were hit and wounded.

It was evident that the tribune was reluctant to apply the sword. But as it seemed inevitable, Nereus forcefully gave the command, and the soldiers rushed upon the armed crowd.

Pancras watched from his vista, at once fascinated and appalled. The cries of men mingled with the clashing of swords. It was utter chaos; it was choreographed elegance. It was brutal and ruthless; it was necessary and just.

The foreigners numbered well over a hundred, and the guardsmen were less than half that number. But the superior training gave the Romans an advantage over these peasants.

The torches that garishly lit the battlefield also sparkled upon the rivers of blood beginning to pool on the ground – Roman blood or foreign blood, he did not know. He could see a few men fall to the ground, their life-force drained from them. It disgusted the young servant-boy, but he could not turn away.

Nereus stood away from the fray, still weaponless and directing the battle. Periodically he would shout instructions to his men, who heeded him over the din of shouts and clangs.

Would he ever be free of blood? he wondered as it poured over him once again. The sights brought him back to the arena. His stomach wrenching, his pulse pounding – was it for the carnage unfolding before him, or the memories it induced?

More blood rained down, watering the cobblestones, mixed with the innards of a man who had been sliced through the gut. The shrieks of the dying were an awful cry.

And then, from the corner of his eye, movement arose from the west, a man approaching Nereus from behind.

Pancras cried out, and Nereus glanced behind him in time to see the man's sword lifted high to strike.

A deft dodge allowed Nereus to escape the blow, but the man quickly abandoned the sword and seized him around the neck, intending to choke the life from him.

Without a thought Pancras was descending the stairs. He quickly drew the dagger from his breast and, with a bestial cry, lunged toward the attacker. The blade found its way deep into the back, cutting through rib and lung.

A muted exclamation escaped the wounded man's lips, as he lost his grip and tumbled to the ground, his essential fluid draining quickly. Within seconds the man was dead.

Pancras looked down to his hand, still gripping the crimson blade. The blood had crept up onto his hand, his arm, his sleeve, his very soul. He had now become that which he feared – and a manly bravery began, in seminal form, to grow within him.

It was as if the battle had faded into a muted whisper. Time seemed to slow as Nereus stood and shook himself off, looking deep into Pancras' eyes with a mixture of pride and sadness. The soldier suddenly looked very tired and worn, a man whose time had passed.

"Thank you," he said, gruffly.

Pancras nodded his acknowledgement.

"Now, go home. You have had enough for one night."

"I will do no such thing. I will stay and fight with you."

But the battle was over. The men of foreign tongue were surrendering. The clatter of swords falling to the ground echoed, as the shouts subsided. The remaining Praetorians encircled the men with swords drawn, forcing the submission. Heavy chains were applied to some of the men, lest they seek to flee.

"Now we shall do to you what was done to the men of Nisibis," they were told, leaving them quaking with fear.

The condemned men seemed already dead in soul, Pancras thought. He tried to feel hatred for them, but they had families and children, too. Heads hanging, they were seeking justice for their countrymen – justice that the murderous Empire handed out to all, regarding none with compassion.

As he watched them led away, he looked back down at his hand. It was still warm and wet, as if the blood still had vitality in it. That man who lay at his feet would never rise again – and Pancras was as ferocious and guilty as the Empire he loathed.

He could overhear his master speaking with an underling about disposal of the bodies – a clinical man performing his obligatory tasks. Surely *he* no longer looked at blood with horror. Perhaps shedding enough of it makes one immune.

Was it right? Was it wrong?

He had taken a life.

Killed a man.

The realization had yet to burrow into his mind.

Nereus returned and gave a light pat on the back. "Time to go."

They walked in silence all the way home, Pancras' mind swimming with sleepless and disjointed thoughts.

He noted, as he stumbled into bed, that the horizon had just begun to crest red with the dawn. The color of a new day. And the color of blood.

~~~

He slept far into the afternoon, when he was awoken by the sounds of bustle in the domus.

Coming into the kitchen, he was drowsily surprised to see Aquila and Achilleus packing all of their pottery into a tall wooden crate, with strips of linen between each fragile dish.

"What is this?" he queried.

"Oh, Pancras! You must be hungry." Aquila began to fuss about the kitchen. "Some bread? Figs? We have some milk…"

"Yes, thank you."

Meanwhile Achilleus continued loading the crate, item by meticulous item.

"Why are we packing?"

Achilleus gazed thoughtfully at him, but did not answer.

A plate of flatbread with a cup of milk was brought forth. "I will put this in the triclinium," Aquila commented. "You should wash up."

Pancras looked down at his hands and a shiver of shock overtook him. The blood had dried a rusty maroon. His hand was still caked in it, and splatters dotted his tunic.

"I...I...yes, I must," he stuttered, shaking.

"Go quickly."

He fled.

~~~

The blood comes off the hand easily enough; it is the bloodstains in the mind that remain. Did he want to think about what he had done? No, it was better to keep it out of his thoughts.

It had been a while since his fragile grip on sanity had begun to slip. When was it? – oh yes, Antonius' death, when he lost everything for three days. But here he did not have the luxury of three days of insanity. By that time he might be dead. Who would kill him? The Persians, the Emperor, the lions?

To stay sane was to stay alive. He would push all those memories to the brink of existence, off the cliff where forgetfulness may swallow them whole. Especially the memory of last night.

Returning home, he ate and drank until he was fortified. By this time, Achilleus had moved on to the library, where he was sorting the scrolls into another wooden crate. Curiosity ate at Pancras as he ate his bread, and when he could take no more of either, he demanded an answer.

"Achilleus, why are you packing?"

The rotund man looked up, his grotesque features still bringing mirth to Pancras' countenance.

"Take what you need. We leave on the morrow."

"Leave? Where are we going?"

"We are taking Domitilla to safety."

"And where is that?"

"Pontia."

"I have never heard of this place."

"And that is what we are counting on. May the Emperor be as ignorant."

Whether he meant that as a slight, Pancras was unsure. "I see."

"Will you help me pack?"

Pancras nodded, and the two worked in silence for a while. Quills and ink, parchment and papyrus, scrolls and vellum were carefully stacked inside the wooden crate.

"What will we do with the desk and the scroll rack?"

"We leave it here. No space on the cart."

They continued, moving along to another room.

Time passed, and the task was helpful at keeping the memories at bay. Until Achilleus decided to reopen the wound.

"I heard about last night. I am praying for you."

No! Stay far away from that territory!

But Achilleus continued, "It is not easy. You are far younger than I was when I first witnessed such atrocities, let alone had my hand in one. But let it not trouble your heart. You have done nothing wrong. Your deeds were courageous and just – you must not regret them."

Nothing wrong! He spilled blood. Who made him the arbiter of right and wrong, life and death?

"Nevertheless," the big man continued, "I pray for you, for the memory of such bloodshed does not heal easily."

What good are prayers? Have any of the gods ever responded?

Pancras pursed his lips, angry that the topic was broached. He would not cry, no, hold back those tears...but flow they must, of anger and shame and disgust at himself and this wretched Empire that forces men into such barbarism...

"Lord, heal our brother," Achilleus prayed aloud. "Heal this young man's heart. Heal his memories. We commend his soul to you."

This was too much!

And Pancras stormed out of the room, into his own alcove where, drawing the curtain, he could be alone with his torturous memories.

~~~

From his perch atop the bouncing mountain of crates, Pancras watched the horizon begin to glow, illuminating the city that was quickly fading into the past. A caravan of four carts, hitched to horses, formed a procession along the cobblestone road. Pancras kept the boxes company behind Nereus and Aquila, while Achilleus commandeered another carriage, accompanied by Domitilla. Other families, whom Pancras recognized but did not know personally, pulled up the rear.

The wooden chests, packed tight with every last item in the house, were held in place with carpetbags, blankets, mattresses, and all the flotsam of human existence. It had been loaded in the darkness before the dawn, as if slinking out of town in the shadows would offer some protection to the condemned. The mission was dangerous – if caught trying to save her life rather than take it, it would be their blood required.

But as the distance between their caravan and the Eternal City grew, so did the realization that these dishes and blankets and clothes were not meant for a three-day trip. Was this exile to be permanent?

The sun weaved in and out of clouds, threatening rain.

Where were they going? The road led to Ostia, and points beyond. But where was the *beyond*?

More importantly, what was he leaving? He hated the city, its rivers of blood and the foul stenches and the corruption of its people. But he also loved the city, the city of his youth and his friends. And his *together* – would he see her again?

Conflicted as he was, he faced backward until the city disappeared from view.

What was his destiny? Was it back there, where he had been promised the world? Or was it towards an uncertain future?

Hours upon hours passed, along with periodic smatterings of rain from the overcast skies. In silence they traveled, pressing on farther than comfortable to put more distance between themselves and the Emperor who wanted the girl dead.

At a roadside fountain, they disembarked and took long draughts, allowing the horses a rest. Nereus reclined beneath the shadow of a holm oak pregnant with acorns, evidently grateful that the bouncing had subsided for the moment. His face still characteristically grave, he must have been acutely aware of the danger.

Pancras sidled up to him, sitting on the grass. Much to the boy's surprise, Nereus gave his shoulders a paternal pat.

"Do you fear for our success?" the boy asked, the tension palpable.

"I fear nothing," he replied gruffly. "I trust in the Lord. If we live, we live. If we die, we die."

"Even so, I wish to live."

The soldier plucked a blade of grass and clenched it between his teeth.

"I see that we have packed everything. The scrolls, the armor, every last dish in the house..." Pancras observed.

"Let us hope they arrive in one piece! They were imported from Neapolis!"

They shared a muted chuckle.

"I fear to inquire, though," the lad continued, "Is this relocation permanent?"

The man squinted thoughtfully. At length he replied, "There comes a time when a man must abandon his beloved, all that he fought for, when this beloved becomes corrupted beyond recognition. He will always love the ideal; that which she could be. But the virgin has become the whore. Fallen, fallen is Babylon the great!"

"Your home? Your city?"

"It goes down in flames."

And the reality began to sink in – the permanence of this move. He would never stroll along the Tiberis, his hand melting into hers. He would never take his beloved into his home, he would never rise in society to the upper echelons. All of this was slipping from his grasp, like a leaf cast upon the river flows onward until it is beyond reach.

"And as for me..." he croaked out, choking on the words.

"Pancras, I offer you a better way to live. There are some things that, once stolen, can never be returned."

He looked down to his hands, the hands that slew a man. Nothing could undo such brutality – he had become what he feared.

But Daphne!

"And if I wish to remain in Rome?"

"You are not my slave; you are free to return."

"But you think it imprudent."

"Few could remain without drinking of its poison."

"Yet you have remained unscathed."

His look spoke volumes of the wounds he bore, wounds upon the soul. "My calling is – or was – to fight, that those beneath me might be free. Your destiny is different."

"You speak of my destiny, but I do not know what it is."

"The elder said you were among the Lord's anointed."

The understanding was so instantaneous that a shiver ricocheted through his spine. "So this is why you have tried to protect me from evil? Because of the prophecy of some condemned criminal?"

"No, Pancras. You judge me wrongly," he replied severely. "I seek to protect you because the evil of Rome corrupts all men, no exceptions. Only misery awaits those gluttons, drunkards. Brutes! All of them!"

"And you have discovered a better way?"

"Love. Love, Pancras, is the better way."

"I have a love, Dominum. She awaits me back in Rome."

A lengthy look, but nothing more from the centurion for the time being.

The horses having drunk, the women having taken care of their needs, the rain started in earnest.

Nereus rose with a harrumph and began to hitch the horse again. "We must work in the daylight, for nightfall is drawing nigh."

But Pancras sensed a double meaning in his words. "If I may speak freely - for a soldier, you are quite a poet."

"Poetry…" he grunted, lifting the harness upon the girdle.

"…helps me…" he continued, adjusting the bridle.

"…forget…" The man hoisted himself up to the seat.

"…the blood."

~~~

Periodically the rain would fall, light showers that chilled them to the bone, before the sun would peek its brilliant head out, lifting their spirits and filling them with warmth. Pancras recognized the landmarks along this road. He had traveled it many times with his uncle to the beaches of Ostia, during better days when their hearts were light.

And oh! The memories returned of his journey along this road, yes, this very same road! – when he first arrived in this land, as a young boy. Half-crazed, aching with grief, alone in the world – it seemed a lifetime ago. Now he was no longer a boy, but a man. He had been through the crucible and had come forth stronger. He had seen the depths of prison, mourned his dead, fallen in love, killed a man. What had transpired in these past three years!

And yet, as the cart leapt and vaulted over the uneven cobblestones, the bulla bobbled on his chest as his link to that young boy. He gripped it once again, as he did a hundred times each day, remembering wistfully the man who had given it to him. The grief was not as piercing as it had been on that same road three years ago, but it dwelt in the background, awaiting the unexpected moment to drag him into the past. Reminding him yet again that he was alone in the world.

All this will be yours, echoed in his ears again. But he would always respond – *all this has been taken away!*

This time, no one could take it away from him. No, the glories of Rome would not be denied him. His beloved would be waiting for him. The decision had been made – he would return.

If he could not have Phrygia, at least he could have Rome.

His heart was resolved.

He needn't become as bloodthirsty as Nereus believed. Did not this city have a noble past, ruled by men of honor and culture? His master was wrong – some things that were lost *could* be restored. And he would be a part of the restoration.

There was another pause, as the journey had become exhausting and the people were as shaken as marbles in a bag. This time, the disembarking featured Nereus sitting by Aquila, wrapped in an embrace of love, speaking of practical matters. Achilleus was busy drawing water for the horses.

And then there was the princess. She had wandered into the field, picking the last of the autumn flowers to accentuate her simple braid. Despite the bruises and scars – now healing – she struck him as a paragon of virtue, a source of sunshine on this overcast day. Why was his heart stirred towards her, albeit in a different way than his Daphne? He would never know. Better to forget her – he would not see her again!

With an unwavering intent, he marched up to his patrons.

"Sir, my lady, please pardon the interruption."

They ceased their conversing and gazed upon him.

"I have decided, as a free man, to return to Rome. I thank you very much for all of the tremendous kindnesses you have shown me during my time with you, but my life is in Rome."

Aquila was unsurprised, as they had evidently been discussing this among themselves. "Where will you stay?"

"Nereus, is the tetrarch serious about his offer?"

Nodding, he said nothing. But his silence was loaded with disapproval.

"Then I shall take my destiny as the son of the Emperor."

"My son, I warn you again – there is no greater tragedy than being assassinated as the Emperor's son."

"Shall I not enjoy the protection of the Praetorian Guard?"

"Do you not know your history? How many of our Emperors have been betrayed?"

"Yet they were wicked men. I will bring back honor and dignity to the public life."

"A noble task to be sure. But to them, you will merely be fresh meat, thrown to the wolves."

"I thank you for your concern, but I am not afraid. I have seen the world, and am ready to be a part of it."

"You have seen nothing!"

Pancras took a deep breath, steadying his nerves. "When I was a child, my father promised me that all this would be mine – the homestead, the joy. When I had lost him, my uncle took me to the Temple of Jupiter and promised me that all this would be mine – the glories and wealth of Rome. This, too, had been stolen from me. I will not surrender this third chance."

Aquila spoke. "What if…what if all that you were promised is yet to be fulfilled?"

"It will be – by my own hand. Nereus, you spoke of my destiny. I know what my destiny is to be – to be the son of the Emperor, to rise up, to restore the noble glory of Rome."

Aquila, concerned, addressed her husband. "Dear!"

He replied with a sigh of resignation, "I shall not object. Go with God, then."

"I need nothing from your deity, nor any other. Thank you again – I wish you the best on Pontia." He turned and set his face toward Rome.

"If you wish, ride with us further. We are only a few stadia from Ostia. Then, I will give you a horse to return to Rome."

Yet another act of generosity! Knowing this would save him hours of walking, he nodded gratefully, and climbed upon the cart once again as the journey began anew.

~~~

Arriving in Ostia toward the end of the day, they unloaded the cart amidst a chilling fog that blew in off the sea. A ship had been prepared for them, and a crusty sea captain greeted them when the first crates came aboard. Although anxious to return to the palace, Pancras carried his share of luggage, in gratitude for their gifts.

Within the hour, the task was done, and unsentimentally the passengers boarded. The soldier and the captain engaged in a private discussion, resulting in them trading horses, for Nereus' steed had tired hauling the cart.

As the rest of the family settled into the ship, Nereus stayed aground to teach the basics of horsemanship to the boy, who had never ridden before.

"Balance well, Pancras. There you go! Hold tight to the reigns. This old mare loves to gallop, I hear. She is a fast one, and do not be afraid to ride her hard. You can cover those stadia in no time! I hear Galerius is hosting a celebration tonight before departing for Tivoli tomorrow – arrive quickly and you shall find a warm welcome. Stay in the saddle – now you've got it! Let me see you trot around…well done. You are adept at this – it is as if you grew to manhood on the hide of a horse! Fare thee well, and I wish you Godspeed."

Mounted on the back of a majestic beast, Pancras felt a surge of pride. Straightening up, he said, "Nereus, I thank you with all of my heart. You have been kind to me beyond any other. You will always have a friend in the court of the Emperor."

Nereus acknowledged this with a solemn nod.

And with a kick of his heels, Pancras left only dust and mud in his wake as the port of Ostia became merely a memory.

~~~

The stadia continued to tick away, one by one. The lad was enjoying the ride, despite the gathering darkness. He was one with the wind. He was a bird, he was Icarus, he was alive and free and heading toward the most enviable position in the empire.

He knew not what awaited him, but it would be wrapped in gold and silk. Never again need he serve, never again would he hunger. He would be a burden no longer.

The Porta Aurelia was barely noticed as he passed through the city walls into Transtiberim. His old neighborhood! The insula where he spent those long years with his uncle, now flying by in a few long strides. There was the public fountain where he drank on his first morning in Rome. Up ahead, the marketplace where he used to buy bread, now shuttered. The late hour was a benefit, as the streets were vacant, allowing him to make haste.

He knew the way without aid. How often he had passed the palace, longing to be invited in – and now it would be his home forever!

And there it towered, a black figure against a black sky. Cries of revelry flowed from every open window.

He approached the gate, where a Praetorian guard stood watch. Upon his signal, Pancras brought the horse to a stop.

"I have come at the invitation of the Emperor."

"Who art thou, pray tell?"

"I am Pancras, the friend of Nereus. Surely you know him?"

The soldier nodded, but was unsure of whether to allow this boy further into the compound. After some repartee, it was decided that Justus would be summoned to vouch for the invitation. Pancras waited impatiently until Justus came out, clutching a goblet of wine in his hand.

Even in the darkness, it was surprise – no, definitely shock – that registered upon his face. "You are Nereus' charge, are you not?"

"I was. But he has granted me liberty to accept the Emperor's gracious offer."

"Yes, I recall," he said with great suspicion. To the guard, he demanded, "Frisk him. No weapon of his shall be admitted to the palace."

Pancras dismounted, and handed over his dagger. He began to climb the stairs but was closely trailed by a suspicious Justus.

"Why are you here, boy? Have you come with ill intent?"

He stopped and faced his accuser. "Not in the least. The Emperor welcomed me into his retinue."

"You do not know what you are asking."

"I am not worthy to be the Emperor's son, I know. But I believe it is part of my destiny."

It was difficult to identify the distilled malice coming from the man's gaze. Was it envy? Fear? Suspicion? No matter – with confidence would he walk among the giants!

He ascended fearlessly and, recalling the layout of the building, quickly found the grand atrium. The sound of merrymaking guided him, thrilled him. But he was completely unprepared for the scene that unfolded before his eyes.

For at the moment he turned the corner and beheld the room overflowing with guests, every sort of vice was on display before him.

There, off to the side, were men doing unnatural things with men. Likewise were the women lying with women, in a manner foreign to humankind. There, visible to all in the room, were several people gouging their throats to forcefully vomit into bowls held by servants. Several times their aim was poor, and the servants found themselves covered by the rank vomitus. A man was pouring strong wine all over the face of a drunken man, whose gaping mouth caught little of it.

Here and there lay the bodies of those who had passed out – or perhaps died, he was unsure. The entire room reeked of bodily odors and vomit, alcohol and the finest foods which were strewn half-eaten across the room. Upon a low table pranced a woman whose clothes had been replaced by a flimsy loincloth of beads, her nakedness available to the many who peeked beneath. A raucous and feverish dance overtook the men and women, who gyrated as if possessed by demonic music. A man found a stuffed pastry to shove into the face of a woman beside him, who laughed hysterically.

And then there were the heads.

Stationed as sentries around the room were numerous severed heads, grotesquely mounted upright on poles. At least two dozen of them stared sightlessly, their mouths agape, their pallid flesh the color of death. A rusty ooze dangled beneath their necks, as brain matter and blood mingled and dripped forth. The few whose eyes were open stared sightlessly at the shameless partygoers, who seemed unconcerned by the grotesque decoration.

In horror, Pancras could not take his eyes off of them. They looked familiar, but he could not understand why, overwhelmed as he was with the disgusting panoply of evil that was shamelessly taking place.

Above the din of this portal to the underworld, he heard his name ring out.

"Pancras! Oh Pancras, I knew you would come!"

And Galerius – drunken, filthy, half-naked Galerius – approached from out of the crowd and put a sweaty arm around him.

"Welcome to my home! No, to *your* home! You have chosen wisely! I would have taken you by choice or by force; you have chosen the better. Allow me to introduce you to my friends!"

He threw up his toga-less arms, wrapped as he was in merely a thin linen sheet, and announced to the crowd:

"Behold! My son has arrived! My dear court, my friends, come and meet Pancras!"

But no one could hear him over the music, which he did not seem to notice. He poured more wine into himself, sputtering and choking and spilling much of it down his chin.

"Do you like my décor?" he demanded, sweeping his arms about the room in broad gestures. "These ornaments – brought to me all the way from Persia!"

And the faces of the dead were no longer a mystery – he had seen them alive two days prior. This was the penalty for rebellion in this empire?

A wave of nausea came upon the boy. He gave up the peace of a tranquil household for this? What had he done?

"Come in, Pancras, you must be hungry!" exclaimed the Emperor.

On the contrary, he was sickened to the core. As much as he blinked his eyes, hoping this was a nightmare, the orgy continued. From every corner, the lust, the gluttony, the malice threatened to overcome him.

Shaking, he turned and vomited. He could no longer stand the assault on his senses, on his mind, on his very soul. Turning, he fled from the palace faster than the daemons could chase him.

~~~

His horse had been tied up, but he loosened the reigns in great haste and galloped away to the questions of the guardsmen.

Out of this city, out of this city! Nereus was right – the heart of Rome was the pits of Hades! Oh why did he have to see it with his own eyes!

292

Down the streets, out through the gate, and into the countryside. The clouds had parted, allowing a half-moon to cast shafts of light upon the ground.

"Oh, please," he pleaded with the night, "Please be docked in Ostia!"

Once again, his only hope lay in this family. He had learned his lesson and would come back contrite and humble. He would grovel, he would beg. The first time he returned to the household, he was innocent, but this time he was guilty. Who was to say if there would be a third chance?

He pushed the horse to its limits. The perspiration became as clouds on the clear night, its muzzle huffing and snorting out bursts of mist as it raced home to the port city.

Through the saddle, Pancras could feel the beast's heart racing, and keeping time with his own thundering heart. The full weight of his own folly, combined with the horrific memories of the evening's debauchery, mingled into despair.

"What have I done?" he cried out. "What have I done?"

All was a blur. Those tears obscuring his view – was it because of the breeze in his face, or the bitter shame of his mistake? This could be the end for him!

As the horse ate up the ground, consuming stadium after stadium, he began to whisper his only hope.

"Oh God of Nereus and Aquila, oh God of Achilleus and Domitilla, if you are true, I beg you to hear my plea. Save me from this destitution. Reunite me with my family. Take pity on me."

His only hope – that this mythical god of the Christians would somehow answer his prayer.

~~~

The city of Ostia was likewise a blur, asleep in the deeps of the night. He was alone on the cobblestone, racing like a madman through the maze of streets.

As he approached the dock, a solitary lantern cast its glow upon the sea. In the fog, he could not decipher if the ship was still docked. The end of the mooring had disappeared into the mist.

Leaping from the horse, he started racing toward the pier when a man instantly materialized from the vapor.

"You have arrived," Nereus said plainly. Not happy or disappointed – merely an observation.

Pancras knelt at his feet. "Once again, I must ask for your compassion."

"I knew you would come."

"You were correct – in everything. The city is totally depraved. Galerius is…"

Nereus cut him off by helping him to his feet. "You needn't say anything. Come, let us be on our way."

~~~

The rhythmic rocking of the ship was cathartic, somehow. He did not bother to lie down, knowing that sleep would be elusive. Too many disturbing sights, and he was unable to rid his mind of such images. He wished that they would not follow him into his dreams. But knowing that they would, he decided to avoid dreaming altogether.

Nothing was visible from the prow of the ship, as they sliced through the fog. A fitting metaphor, he thought. They were sailing, but to where? He was trusting his life to this man, this group. Faith alone must suffice, for he had nothing else left.

A sailor or two kept watch, up in the crow's nest. But futile was their task, for nothing and no one could be seen. They sailed by faith, as well. That, and a fine compass.

His musings were of the darkest kind.

Perhaps Nereus was correct, that some things, once lost, could never be regained. But what did that mean for him? The innocence he lost when dagger plunged into flesh – could that be cleansed? The loss of family and homeland – could that be recovered? Doubt was fighting with hope, and the battle was being lost.

Looking down, he saw that his hands, moist in the mist, were gripping the railing like a lifeline.

Oh well, no matter. Perhaps he needed this railing to be the only stable thing in his life. Everything else seemed as storm-tossed as the chaotic waves.

Oh, these mighty waters, frothing and churning! The chaos outside echoed the chaos inside. Beneath the surface of these waves was nothing but the deeps, where Leviathan reigned supreme. Beneath the surface of his life were the pits that yawned wide to Sheol.

His anguish began to give way to a yearning. It was a reprise of the mysterious longing he felt that day, when the sun was shining and he and Daphne lolled by the river. At the time, the longing was unsettling, but now it had become urgent.

But what words could describe the longing? Was it a search for love? For meaning? For belonging? For innocence? This hunger must be a sign that there really is food for the soul. This ache demands a medicine that must exist, somewhere. For if the search is nothing but vanity, if the longing cannot be satisfied, then what is to prevent him from stepping forth from the railing and abandoning his body to the sea?

No, he was convinced that there was a hidden truth beneath the veneer of life, beyond the trite conversations and mundane tasks. But where can he search for this truth? Perhaps the Greek philosophers? An esoteric mystery cult? Will he find it in friendship, in marriage, in work, in play?

Hope and doubt played each other's adversary, as no answers presented themselves that night, in the mist and the fog, with the breeze at his back.

But something else was at his back – footsteps through the fog.

Domitilla approached and edged beside him. He noted that she, too, looked sleeplessly tired, her bearing weary as the breeze caught her garments and wrapped them around her.

For a while they were content to stare into the darkness together. The cold mist began to bite into them.

"You must be tired," he began. "Your accommodations these last few days are not conducive to rest."

She smiled at him, an unexpected ray of warmth in the chill of night.

"Do you fear this journey?" she asked him simply.

Which journey? The journey to Pontia, or the journey of life?

He chuckled mirthlessly. "After everything I have seen, how can I fear this?"

"You have seen much. But not everything."

He looked at her soberly, and noticed a peace in her face. For a condemned woman, she had remarkable poise. He was unworthy to see such innocence – with his past! – and turned away.

Instead, he asked her, "Forgive my impertinence – but I am very curious. For what reasons did you refuse a royal marriage? I would imagine that it would prove a tempting proposition."

"Not at all," her silky voice replied. "I was already betrothed."

"Ah," he understood. Cheekily, he added, "A regular Aphrodite, eh?"

"My beloved was no mere demigod. He is the Lord of Heaven and earth."

"The Lord of Heaven and earth? I have heard of lovers deifying their beloved, but does that not stretch the imagination a touch too far?"

She laughed, the sound of bells and birdsong. "I know that you do not yet know him. But when you meet him, you will understand."

"Oh, I will have the chance to meet him?"

"I pray this is so. If you do not meet him in this life, then you certainly will in the next."

"I do not understand. What is his name?"

"He is the One that you seek. The One your heart yearns for."

Pancras was tempted to dismiss this as the ravings of the deluded, but her words pierced his heart with surprising accuracy.

Straining to have vision in the darkness, he asked, woundedly, "What do you know about my heart's yearnings?"

"I only know that you share the yearnings of all the sons of Adam. For I have felt them too."

He knew not who Adam was, but it was a strange comfort to know that his burden had been shared by all of mankind, from princess to pauper. "Do you still feel this longing?"

"No, for I have been satisfied. I have tasted and seen."

"Then share with me the banquet! For I hunger still!"

"When you returned to Rome, what did you see?"

"Unspeakable things. I would rather not discuss it..."

"You saw evil."

He considered the simple summation. "Yes, it was evil."

"And evil needs an answer. The answer is love."

"I have seen men do awful things in the name of love. They love themselves, and they fill their coffers on the backs of the poor. They love their country, and they murder those who dare raise their voices against it."

"Love is not an idea, Pancras," Domitilla said, surprising the boy that she knew his name. "Love is a person. Love is the God who created the heavens and the earth. Love is a man who took all our punishment upon himself, the punishment that we deserved for our evil. Love is everlasting life."

"Myths! All myths!" he exclaimed bitterly. The image of a friend burning on a stake...it was too much to bear.

"Joy, peace, patience, love – are these myths?"

He turned and studied her face in the dismal light of the solitary lantern hanging from the mast. Yes, she had these qualities. He could not deny that this myth has brought her an envious peace. He craved it, but feared it.

The sloshing waves drew his attention away. Being in her presence was both a delight and a torture. A delight – for she possessed the banquet. A torture – for it was a reminder of all that he lacked.

"In any case," he muttered, "I cannot believe in your God. The cost is too much."

"The price is always high for that which is most valuable."

"To find your peace, I have to be ready to die?"

"Nothing less than the Cross."

"Oh, I have seen crosses. Those bloodied, emaciated men who hang outside the city walls, screaming as their torture drags on for days...there is nothing peaceful about that."

"Unless it was embraced out of love."

"If it was a choice between the longing or the cross, I would rather suffer the longing until the end of time."

"Then suffer it, you will." Nary had a trace of harshness entered her words; she was as sweet and fresh as the morning dew.

He did not respond.

In silence they stared into the darkness for an eternity – her with hope, him bordering on despair.

At length she bid her goodbye, and headed beneath the deck for a time of rest.

Pancras stood by the rail until the night watch was over and the first feeble streaks of dawn arose over the ocean, casting a haunting glow upon the island of Pontia.

PART FIVE: *Lessons of the Sea*

The dawn burned off the last of the fog as the ship set down anchor. They were still a good ways off from a wave-swept shore, facing a crescent of cliffs towering over a significant beachhead. Froth and swell lapped at the brilliant white sand, as swallows torpedoed in and out of caves etched deeply into the cliff face.

A smaller fishing skiff was coming out to meet them, tacking in the wind. The weatherworn sailor waved up to the passengers, evidently with some excitement.

They began to haul crates and carpetbags from the hold onto the boat, filling every cranny with items or people. Pancras did his share of the heavy lifting, and was left on board to await the small dinghy's return.

Two more trips ensued, ensuring safe passage for all passengers and luggage. Once everyone was safely aground, the larger sloop slunk away and their exile began in earnest.

"Welcome, Nereus. Your arrival has been much anticipated," the leather-faced man said, as he hauled the boat ashore and secured it to a pylon.

"Thank you. I pray that the others have enjoyed safe passage?"

"Indeed. Most are lodging in points north, but this beach should provide you with ample seclusion."

"I am grateful. I know you have little to share; we have brought gifts from Rome."

"We have more than enough. And we are happy to have you."

Turning to Pancras, Nereus said, "Pancras, I wish you to meet Miletus, our presbyter. You will be working with him on the morrow."

With great respect for his dignity, well-earned through decades of hard labor, Pancras nodded deferentially. The old sailor appeared to possess the enviable combination of physical strength along with the wisdom of an aged one.

"Pancras, welcome," the old man said. His beard turned up in a smile, even as it flowed to the center of his brawny chest. "I work these seas, taking in whatever the Lord provides. But my strength has begun to falter as my fires have dimmed; it will be a welcome relief to have strong hands on my boat."

Ah, a fisherman. Pancras had no experience here – but he was grateful to be far away from the ever-hungry noose of Rome, and was open to anything.

Along with the other men, they began to haul the crates further onto the beach, to the mouth of the largest crevice in the cliff.

"It is not the Emperor's palace, for certain. But it is the best we could find for now. We will work on building once you have settled."

Nereus stooped briefly to enter the cavern. Perhaps three paces wide and twelve paces deep, the floor was pockmarked with stones in between the sand. The roof and walls jutted at odd angles, and there was not a scrap of privacy, save a single boulder that protruded from the side.

Pancras watched intently as Nereus sighed, resting his hand on the wall and laying his head upon it. From the glories of a villa on Avetine Hill, to a cave barely fit for a beast! Surely the humiliation would be too much to bear!

But to the boy's surprise, the former soldier turned and, with stoic resignation, said to his family, "Welcome home."

~~~

All it took was a woman's touch. The cavern, while still cramped, took on the semblance of a home. A sheet was hung from the entrance, blocking the wind and providing a retreat from the pounding surf. Beds were quickly assembled, with Pancras and Achilleus dwelling near the entrance as the married couple took up residence behind the boulder. Miletus had brought bread and dried fish, and stood at the entrance while they swept and tidied and found spaces for their copious crates.

"You know this island has quite a history – as does this cave! Legend has it that this is the isle of Aeaea, where Odysseus stayed on his journey. Yes, Homer! This cave, this very cave, was where the sorceress Circe lived. No one knows exactly where, of course; it could have been the beach on the other side of the island, you know, but legend has it that this is her very cave! You know of the story? Of course you do, who has not read the Odyssey! So you tread on hallowed ground. But do not fear the sorceress' powers, I have blessed the whole island, especially this cave, in anticipation of your arrival. May this island remain unmolested and undiscovered by the eyes of Rome – and Circe!" He chuckled at his own jest.

An interesting legend – this was the island immortalized in the greatest of all Greek epics? How often had his father read to him the story, and Pancras had dreamt of visiting these places. Troy, Ismaros, the Island of the Lotus Eaters…and here he stood, on the sand where the legendary heroes of ages past set foot. He paused his work for a moment to savor the timelessness.

"Ah, yes, I pray this island will forever remain untouched by these pagan men. For decades we have lived here in peace. Diocletian's edicts have no force here. We are a small community, perhaps seventy or so, poor and insignificant. May we always remain thus."

"I pray that our presence here may not bring trouble to you," Nereus said.

"We pray so also, but are prepared to do whatever necessary to protect you."

"For this, we are grateful."

"Now, I will leave you to your rest, for your journey has been harrowing. We will have food for your supper – you needn't worry."

"That will not be necessary."

"Nonsense! We have slaughtered the finest lamb. It roasts as we speak. Your arrival is a reason to celebrate!" With those joyous parting words, the fisherman departed.

The crates stacked, the beds laid out, the floor swept free of driftwood, they set about exploring the island.

Pancras followed the fisherman's footsteps. The other families, including Domitilla, had found lodging in other caverns along the cliff, and Pancras passed them by, greeting them with a nod. His eyes lingered upon the Emperor's niece. From palace to pauper, how she had fallen! But he noted that she went about her duties with a secret smile on her face, humming a simple tune. Her degradation seemed not to bother her in the least.

Mystified, he continued onward to the path that led up the side of the cliffs. He felt surprisingly fresh and free on this sparkling morn, as the sea shimmered as on the first day when the gods created the world. It was as if the island, with its blindingly white cliffs and pristine sand, its salt-spray smell and low scrub-pine, offered a baptism of the soul, a chance for a new start.

The trail wound up the cliff-face to an overlook. The view was breathtaking. The horizon stretched on as far as the eye could see. Cerulean water mingled with the silver sheen of the sunlight. He almost had to shield his eyes from the brilliance. The cliffs shone as a blank canvas, awaiting the work of an artist. Overhead the gulls cried aloud, and up along the path, sheep grazed lazily.

He inhaled deeply, feeling a surge of energy. This was the right decision. A simple life, to be sure, but a happy one. So long as he did not think of what was left behind, he was able to enjoy the view, overwhelming the senses.

And then, in the midst of such rapturous beauty, the dart of longing pierced his heart with a vengeance.

All this, and still something missing? What did he still lack?

~~~

It was a welcome odor, the roasting flesh of the lamb. They inhaled deeply, smelling its scent before catching a glimpse of the bonfire that raged.

But when they arrived over the ridge and saw the soft glow and the dozens of people gathered around it, there was a cheer in the air that dispelled their exhaustion from the trip.

They approached the group, and Miletus met them half-way. Extending the handclasp of greeting, he welcomed Nereus.

"They have been anxious to rest their eyes upon you," the sage greeted with a broad smile.

"Your hospitality is most appreciated."

"Come, sup with us."

Nereus and his family drew near to the animated crowd, whose conversation and laughter dispelled any nostalgia for their home country. This was a new life, with new kin – a fresh start.

Pancras looked around in the dim twilight and noticed a few other lads his age, whom he promptly went up to greet. They were friendly but rustic, uncultured in their manners and roughshod in their attire. Nevertheless Pancras was grateful to find peers on the island, peers who were welcoming. They immediately shared their bread and roast meat with the Phrygian, and passed around a communal cup for drinking. They spent a while chatting about inconsequential things.

The conversations wore into the evening, interrupted only by more feasting and laughter. Large and succulent slabs of roast lamb were sliced off and handed around, seasoned with a local spice that Pancras had never tasted before. Wine flowed freely, yet all stayed safely away from the threshold of intoxication. The laughter sounded pure, not at all raucous like the prior evening.

Was it a mere few hours ago that he was at another party? The two differed so drastically that they could barely share the same name. Rome was an indulgence of every pleasure known to man and beast; this gathering was one marked by temperance and joy, true conviviality and the enjoyment of wholesome friendship. Even amidst the trivial discussion with these fellow boys – the games they like to play, their siblings, their provincial lifestyle – there was a lack of guile that Pancras found refreshing, with none of the cynicism to which he had grown accustomed.

At a certain point Miletus got up to offer a toast to the health of their new refugees, which the crowd lustily drank to. Nereus himself offered a short speech of gratitude, which was warmly appreciated.

Despite having never met this group, there was a surprising affection towards the newcomers. What was this bond that brought such disparate strangers together?

After the speeches, the music began. Lute and harp, panpipe and flute combined to provide a melancholy tune. He expected the bawdy lyrics and vulgar dancing to begin shortly – and hence was shocked when it was something else entirely.

The voices soon rose, but instead of a drinking tune, it was a solemn hymn to their deity, praising the Christ. The elderly among them closed their eyes, a tranquil smile on their lips as the anointed words poured forth. Many stood, their hands raised in an act of surrender, as their voices rose together in a sacred offering. Pancras could almost imagine the sounds penetrating the heavens, flowing upward in an incense of love and worship.

Although an outsider, Pancras could only wonder in amazement. Even the boys with whom he shared the *cena* together, these young lads who enjoyed knucklebones and races and could barely sit still in their lessons, stood in their rough woolen tunics and reed-woven sandals, their hands and voices raised together in praise. It was a current of love and unity, the likes of which he had never encountered before.

He sat on the outside of the circle, listening intently, watching the flames dance as the remaining fat of the sheep dripped upon it. They praised this Christ as a god, speaking of his death and rising from the dead. The beauty was captivating. None of the traditional myths – oh, those ancient stories of Mount Olympus! - could inspire such devotion. It is as if the island and the ocean itself became a song of praise on a night such as this.

The song changed, and another one began. The singing continued, even as the air began to crisp and the fire settled down to a bed of coals. By the dim firelight Pancras noticed Domitilla seated by herself, some distance from the inner circle.

He went and sat beside her upon the rock, still warm from the now-hidden sun. With eyes closed, she remained silent, her face radiant with peace.

"Do you miss it? Your family, your position, your city?" he felt he must ask, though he regretted breaking her stillness.

"Miss it? Pancras, do you not feel it? This is my family – this is where I belong."

"I do feel it…a love here that I have never…" his voice trailed off, lest he disparage the memory of those he had lost.

"Grace has brought us together."

Grace? What did she mean by it – what free gift?

She continued. "Do you not sense his love? That is the grace."

And they fell silent before the mystery, as it continued to unfold through the singing and the praying. Some of the assembled throng began speaking in unintelligible tongues – even Achilleus began to babble. Such a display merely added to the mystique.

Yes, it was a grace – a free gift of love. Pancras could feel it, sense it. This eclectic collection of people was not accidental – they were drawn together, held together, fortified with *something*. It was in the air, penetrating their hearts, and Pancras could feel it knocking for entrance on his heart as well.

The song finally drew to an end, and the night was concluded with murmured greetings and well-wishes. With overflowing hearts, they dispersed, each to his own home.

And Pancras returned home with his makeshift family, perplexed but at peace.

~~~

That night, he dreamt of blood and fire.

~~~

A good shove from the pole oar, and they were off!

They set out a couple stadia from the island, far enough that the white crescent cliffs were a mere fingernail on the horizon. Once Miletus was satisfied at their location, they heaved over the gillnets, one on each side of the boat.

The dawn promised to be unseasonably warm, and soon the boy and the man were stripped to the waist as their tasks were completed in silence. His bulla stuck to his bare chest, plastered by the humidity.

A quick heave of the net, sending it deep into the blue, followed by a brief trawling. The boat drifted aimlessly on the current, sweeping up bass and carp, along with the detritus of the sea. Once the hemp-woven net showed signs of filling, they would haul it in, dragging it hand over hand to examine the catch. Worthwhile fish would be tossed into the wooden cask, while the driftwood and seaweed would be sent back to the sea.

They worked in silence for some time, enjoying the placid sea. Small rivers of sweat began forming, carving tracks down their backs and arms, as the sun beat down on the laborers.

Though Pancras had never fished before, it was uncomplicated and he was quite apt at it. But his back and arms began to tire quickly, unaccustomed as they were to such toil. Nevertheless, he could hardly complain, considering the venerable age of his teacher, who was able to heave the heavy nettings without so much as a groan.

The lad had let loose another throw, and he paused to wipe his brow and admire the sea, as still as an undulating plane of glass could be.

"You work well, Pancras," the man said, resting on the flank. "We will have a catch before midday."

Pancras had to squint in the sunshine to see his teacher. "I thank you, sir."

"You have never fished before?"

"With a line and hook, we used to catch carp in the Tiberis in Rome. But rare were the days that we caught one large enough to keep."

He chuckled, remembering the frivolous days of his own youth. "More to pass the time than for food, eh?"

"One could say that."

He watched as the old man, full of years, dipped the oar into the water to drag the nets further into the deeps.

"If I may ask, sir," Pancras began, as he watched a couple fish wriggle helplessly in his trap, "You were introduced as a presbyter. An elder. Is that a title?"

"Oh yes, yes indeed," he answered, leaning on the oar as if a cane. "I lead this small flock, oh yes. We are small in the eyes of the world, but mighty in the Spirit."

Pancras snorted a cynical smile. So this was no mere chance that Nereus assigned him to this fisherman.

"I think you will find me a difficult convert," he replied.

"I do not see you as such."

"But certainly this was Nereus' intention in assigning me to you, when he needs my help in building a domus."

The old man did not immediately respond. He rose and looked out over the vast expanse of sea, unbroken save for a small speck of an island that they called their home.

Finally, he said, "The ocean teaches you many things."

Here their brief exchange ended.

The sun began to tend toward midday, and their catches became sparser. A dogfish here, a hake there. Mostly the nets were drawn up empty, as the creatures sought out the cooler depths, away from the sun-warmed surf.

"Come, we shall sup together," Miletus said, opening a sack with bread, dried fish, and skins of water. "We will head to shore, and if the tides are in our favor, I shall show you the art of collecting mollusks and abalone."

"I am grateful," he replied, tearing into the bread with polite restraint. The old man bowed his head before consuming his.

"My dear Pancras, tell me about yourself. You are not a Roman, I am certain."

"After all these years, my accent betrays me?"

"Not only that – but there is something uncorrupted about your soul."

Uncorrupted? Hah! Pancras was forced to look away, lest his guilty conscience be revealed.

"So all Romans are corrupted?"

"No, no, not at all. Some have escaped the coming wrath by the grace of the Most High. Others by fate, or by

310

ignorance. But for any man who seeks the truth, he is confronted with a choice: hedonism, despair, or faith."

"This seems far too simple."

"And yet have you not seen it?"

The man's piercing eyes, squinting in a bronzed and wizened face, had seen many things, more than Pancras could fathom.

"You ask where I am from," Pancras evaded, changing the topic. "I hail from Phrygia, in the east. You have heard of it?"

"Heard of it?" he harrumphed, in a pantomime of mock-offended. "I am no provincial backwater fisherman, no! I have seen such lands and traveled all over the known world!"

"What brought you to the ends of the earth?"

"Before I was a fisherman, I was a fisher of men. I cast far and wide the net of love and truth. Many large fish I brought in to the quiet waters of his love!"

This mixing of metaphors only served to confuse the boy. "I do not understand. What was your quarry?"

"Souls, my boy!" he laughed, his beard bouncing up and down.

"So you preached your religion to the corners of the earth?"

"Indeed. Many were added to the Lord. Ephesus, Antioch – even up to Dacia, and *nobody* goes that far north!"

"Did you encounter barbarians?"

"Not quite, although those Carpians could be rough. The outskirts of the empire are barely more civilized than barbarians. War-hungry, they were. Had no use for learning or public order. But once we had brought the *evangelion* to them – they were like angels. Angels, I tell you." He smiled wistfully, remembering the good times.

311

"What is this *evangelion* you speak of? What good news?"

"That it is possible to be forgiven."

"Forgiven for what?"

The smile faded. In its place was a somberness that was unnerving to the boy.

"All have sinned, Pancras. All are covered in the filth that stains every conscience. Woe to us if we die unclean! But our faith in the Christ can cleanse every blot."

This proselytism was an irritation that continued to fester. If he could, he would end this conversation and walk away…but being surrounded by fathomless depths of ocean made that rather difficult.

"I do not believe in your Christ," Pancras rebuked. "Does that mean I am still in my sin?"

"Look at your hands, and tell me yourself."

Pancras looked down, and the image of bloodstains reappeared on his tanned flesh. He quickly shook himself, recognizing this as a mind-trick, and eyed the old man with suspicion.

"You know nothing about me!" he cried out.

"Only that we share the same fallen nature."

"And your Christ is the solution?"

"The only way. The only truth. The only life."

"What makes him different than the tinpot saviors who end up lining the Appian Way?"

"Oh, no political champion was he. No, he came to proclaim a kingdom not of this world, for he himself was not of this world."

"Not of this world? As if he was some deity in bodily form!"

"Precisely."

Pancras waited for him to qualify his answer, but the word hung in the salty air, full of meaning and demanding a response.

"You believe this Jesus was a god?"

With a broad sweep of his arm, Miletus pointed out the grandeur around them – the empty sky, the profound depths that lapped the sides of their craft. "Does not the creator love his creatures? And when his creatures had fallen into captivity, would he not rescue them? He paid the ransom for our freedom upon the cross, but life itself could not be killed. Three days hence, and he rose again."

"Yes, I have heard the legends."

"And I have known the eyewitnesses."

"Surely that is impossible! Centuries have passed..."

"I do not know them personally. But I am a priest in the lineage of the Twelve, who touched his risen flesh. I have read their recollections."

"Must you rely on the testimony of dead men?"

A wistful look crossed his face. He did not respond immediately. Instead, he stood up and set the sail toward home.

Pancras watched in silence, chewing his bread thoughtfully. He wondered if he had won this argument – and why did he feel a profound sadness at doing so?

The canvas caught the wind, and they began to cross the vast depths toward Pontia.

After a while, Miletus spoke – barely audible over the laughing surf.

"Yes, I know that he is alive. I have needed a savior more than most, for I have sinned more than most. My younger years were full of the lusts that snare all men – lust for women, lust for blood. Indulging every appetite, seeking to fill a void I never knew...I was Galerius."

Certainly not! This kindly man, balding and wrinkled, could not have thirsted for blood as the tetrarch who displayed severed heads as party decorations.

"Doubt me not, Pancras. I was no different from him, but as a matter of scale. As the Emperor, his sin is writ large – but our hearts were the same. I grew up in Rome, a product of the same corrupt soil that produced our leaders. And as a young man, I lied, cheated, stole, murdered…whatever I pleased.

"And yet, when I met him…when I met him, everything changed. I have been made new. I have experienced forgiveness. And most of all, the emptiness in my soul has been filled – with a love I never deserved."

Free gift, Domitilla had said. A gift of love.

They sailed in silence until their feet touched solid ground.

~~~

That night, he dreamt of blood and fire.

Shivering, he awakened in a tunic soaked in sweat.

Why? he wondered. Why did these nightmares plague him? He remembered little but the anxiety remained. His heart hammered, as goose-bumps arose on his skin.

The bitter bile of fear gnawed at him as it hadn't done since those awful days of his youth. But he had nothing to fear – or did he?

He rose in the night, and carefully picking his way out of the cave, went to the seashore. The tide was out, and the pungent odor of seaweed and rotting fish assailed him. Finding a patch of dry sand just out of reach of the endlessly-thirsty waves, he sat down and stared at the starlit sky.

Blood.

Fire.

The wrenching, twisting, agonizing anxiety churning in his stomach.

Blood – staining his hands, soaking the arena floor.

Fire – watching his father's body consumed, his friend hung in a blaze of humiliation, the flames a foretaste of his own eternal destiny.

And the fear that there was nothing he could do to cleanse the blood; nothing he could do to quench the fire.

~~~

They had come in to dock at midday, the hot sun making fishing fruitless. Yet a series of dark clouds rolled across the horizon, promising liquid relief.

Pancras left the boat to help Nereus with the house. The soldier had been granted a plot of land on the far side of the island, a couple furlongs away. The boy climbed the path to the top of the cliffs, still finding the view from the top to be breathtaking. A light canter brought him quickly to the hilltop where Nereus was packing stones one by one, securing them with a mortar made from ash, lime, and seawater.

Nereus looked up, still crouched as he pasted another stone atop the foundation. He nodded a somber greeting.

"Dominum, I have come to lend assistance. Miletus has finished fishing until the late afternoon hours."

"I thank you," he replied, but looking deeply at the gathering clouds on the horizon, added, "Your help would be of more use to Domitilla. She is tending a flock on the east end; with the approaching storm, you must help her drive the sheep into the pen for their safety."

315

Pancras nodded, eager to offer his help.

The trek was again brief, and he came over a rise to behold the pastoral scene.

From the rock that served as her perch, Domitilla kept a watchful eye on her flock of thirty or so scattered ewes. Surely they belonged to another in the community, but she guarded them as if they were her children. The love in her eyes was touching.

Pancras descended upon the short-cropped grass, wading in between the grazing livestock. Domitilla flashed him a smile as he approached.

All of a sudden, he was back in Synnada, helping his father with his flock of sheep. It was a misty autumn day, and the butchering needed to be done before the snows came and shut down the road to the market.

The young lad had watched Cleonius wrestle the sheep into small stone shed out back. The lamb fought with all its might, knowing what would come. Pancras, for his part, had his small hands on its rump, pushing with all the force a seven-year-old could muster. But with father and son working together, the sheep was soon dragged through the low door. With haste and mercy, Cleonius unsheathed the knife and slit its throat, catching its fast-spilling blood in a basin.

A pang of pity washed over Pancras, for its bleating was frantic and agonized. But this was a necessary part of life, he knew – for he too enjoyed a fine cut of lamb for dinner as much as anyone!

The poor animal collapsed upon its side as its life bled out.

"Father, it is dead," the boy observed.

His father nodded with great solemnity. "It has given its life for you."

"We shall feast tonight!" he exclaimed, smacking his lips with boyish enthusiasm.

"But first, we shall offer a barley cake to the Lares."

"But why?" For the lad liked barley cakes. To waste one was akin to a minor tragedy.

His father began to make quick work of the carcass. A few deft strikes separated the fine woolen hide from the bloody meat underneath.

"Oh Pancras," he chuckled, knowing his son all too well. "Everything we have is a gift from the gods. We must thank them."

"*Everything* is a gift? But you work so hard!"

"And it is the gods who give me the strength to do so. Do not fear the loss of a barley cake, son – if the gods are pleased with us, they will give it back to us a hundredfold!"

The boy smiled giddily at the thought.

"Pancras?" Domitilla asked, standing a few paces away.

Pancras shook himself out of the memory. "All is gift," he murmured. "You said so yourself – all is gift."

She smiled at him, brimming with subtlest joy. "It is all a gift – from a Creator who loves us."

Was he ready to believe that?

With a deep breath, he addressed the matter at hand. "We must bring the sheep in for now – storms threaten."

They quickly got to work and drove the beasts through the dale, to the pen. Domitilla opted to stay in the adjacent cottage, for she had arranged to help the matriarch to spin wool. Pancras took his leave, and the walk back to his cave-home was ponderous indeed.

~~~

That night, he dreamt of blood and fire.

He awoke with an inarticulate cry, his garments soaked with sweat.

Along the far edge of the cave, shadows pranced ominously. Whirling around beneath his blanket, he saw Achilleus standing over him, holding a candle. Profound pity was in his eyes.

"Trouble sleeping, Master Pancras?" he asked.

Pancras rubbed his face. "Dreams. Meaningless things."

"You were crying out – I was concerned some cave spider had swallowed you alive!" He chuckled softly at his own joke.

"Thank you for coming to my rescue," Pancras replied drily. "But I am fine."

"This is the third night for these nightmares, is it not?"

"How did you know?"

"I am a mere cubit away – I hear your murmurings throughout the night. You are not at peace."

He sighed. It would be futile to hide his interior angst. Sitting up, he leaned against the jutting stone wall. "I fear I am not. These have been trying days."

"Miletus can help."

Quietly laughing in scorn, he replied, "The fisherman? I know he is revered as a holy man, but..."

"Come with me." He led the way out of the cave, allowing no riposte.

Frozen, he pondered for a moment – did he want to follow?

Well, he certainly did not want to continue being disturbed by such dreams. Their specific content was inaccessible during waking hours, but his racing heart knew that the fire was consuming him, the blood drowning him.

Reluctantly he rose, hoping that this eccentric shaman would be able to find a cure for the ailments of his mind.

Achilleus led the way, his candle-flame barely able to push back the oppressive darkness. Up the cliff path they went, across the upper fields, and through a collection of grapevines which whispered in the night wind. Their feet led through a forest of massive oaks – some larger than a man's embrace could encircle. At the edge of the forest, perched atop the highest crest of the highest hill on the island, was a small stone hut, simple and without extravagance.

The solitary window glowed, indicating that the resident still stirred. What watch of the night was it? Pancras tried to determine from the few stars that peeked through the clouds.

Without hesitation Achilleus rapped on the door, but received no response. Leaning in close, he evidently heard something, for he opened wide the door and motioned the boy to enter.

"I trust that you know the way home," he said kindly, before beginning his own descent.

And so here he was, outside of the fisherman's hut, alone on a strange island in the middle of the night. The absurdity of it all struck him forcefully, but, with nothing to lose – he fearlessly crossed the threshold.

It was perhaps the simplest home he had ever seen. Barely tall enough to stand erect, he noted that it was perhaps two strides across and the same lengthwise. Lit simply with two small oil lamps, the presbyter was upon his knees with his arms extended, facing a wall upon which a simple painting had been hung. The portrait was unrefined, lacking artistic merit. It featured a woman in a veil, looking downcast. She held a young child in her arms.

"Forgive me, Dominum. I do not mean to intrude, but Achilleus had mentioned that…"

"Silence in the presence of the Lord!" he roared without a flinch.

Pancras was taken aback by the outburst. His heart hammering, he slunk upon one of the two stools in the hut, leaning his weary head against the stone. Watching, respectfully, whatever would transpire.

The fisherman was immobile, his hands extended as if nailed to a board. A continual, rhythmic drone provided the background. At first the boy strained to make out the words, but they were spoken so low as to be inaudible. It was some Greek prayer, he realized. Oh well. He would wait.

There was not much more to notice in the hut as he waited for the presbyter. A blanket hastily thrown upon the floor, a sack of some food – beans or rice, perhaps – off in the corner. But that strange and uncouth portrait – why did it draw his eyes again and again? He would try to look away, but there was something tethering about the gaze of the woman in the kitschy painting.

His heart returned to its normal pace, and his metaphysical heart was beginning to lap up the tranquility in such simple surroundings. No, it was not the simplicity. It was something different – a sanctity, perhaps? He felt an awe that he had never felt in the grandiose temples of Rome.

Time seemed suspended – he did not know how long he sat there, content just to be aware, watching the man pray, and somehow trying to reach out to the divine himself.

In such a setting, the claims of this mystery cult did not seem so farfetched.

At length, the fisherman seemed to be concluding his litany. With exaggerated gestures, Miletus bowed three times to the floor, his forehead touching the ground in humility. Rising, he turned to his guest.

"My dear Pancras, it is good to see you. I have been praying for your visit."

The boy nodded.

Seating himself, he leaned forward and diagnosed plainly, "You are troubled by something."

Again, Pancras nodded. Where could he begin? There was too much to say!

But Miletus filled in the silence. "You carry something on your conscience that you wish to lay down. You have not been wholly corrupted by Rome, not yet. But perhaps its foul stench has filled your nostrils, its vile wickedness has weaved lies into your mind...and forced your hand to become what you abhor."

"I have been having dreams, Elder," the boy blurted, his head hanging in shame. "Blood and fire. I know not how to scrub the blood from my memories."

"This blood was on your hands before it was in your memories." The analysis was painfully correct.

Pancras tried with great effort to hold back tears. "Before we left the mainland I...I killed a man."

"That was not your sin."

Shocked, he looked up. "What do you mean?"

"It was not malice or hatred that led the dagger into the flesh. You did so out of loyalty to Nereus."

"How do you know this?" he whispered.

Miletus merely smiled and continued. "No, your sin was not slaughtering an attacker. Look within your soul – and tell me what your sin is."

The boy was quiet for a moment. Was it not the blood on his hands that troubled him so? Or the horrific blood-scenes that had so often filled his young life.

"Why did you turn back?" Miletus prompted.

"Turn back? From what?"

"Nereus offered you a better way to live. Why did you return to Rome?"

Surely Nereus has explained his situation, Pancras reasoned. He wished it were not so – for he was deeply ashamed of that ill-fated journey! He remained silent, not wishing to discuss it.

But Miletus was willing to wait.

Time stretched on. Nothing stirred within the hut or without it.

If Miletus was the holy man that Achilleus claimed, then he could tell Pancras what he did wrong! There was no need for the boy to explore that region of the soul. Let the soothsayer speak first!

But Miletus continued to gaze at him in silence.

Pursing his lips in frustration, Pancras knew he had to speak – or leave.

"Miletus, you know why I returned to Rome. I wished to take my place in the Emperor's house. I am ashamed of it now – what a fool I was!"

"And what did you desire?"

"Who would not desire a life of riches or pleasures! There is nothing wrong with this!"

"And what would you have had to do to acquire such riches or pleasures? You were willing to become like Galerius."

"Never!" he declared adamantly. The thought filled him with disgust.

Unexpectedly, Miletus stood and motioned for the boy to follow him. In silence he obeyed, leaving the hut behind.

The elder led him to the brow of the hill, overlooking the ocean. He could not see much, for the darkness was overwhelming. But the sound of the waves could be heard, steadily beating against the seashore.

"Have you ever felt a longing, Pancras?"

Yes, of course. He needn't say anything. It lay just below the surface of his workaday life, bobbing up whenever an undistracted moment arrived.

Miletus continued. "More torturous than all else is the human heart. Its desires are all-consuming. It is a gaping chasm, an infinite hole."

The entrance to the underworld, Pancras mused. Such was the heart – such was *his* heart. The darkness of the night reflected the darkness inside.

As they stood beside each other, allowing the sea breeze to rustle their clothing and tousle their hair, Miletus put an arm around Pancras' shoulder. "This desire is meant to be fulfilled by the only infinitude in the universe – God."

"Which god? Oh, forgive me. I forgot you worship only one."

Miletus snorted. "Pancras, my son, you have tried to fill this chasm with the things of this world. And as much wealth and pleasure as you pour into yourself, the hunger will grow. It will consume you. And soon you will do anything to pour more wealth and pleasure into it – you will do anything, including walk in the footsteps of the Emperor. There is no end, Pancras. Like the grave and the Emperor's treasury, there is a hunger that can never be sated."

Pancras smiled at the jest, but was troubled in spirit.

"You have described it accurately," he admitted, humbling himself. "I have felt the longing you speak of. And I have indeed pursued wealth and pleasure, as if they were my missing birthright. Is this my sin?"

The silence in the night wind affirmed it.

"But then," he continued, still steeped in a breathless despair, "is there anything that can satisfy the longing? And is there any forgiveness for the sin?"

Pancras could sense the intensity in his mentor's words as he spoke. "Believe in him, Pancras. It is he that you thirst for. It is he who can heal your wounds."

Wounds. The word brought back blood, drowning him in images too disturbing for words. Severed heads, hands covered in blood, crucifixes and wild beasts and the endless sea of blood that drowned the city of man.

The darkness around him, the darkness within him. That yawning chasm opened only to a deep gloom.

But perhaps Miletus held out a lantern?

"I...I do not know..." Pancras stuttered, stricken. The tears were flowing freely now, unseen in the night.

"His blood can cleanse you."

"How can blood cleanse blood!" he shouted, though his words were carried away by the wind to the four corners of the earth. "Must everything I see be death!"

"His death is different, my son. It was death for him but life for us. His blood washes away our blood."

Pancras could barely see him through the tears and the blackness, but he felt warm hands on his head.

"What are you doing?" the boy objected, but did not shake free of the hands.

The presbyter began speaking words in Greek, words of praise to his God.

No! He must not invite this god's blood into his soul! It was enough that human blood was invoked upon him on, the blood of a so-called divinity would curse him for eternity! This must stop, this must stop!

He was sobbing now, breaking down. He had tried to hold it together, but could do so no longer. He was weak, he was dissipating, he was...

...he was filling with peace.

As if a warm current of oil was being poured into his flesh, he felt a gentle shower of peace radiate through him.

The tears dried as quickly as they had sprung. His frantic gasps had become calmer, even as the presbyter began invoking the blood of this Jesus upon him.

What kind of power is in this blood? He was filled with wonder and light. A glow began to ignite in his chest, a fire so sweet and unlike the fire that plagued his dreams. The despair abated, replaced with hope.

The prayer lasted but a minute, a minute that stretched suspended in time. It felt as if the sun had revolved three times around the earth by the time the elder lifted his hands, and Pancras lifted his eyes.

They stood for a moment, without speaking.

Refreshed, as if he had drunk deeply from a spring of living water, Pancras wondered at what he had just experienced. No longer troubled, he felt a new hope and strength taking root within him. He eagerly anticipated Miletus' explanation of this prayer.

But Miletus said simply, "Rest with the angels. You know the way home." And he turned and walked away, leaving Pancras alone on the crest of the hill.

Following the dim light of the crescent moon which had peeked out from behind the clouds, the lad went home, reveling in the peace. Oh, the memories of blood and fire were still there – but there was another memory now: of blood that covered him on a hill, protecting him, washing him clean.

That night, Pancras slept soundly.

~~~

Weeks slid by, merging into one another with little to separate the days. He was steeped in a serenity that had so often eluded him in his life. It was not an easy life, by any means – the days of endless toil, the nights of sleeping on a rocky bed in a cramped cavern. Unaccustomed as he had been to such work, his muscles had suffered from an initial soreness, which had since worn off. In its place arose a strength he never knew he possessed. His skin – the skin of all, including the usually-translucent Aquila – had taken on a sun-bronzed sheen.

Oh, Aquila, Nereus, Achilleus, Domitilla – what a family they had become! The cave was a home, expanded by love and decorated with peace. He was overwhelmed with gratitude every time he would drag the boat ashore, his feet splashing through the surf, when he would catch sight of Aquila beating their soaked tunics against a rock to cleanse them. The odor of roasting tuna, turning slowly on a spit over a charcoal fire, was but a simple thing that infused the days with happiness. A kind word from Achilleus, the demure smile he shared with the princess, a gruff nod from Nereus – it all became something so familiar that he wondered if this was the home he had always longed for. Was this Synnada, after all?

His days were filled with rich conversations with Miletus, as the two of them brought fish from *Mare Nostrum* – which seemed to be a sea teeming with life, solely for their

326

own pleasure. The fishing kept the island well-supplied, but it was never sold at market – no, this island operated on an exchange system only. Perhaps a few fish were exchanged for a half-dozen eggs, some olives, or a handful of figs.

It was hard work, leaving before dawn and returning by mid-day, when the fish departed for deeper waters. The afternoons would be spent on various tasks. Sometimes, he would help Nereus lay stone upon their small home upon the brow of the hill. If the old soldier preferred to work as a solitary – which was often – then Pancras would assist Domitilla with the care of the sheep. As the sun progressed toward the horizon, the boy was usually able to steal away for a few games with the other boys on the island, the lads he had met that first night and some of their friends. Their kindness and welcome prevented the loss of his former friends from chafing at him.

Every seventh day, and frequently throughout the week, he would join his surrogate family for a worship service at the largest home on the island. It was not grandiose, not when compared with those villas back on the mainland. But it was large enough to hold the congregation, compressed cozily within heavy stone walls.

And the singing! It rose to the skies, echoed off the four walls, and never failed to baste him in a tranquility that was nothing short of divine. The recollections of their apostles were full of an elegantly simple wisdom, and Miletus would exhort the people with a passion that no man would possess for Jupiter. They came from every side of the island: filthy, weary, and with the odors of the earth – but when they entered into their temple, it was a portal to the heavens.

Now, *he* was not ready to believe, he told himself. He was merely attending these services for companionship. It was a beautiful, peaceful cult, but a cult nonetheless! And he, the proud and educated and urbane soul that he was, would need no backwater sect – so he declared to himself!

But in his quieter moments, he wondered if this was true.

And thus life progressed in a rhythm as steady as the seasons, as faithful as the sunrise. It was peaceful, joyful, and without strife. It was simple, but it was life.

~~~

Another day upon the sea.

"Miletus, why is it that Domitilla refused marriage? Marriage is the natural way of all men and women."

A mighty grunt was the response, as the old man wrestled with his net, teeming with fish. Pancras came over to lend assistance, and with their forearms burning with the strain, they hauled it over the side of the boat and splayed their catch upon the deck.

"Marriage is indeed a great gift," Miletus replied, stooping to sort their prey. "But some are called to a higher life. To give one's heart to God is a sublime dignity."

"So, is she like one of the Vestal Virgins?"

"Similar. She has consecrated herself freely to Him."

"It seems like such a waste."

"In the eyes of the world, perhaps. But from the eyes of eternity, she is wedded to a finer Groom than could be found in all the land. Jesus Christ is her Bridegroom, and He has invited her to the deepest love."

"I wonder if she does not regret this decision. For every woman longs to be a mother."

"But she *is* a mother – a mother to the soul. Her prayers and her love have brought many souls to rebirth."

328

"How does a soul become reborn?"

"Three hundred years ago, a man asked our Lord a similar question. How can man be born again? Surely he cannot reenter his mother's womb, can he? And yet our Lord revealed to him that the rebirth comes through water and the Spirit, not in the physical realm."

This mysticism seemed, to Pancras, to be a jumble of symbols and rites – a puzzle whose solution escaped him.

"I do not understand. You speak of many things – water, spirit, bridegroom, bride. But clearly these words mean something different than how they are ordinarily used."

"Ah yes, Pancras. These are the *mysterion* of our faith. Symbols point to deeper realities; the physical reveals the spiritual."

"This water, then," Pancras said, leaning over the edge and bringing up a handful of saltwater. "What does it reveal?"

Miletus looked at him evenly, a sly smile playing on his lips. "You tell me."

"Water can cleanse, and it helps all things to grow."

"Precisely. Now what can it do for the spirit?"

Pancras thought for a moment, not wishing to give the wrong answer. "Perhaps…perhaps it can, in some way, cleanse the soul of wrongdoing and bring it to spiritual growth?"

The fisherman stood and grasped the boy's shoulder. "Well done. Our initiation into Christ is a baptism by water – what water does for the body, the invisible power of grace does for the soul."

They continued sorting fish, while Pancras continued sorting out the mysteries. All of these new ideas were cluttering his mind – he had to somehow make sense of them all.

At length, he offered timidly, "So does the virginity of Domitilla point to a deeper reality? Is she one of your *mysterion*?"

"One could say that," the presbyter responded thoughtfully. "Her life shows the world that the Christ is real, and that intimacy with Him is a far greater blessing than the physical love of husband and wife."

The convictions that drove these Christians to adopt such countercultural ways of life! Apart from the Vestal Virgins, there was no one who would voluntarily give up the consolations of the marriage bed. Such sacrifice was unheard of in his old world – *their* old world. But this island – this faith - was a new world, and Pancras was still adapting to breathing the fresh and cleansing air.

"And you, Miletus," Pancras began boldly, his curiosity overtaking his natural reticence, "Have you forsaken marriage as well?"

"Nay, my boy. I had a bride in my youth – for seven fine years we shared a home."

And then she died, Pancras verified in his mind.

"I am sorry for your loss," the boy murmured.

"Be not sorry!" Miletus answered, shocking him. "Her death was beautiful, beautiful! Her heart was prepared, for Christ dwelt in her as He dwelt in me. We will see each other again – of this, I am sure."

"But surely it must have been difficult, at the time."

"Pancras, we walk by faith – not by sight. She is gone from my side, but not from my spirit. I pray for her daily, and eagerly await our reunion."

"You are so sure of this?"

Soberly, he replied, "Of the coming resurrection, I am willing to stake my life. For if the resurrection will not take place, then we are the most foolish of men! Without the resurrection, then eat, drink, and be merry, for tomorrow we die!"

A brief vignette of the party at the palace flashed before the boy's mind. Yes, he had seen that ethos. He quickly shook his head and deeply inhaled the salt air to regain his equilibrium.

"You remind me of Antonius," Pancras mused, continuing to work. "He, too, believed in the Christ. He, too, faced death without fear. I wondered how he could do so."

"He knew the One who conquered death. Those who are in Christ will never die, for they fall asleep in the hope of resurrection."

"So you do not fear death?"

"Imagine that you were born into a prison and unable to see the world outside. A door separated you from the fine things of the world: the sunlight, the banquets, the games. But you had no concept of these things, for your world was only a prison: dark, musty, filled with decay. Every now and then a person would leave through the door, and never come back. You would miss them – for they were your friend! You had known them for your whole life!

"But now," Miletus continued, "Imagine for a moment that someone from the outside comes in. He tells you of all the good things that you can experience outside of the prison. He knows of these things, for he has been there himself. And because he loves you, you can trust him. He promised you that he would walk through the door with you. Would you take his hand? Would you stand up and walk with him through the door? It would be frightening, for you do not know what is on the outside – but he does.

And if you know him and love him, then you will have the courage to take his hand and walk through the door into the sunlight, into the grand world outside. It is frightening – but there is trust and hope."

A beautiful thought – but a more sinister one pressed upon Pancras. "But – but what if – what if the door does not lead to paradise, but instead leads…to the underworld?"

"Ah. The underworld." Miletus furrowed his brow, seeking to express the truth in a way comprehensible to the pagan young man. "Yes, the underworld exists. But it is only for those who refuse to take the hand of the Christ."

Like waves crashing upon the shore, tossing up surf and sand and leaving a froth of chaos in their wake, memories poured down upon Pancras. He tried to forget the death he had seen, to focus on this message of hope – but he had seen too much.

"What if…what about…" he choked, remembering. "My father. He did not know your Christ. Is he…?"

Miletus put down the nets and came over to him.

The boy's chest heaving, he was trying with all his might to avoid falling headlong into the pit of despair. "If what you say is true, then my father…"

The fisherman comforted him with a paternal embrace. "Oh, Pancras, Pancras, my son. Your father did not reject the hand of Christ. He never saw Him; He stayed hidden from his eyes."

"And so…?"

"We must hope. We must pray."

Pancras nodded, understanding.

"But as for you," Miletus continued, "Christ is offering you His hand. Will you accept?"

"I don't know!" he exclaimed, frustrated. He turned away, returning to the sea, to check his nets. "I don't know what I believe. Your prayers are beautiful, your teachings are fine, but I do not know if I can abandon the gods of my father. Oh, who am I fooling? I do not believe in them either."

"What is preventing you from turning to the true God?"

"Your god demands so much!"

"Nothing less than your entire self."

"I do not know if I can offer that," he retorted, growing aggravated.

"You have sensed His peace, have you not? You know that your heart is aching for Him." Pressing, always pressing.

"My heart is aching for *something* – but I do not know if I can offer what he demands." A sharply defensive tone entered his voice.

Miletus doubled down. "Then for what shall you live? For yourself? For a few years of pleasure? For the honor of being the Emperor's son?"

"Enough!" Pancras cried out. He could take no more of this.

Miletus, silenced by the outburst, looked at him with pity. The boy had slunk to the deck, his arms crossed over his knees and his head resting upon them.

A minute passed, where only the soft and rhythmic lapping of waves broke the stillness.

At length, the fisherman spoke. "Let's go home."

~~~

The cock crowed, and reluctantly Pancras was dragged awake. He forced his eyelids up, seeing nothing, for the sun was hours from rising.

He hoped that there would be fresh water in the jug, for the night had brought on an intense thirst. Sitting up, he felt around in the darkness for the jug of water, hoping to slake his dry tongue. There it was – and, sloshing inside it, was a bit left to satisfy the craving.

Taking a drought, he wiped his mouth and keened his ears. A low conversation was taking place outside – he recognized the voices of Nereus and Miletus – but the topic was indecipherable.

Exiting the cave with a bit of bread in hand, he prepared for the day, untying the rope to free the boat from its mooring.

"You are not going out today," Nereus rumbled with a scowl.

Pancras bowed his head deferentially. "My apologies. What will you have me do instead?"

"You will assist me. There has been an outbreak of Roman fever on the northern point."

"Your master knows medicine from his days in the Guard," Miletus chimed in.

"As you wish," Pancras replied. A day's respite from the backbreaking work of fishing would be a great gift.

"We leave at dawn."

Even better – another hour of sleep.

Or so he thought. Nereus picked up the empty water jug and thrust it into the boy's hands. "Fill this up. We will bring them food and water."

The tasks seemed to multiply from then on. Upon returning to the cavern with a full jar, they busied themselves with building a fire and baking flatcakes. Aquila tore strips of linen into bandages, stacking them cleanly. Achilleus claimed knowledge of herbal remedies, and he set off into the underbrush to collect flora.

As the darkness melted away into an overcast sky, Nereus and Pancras gathered their supplies and set off.

Not one for superfluous words, Nereus kept a stony face as they traipsed in silence across the landscape, dotted with small brick and stone huts staggered across a central lane. Through fields and across rocky hilltops with the most spectacular views of the sea, down quiet paths and past sheepfolds surrounded by ancient stone walls.

For over an hour they walked, further than he had explored this island outpost. The new scenery continued to overawe young Pancras. The wind, crisp now with the full-throated voice of autumn, whiffled with a salty freshness. The rippled silver sky answered back to the whitecapped water, visible from the trail that took them along cliffside and up closely-cropped hills of emerald grass.

"Does this island have no doctor?" Pancras asked, wondering when this trek would reach its terminus. The water jug felt as if it were growing heavier with every step.

"I fear they do not," he grumbled. "And Miletus tells me that the Roman fever strikes every year. But no doctor from the city desires such an outpost as Pontia."

They crested yet another hill of low scrub pine and holm-oak, with an occasional cactus shivering in the sea-breeze, and beheld a small gathering of cottages. They were much too sparse to be called a town – a mere crossroads at a convenient location. A thin stream of smoke arose from the chimney of several houses.

From the path, moans could be heard eerily filling the silence. Pancras was fairly dreading this – during those few times his uncle fell ill, the lad would be pressed into the most disgusting service: changing soiled bed linens, cleaning up vomitus, or washing oozing sores. What awaited them behind these wooden doors?

335

"Miletus said the whole village was stricken," Nereus commented. "You take half of my supplies and take the left side of the street – do what you can to alleviate their sufferings, and come fetch me if the case is most severe."

"Are you not afraid of contagion?"

The censuring look was enough to make Pancras regret the question.

Nereus handed him strips of linen along with some of the herbs, instructing him on their proper use. Some were to be burned for a healing smoke, while others were to be made into a poultice and applied to the skin. A few were for consumption by the sick.

This rudimentary knowledge barely sufficed, the boy knew, as he headed to the first door with trepidation. He was unprepared for what he saw.

A widow with two children stared up at him from straw mats upon the floor. Their tunics reeked of vomit, and the children were shivering uncontrollably. Their sunken eyes and pallid complexions were evidence that it had been a few days since they had eaten or drunk.

Pancras felt a wall of stench and disgust pummel him. How could he help these strangers, when his own stomach lurched and rebelled? He stepped back outside for a breath of air, hoping to find Nereus and explain to him that, although he had no objection to helping the sick, he just simply could not do it. But the man had already gone into a house, and the lane was deserted.

He turned back to the house, and saw the hope in the eyes of the poor widow. Was he the first to visit her in her distress?

With a deep breath to calm his nerves, he plunged ahead, entering the house again.

"I am here to help," he declared, assessing the situation. Those tunics would need to be washed, and they needed food and medicine immediately.

The woman struggled to sit upright. "Thank you, thank you!" she groaned, barely able to make out the words.

Pancras held up the water jug and poured a little into her mouth, doing the same with the children. The girl, perhaps of five years, was so weak that Pancras had to lift her head. He noticed that her forehead was covered in cold perspiration, even as she continued to shake for warmth.

His own nostrils were being attacked with offensive odors; his natural repugnance was nauseating him. He loathed this! He allowed the girl's head to rest once more, feeling the filth of sweat and dirt and who-knows-what-else upon his hand.

But the deeds needed to be done, so he buckled down. Finding wood outside, he stoked together a fire. He found some stale bread in the house, and softening it with water, he gently fed it to each member. With the linen that he brought, he made cloths to clean their hands and faces, moistened with water.

Although no words were exchanged between the four of them, there was an unspoken language – gratitude in their eyes, a smile, a hand that was held. Pancras found a surprising sweetness to the tasks, and his natural abhorrence began to abate a bit.

Moving to the next house, he repeated the process for an elderly couple who were too weak to move.

Hours passed as he and Nereus continued their charity throughout the village. A couple houses were empty – Nereus told the boy that their occupants had fled for their own safety, for fear of contracting the deadly disease. They encountered the old and the young, those who were recovering and those who seemed to be slipping through death's door. In two houses, only a cadaver remained, which they dragged outside of the houses to be buried at a later date.

This disease had indeed ravaged this small outpost. In silence they worked, in the most remote and rustic conditions. For his part, Pancras was stunned to see the squalor in which these people lived. Yes, he currently resided in a cave, but it was clean and warm. Besides, their house was almost finished! But these people were the true poor of the earth – Pancras' father's animal barns were finer than the shacks these people used for houses!

They worked until the steel-grey sky began to light up with pinks and purples from the setting sun.

Nereus fetched the boy for the trek home, finding him taking out a chamber pot filled with the foulest excretions. Upon cleansing the pot and returning it to its owners, they departed, leaving a word of comfort to the old man who was too weak to return the gesture. But his eyes spoke their thanks.

Grateful that the task was completed – but dreading the long walk home – they set off, leaving the village behind them.

A smattering of fat raindrops accompanied them, keeping time with their sandal-scratches on the well-trampled path.

In silence they walked, giving Pancras a chance to digest what he had seen. Like all men, he shied away from suffering. But he knew the fragility of life could not be avoided forever – it had to be reckoned with.

More than that, though – what had it done to his soul? It was both sobering and a gift.

A gift? Where did this thought come from? Doubtless it was Domitilla's influence – *all is gift*, she had said. Even this. Even this.

The silence was healthy, full. The sky grew dim, then dark. But they knew the way.

As they approached the beachhead upon which they lived, Nereus broke the spell of silence.

"You did well today. I am proud of you."

Pancras relished the praise. "Thank you, sir."

"It was difficult?"

"Did you find it so?"

Nereus did not respond. Perhaps, after a man had seen his enemies disemboweled on the battlefield, a little vomit is a small thing.

He did, however, offer this assessment: "You are learning to sacrifice. This is good. From here, it is only a short step to manhood."

"It was a cost, but it was needed – they had no one else." He was still appalled that their relatives had abandoned them in the time of their need.

"It is in sacrifice that a man's life is proven," Nereus responded gruffly. Surely he knew about sacrifice!

"Will we return tomorrow?"

"I will return alone. You will be needed on the boat."

"The weather looks poor, though."

"Nevertheless, you and Miletus cannot spare a day of fishing. We must store a cache of salted fish before winter falls – and every day it draws closer."

This was true – they had been sleeping in their *paenulae* at night, and would soon need them during the day as well.

Nereus had exhausted his storehouse of words for the day, and fell silent for the remainder of the journey.

~~~

The wind had picked up throughout the night, and the occasional raindrops had graduated into a steady mist, biting through their cloaks. Pancras questioned the wisdom of heading out on a morn such as this, but Miletus scoffed at his worries.

"This is but an autumn squall! I have been out in storms big enough to sink a galley!" he cheerfully commented, loading the nets. "Remember, Pancras – the ocean teaches you many things. It will test the mettle of a fellow, making a man out of a boy! We cannot always have placid seas – either in life or in fishing!"

"I see, I see," he replied unenthusiastically, shivering as he pushed off from the shore. Leaping deftly into the boat, they used pole oars to back away from the sand, into deeper waters where they could hoist the sails.

Out from the shore, the chop was uneven. They seemed to sail into the heights, only to be plunged back down to the depths. Upon waves the height of a man's waist, the small dinghy seemed mighty unstable.

Pancras had to adjust to the rising and falling of the ship. This was more severe than he had ever sailed in, and his stomach was queasy.

But it appeared that Miletus was enjoying the challenge. His bearded smile, flecked with mist-droplets, stretched across his face as he sought to hoist the sail. When he could get his balance, Pancras helped – until another wave threw him across the skiff.

"Trouble with the sea-legs, Master Pancras?" Miletus laughed.

"The sea is a living beast today."

"Perhaps we ride on the back of Leviathan!"

340

"Will the fish be stirred up in such weather?"

"Ah, yes indeed! This is the finest weather – a light rain, a choppy surf. The fish have a harder time seeing our nets, and they all come to the surface to investigate if the raindrops are edible."

He found it hard to resist a look of suspicion as he tied the dragline on his net to the metal hook on the prow.

Dropping it in the water, Pancras had to grip onto the sides of the boat with both hands to steady his swirling head and liquefied legs. He had been on plenty of seas in between Phrygia and Pontia, but this was making a fool out of him!

"I heard about your journey yesterday," Miletus commented, passing time as he watched his net fill with fish. "You did well, I hear."

"Thank you," he replied, trying to sit down on the deck. As soon as he did so, the bottom dropped out of him and they plunged several paces as they came off the crest of a wave. His stomach flipped upside-down, and he swallowed hard in the hopes of keeping the inner organs from coming out his mouth.

"It is the fundamental challenge of man – to die to himself, so that others may live."

Pancras was not feeling well enough to wax philosophical. "Yes, it cost a great deal," he replied simply.

"And there is the paradox: the more the gift costs, the more the gift is valued. A man's life is all he owns – and to what shall he give such a gift? He cannot keep it to himself. He must find a cause noble enough to receive his very self."

The trajectory of this conversation was evident enough to the boy. Another attempt to proselytize – but Pancras was not in the mood for it. Not wishing to be rude, he changed the topic.

"Look!" he exclaimed, pointing to the horizon. "With the wind at our backs, we have put out quite a distance from the island."

The speck of land was swiftly shrinking in the distance. Their small craft was cruising – perhaps seven or eight knots, at least. The wind howled harder, flapping their wet garments around them, shaping to their goose-fleshed skin. The rain began in earnest, tiny droplets that stung the skin.

Pancras started shivering from the cold.

"Get up; check your nets," Miletus suggested, noticing his chill.

But the churned-up sea, capped with thick froth, obscured his view into the depths. The rough waves rose and fell, rose and fell, propelling them even further into the sky and into the depths, prompting Pancras to grip the sides with greater fervor, his knuckles whitening in terror.

"And this is why I love fishing," Miletus reveled, standing and shouting over the gale. "It is a perfect metaphor for life. We have days of peace, and days of turmoil – but we must persist through them both. Have I told you the story of when the Lord Jesus calmed the sea?"

"No, but if he has this power, I beg you to call upon him now!" Pancras shouted back. He felt sick, and terrified – he was not a particularly good swimmer, and was hoping that this boat would not capsize.

"And Paul, too," the storm-crazed fisherman continued. "He was caught in many a storm, not far from here."

"Please tell me that he found a happy ending…"

"Well, he did not die, if that's what you mean. But he did have some adventures after he washed up on shore…"

Washed up? Shipwrecked? He did not want to consider that possibility.

The mist had turned into a rain, driven sidelong by the squall.

Perhaps he would die of chill before the sea overtook them, he thought disjointedly. The upsurges crashed over the edge of the boat, filling the deck with a pool of ice-cold saltwater.

"Pull in your line," Miletus directed, as he did so for his own net.

There were a few excellent specimens in their nets, a good catch for such a day. They simply tossed the fish onto the floor of the boat – no need to use the barrel when they stood in water up to their ankles, and rising with every swell that crashed over their boat.

Out they went again, the nets tossed into the sea. They untethered the sail and the jib, not wishing to travel any further. Pancras surmised it would be a difficult tack to come back into port in such a storm.

With a steady hand on the rudder, Miletus navigated them over wave after wave. His years of experience were distilled into a serene confidence that was a contrast to Pancras' terror. The boy wondered at his steady hand – the old fisherman was enjoying this!

"How many years have you been on the seas?" Pancras hollered.

"Alas, too many to count!" he replied.

"And you have seen storms such as this?"

"Many!" he laughed, steering with a deft flick of his wrist. A little line let out here, a small adjustment to the rudder, and the boat was up and over another wave.

Pancras must have been white with terror, for Miletus added, "My boy, when you have reckoned with death as I have, you have no fear!"

He was just hoping that it would end.

His knapsack was soaked, and his food was likely ruined by the saltwater.

Just then, he felt the freezing shower of another crashing wave pour over him. Every muscle tensed up in the cold. How much more of this could he endure?

The contents of the boat – fish, knapsacks, pole oars – sloshed around as if on their own personal ocean. They would slide to one side of the boat, then the other when they plummeted down the backside of a wave.

"How much longer must we be out here?" Pancras begged, trying vainly not to whine.

"You are not enjoying this? This is God's temple! His handiwork is all over this glorious day!"

"Then your God is filled with fury!" the boy retorted, his words overpowered by the thunderous wind.

"Come now, Pancras. Does this not make you feel alive?"

"Nay. A warm fire and a bit of bread makes *me* feel alive."

"A sorry life that is!" he guffawed.

The sky was showing no sign of abandoning its wrath.

"Learn the lessons of the ocean, Pancras," the old man shouted, always playing the sage.

"And what lesson does the ocean wish to teach me?" he snapped back.

The man stood, imposing and fearless, a grizzled veteran of the wars against nature. "We must bow humbly before the mysteries we will never understand. You are so small, Pancras. So small. A drop of water in the ocean of humanity. What does your life mean? What do any of our lives mean? Nothing – unless there is One whose love redeems our nothingness."

Pancras struggled to his feet. Evenly, he gazed at his mentor.

"You wish to convert me. And your belief is an interesting myth, to be certain. But I wish to ask you for the last time to cease."

"I only wish to share with you the greatest gift I possess."

"I am not interested."

Miletus nodded, closing his eyes. Was this a prayer? In his soul, Pancras tried to resist whatever spiritual force was being roused through the holy man's intercession.

The boat continued its lurching, up and down. The wind continued to shriek across the sea. And the man continued to stand immobile, lost in some fool's ecstasy.

"Miletus, please pilot this ship!" Pancras shouted, gripping the mast as they were tossed about like dice in a game.

The presbyter opened his eyes. With a thin smile on his lips, he gripped the rudder and instructed the boy, "Go, check your net."

With a huff, the lad went to the prow to check his net. He leaned far over the prow to drag up the net when a wave crested over him and swept him into the sea.

What? Where? How? The shock of the frigid sea precluded rational thought. Down he went, sinking into the depths. His clothing, soaked, was a weight dragging him downward, down, down...

Vainly he flailed his arms and legs. Which way was the surface? He opened his eyes and was blinded with the pain of unholy saltwater entering them. Pure fear filled his mind – this was the end.

He surfaced for a moment, sputtering and gasping, and saw that he was now drifting away from the boat. But nothing more could he see, for a wave crashed upon his head and once again he was beneath the turgid water.

Involuntarily he sucked some water into his lungs – burning everything as it went down. With every ounce of strength remaining in his frozen limbs he pushed himself heavenward, enough to spew it out, cough, and sink again.

Thrashing, sputtering, utterly panicked, he realized he would never be saved. The sea would be his tomb.

Was he ready to meet his final end? A primal terror resisted the thought. He was not prepared – nor willing! – to descend into the darkness from which no man awakens.

The waves knocked him around, churning and turning in the mighty waters. He was disoriented, frantic. With every second that passed he grew more and more tired, even as the adrenaline poured into every sinew and muscle in his body.

No! I will not go down to the underworld!

A surge of energy propelled him upward once more, where he saw through film-crusted eyes that Miletus was frantically trying to direct the boat towards him. But it was still some distance away, and the mountains of water once again knocked him beneath the surface.

Drowning, drowning, down into the depths…the realm from which no man returns…

His last gasp of air was insufficient, but he continued sinking as if dragged by an aquatic rope.

Fight! I must…

The world was starting to go dim, his thoughts clouded. He strove to keep his muscles moving, but it felt futile. Hand over hand, feet over feet, as if he were climbing a ladder beneath the sea, seeking to climb to the heavens. But this did nothing, as he continued to sink into the depths. His lungs burned, about to burst, starving for air.

This would be his death. He did not have the strength, or the presence of mind, to think about it – it merely *was*. He knew it was time. He had fought bravely, and lost.

He glanced up one last time, through the opaque water and burning eyes, to see a hand extended above him. Could he reach it?

Stretching, pining, he reached up high and suddenly found himself in the trough between two waves, able to catch a rapid breath for a second before he was swept away by the oncoming crest.

Where was the hand? It had disappeared as he sunk once again beneath the surface, tossed upside-down in the vicious surf. The surge had washed away the only hope that could save him. Once again left to the primal chaos of water, he began to surrender to the elements. He would fight no more.

His muscles cramping, his brain starved for oxygen, he gave up the struggle. His fate was sealed. This would be his destiny – to sleep in the unfathomable depths for eternity. Going limp, he waited for death.

And his head was suddenly bashed with…something. Reaching up, he found that it was a beam of wood, thick and sturdy. Grabbing it with fervor, he hoisted himself up, breaking through the surface of the water into the pure air.

Unable to see with his burning eyes, he felt himself being dragged through the water. Coughing and coughing, he spewed seawater from his lungs.

He felt his tunic being grabbed by vigorous hands, hoisting him up and into a boat. He was unceremoniously dropped like a sack of rocks upon the ground, still coughing water out of every orifice.

"My God, Pancras," Miletus breathed, himself panting in fear. "I almost lost you out there!"

The boy could not respond, as he lay exhausted, his heart still racing uncontrollably. He was shivering and hacking, unable to move.

In this state he remained for some time, as the sail swung around and set a course for home. They had to tack into the wind, zig-zagging across the open sea. The rain still poured down, the wind continued to howl, and the boat was tossed up-and-down. But the sickening feeling in Pancras' gut was the least of his worries.

He continued to quiver, from cold and fear intermingled. The realization was beginning to sink in – he had almost died.

He tried to clear his throat, but immediately regretted it as a thousand tiny knives stabbed him. A minute later he retched, right there in the boat, unable to move.

He wished he would die.

Then he realized – he almost *did* die. And he was filled with terror.

Slowly, slowly he opened his eyes. Though they burned, he needed to see if they were anywhere near the shore.

Miletus was looking at him with profound pity. He sat at the helm, hand on the rudder and the sail-rope, masterfully guiding the ship towards the island, despite the storm that continued to rage. Every now and then his eyes would flick up to the horizon, then return to watch the recovery of the boy who almost drowned.

The terror in his heart began to yield to a deeper fury.

"You did this to me!" Pancras croaked.

Miletus regarded him with confusion.

"You prayed for me to drown!" he explained.

"I did no such thing," Miletus answered sharply. "I merely prayed that God would save you in any way necessary."

"I did not need to be saved. I was perfectly fine, until…"

"To save you from yourself," Miletus censured harshly, and Pancras was reduced to silence.

They continued to make swift progress, as the two stared at each other stone-faced through the remainder of the journey. Pancras – terrified from his ordeal, furious at the latest curse of fate. Miletus – stern at the stubborn, prideful young man recovering on his ship.

Soon the waves subsided as they entered the sheltered cove where the boat could be dragged ashore. This time it was Miletus who leapt out of the boat, dragging it onto the sand and affixing it to a rock with a bowline knot.

He came back for the boy, helping him to his feet. They staggered together out of the boat and along the beach, toward the cave that served as a home.

Pancras could not control his trembling, from both the cold and the terror.

As they approached the curtain of reeds that served as their door, Aquila was coming out with a pot. She stopped and stared in shock, amazed at the sight of Pancras' weakness.

Quickly she took the lad and helped him into the home, telling Miletus that she would exercise the maternal care that was needed here. She hastily helped him into a dry tunic, wrapping him in a cocoon of three blankets and stoking the fire until it danced and warmed the entire cavern.

She gave him a concoction of hot water with herbs steeped in it – a bitter drink, he discovered, upon the first sip. But she promised that it would help to put the humors back in him, and at least the bowl was warm in his hands.

"Please forgive me, Pancras, but I was on my way to bring gruel up to the village of those sick with Roman fever," Aquila explained. "Nereus and Achilleus are there as well. We will be back by sundown. I pray that you do not mind being left alone."

The boy shrugged. He has always been alone – what does one more day matter?

With that, she departed, the curtain of woven reed waving her goodbye. And Pancras was alone.

Alone.

Always you will be alone, a nameless voice echoed.

Yes, he answered in his heart. He knew that he would always be alone.

Who was he? An orphan, a fisherman, a friend, a son of an emperor? None of these – he was…alone.

A solitary life, touching few, passes over the earth as a breath. As a breeze dissipates across the land, so his life would be scattered to the ends of the earth, never to be seen again.

Where is Daphne? Where is Decian? Where is Dionysius? Have they forgotten him? If he drowned in the sea, who would be there to mourn his passing? Those few, those precious few who would have mourned, would have held a funeral in his honor and proffered a eulogy, before resuming their workaday lives and forgetting all about the breath that caressed the earth for a time, before disappearing.

Was his life that meaningless?

Yes.

He would leave no monuments to mighty deeds. He would not be listed in the annals of the great men who lived and died. He would leave no footprint on the civilizations that rose and fell, rose and fell, until all civilization ceased and men lay silent in their graves.

This brush with death was but a foretaste of that which will befall all men. For he was spared this time – but next time, there would be no return.

The darkness that had often plagued him came rushing in with a vengeance. Cursed be this life and its vanity! A bitter bile arose within his throat – he wished to curse the world and all that is in it.

Slowly, gradually, his shivering subsided as the fire and blankets warmed his flesh. But there remained, in the center of his heart, a different chill – the coldness of death.

This life was nothing but a living death. Cleonius, Antonius, and the thousand unnamed who met death through the beast, the cross, the sword. He was an instrument of death by his own hand. He was a silent observer of death, unable to stop its creeping tide. He cheated death this time, but his own demise would hang over him like a foul omen, until the final curtain fell and then…

And then…?

Nothing, spat the interior voice.

An awful finality. Nothing. He would join the oblivion.

The vapidity of it all!

And he was unable to object. There were no gods with whom to plead one's case, no Lares for offering sacrifice, no Fates to beg for mercy.

It was he – alone – in a meaningless and ruthless universe.

For quite some time he sat immobile, frozen in thought even if warmed in body. This cave could have been a tomb for all he knew. For every thought was one of the utmost blackness. Every second drew him closer to his ultimate end. The shores of the underworld threatened to consume him once and forever.

The old anxiety, that cursed companion, overtook him. He was sorely tempted to fling himself back into the ocean, to end it all. For at least death would rid him of the anxiety of knowing that there was nothing beyond the veil!

Through salt-encrusted eyes he watched the ocean roar, growling between the thin strips of reed which parted in the wind. He feared it, and he longed for it. The rain-lashed sea, roiling and turbulent, was an apt metaphor for his inner conflict.

He took another sip of the bitter broth, and laughed resentfully. He was saved for this? For terror, for suicide?

Alternating with the anxiety was the old longing.

It is a longing for the wind, he was reminded.

But no…he resisted.

No…

Immediately in his mind's eye flashed the image of a hand, reaching down to a drowning boy. The hand shimmered from the underwater vantage point – was it a mirage? Dare he hope? Dare he reach?

I came that you might have life, and have it abundantly, echoed a stronger, more pure voice.

Hope and despair wrestled within him.

Amidst the annihilation of all things, even his own life, was there a hand held out to rescue him? He knew that to take the hand would be life, while without it he would sink into the abyss, drowned by blood. Could he reach up?

No, he reminded himself. This isn't real. This is just a trick of the mind.

Then why did it resonate within him? Why would a creature, created from chaos and returning to the void, have eternity in his heart?

Beyond rational thought, he closed his eyes and stretched out his hand.

~~~

The rain had stopped, evaporating into a cold mist that shrouded the island. A man walking a few paces ahead would be concealed in the cloud. But no matter – Pancras knew the way.

A brief knocking on the door produced a man who appeared surprised at his midnight visitor.

"Miletus, I wish to be instructed in your faith."

The man's chest swelled in gratitude and he gave the boy a hearty embrace.

PART SIX: *The Shores of the Underworld*

The sun beat down upon the older man and the younger one, but the autumn breeze brought a chill. Another bundle of straw was passed up to Nereus, who knelt on the roof to thatch the last few bundles down, secured against the wind.

A few more, and he came down the wooden ladder with a clap of his hands. He stood back a few paces, admiring his handiwork.

"Well done, Pancras," he said, flashing a rare smile as they both admired the small stone cottage.

"Thank you, sir, but I only helped for a week."

Ever since the near-drowning, the lad had been skittish around water, so he had worked with his master on finishing their family cottage. It was a small, two-room stone structure, held together with Roman cement. Two windows served as sentries overlooking the countryside and the water, while the thatched roof gave the impression that the structure was wearing a fancy hat.

The two laborers sat upon a large rock surrounded on three sides by scrub pine and brush. Grabbing his knapsack, Nereus extracted bread and dried meat, as well as a round of yellow cheese and a skin of wine. They shared a lunch together.

"You will enjoy living here," Nereus began, in an uncommonly talkative mood. "It is a fine home with a spectacular view. Of course, every place has a stunning view on this island."

"It does indeed. I am so blessed to live here."

Nereus gazed at him thoughtfully. "It is my prayer that you will always live in peace here. May no trouble ever reach you on this island of refuge."

"I hope this as well – many years with you and Aquila and Achilleus."

"And then, some day, you will find a beautiful girl, and wed her, and move into a home of your own."

Pancras smiled as he mused of his future. Yes, it will be full of life – he was certain.

"I only wish I could be here to see you grow to be a man," Nereus added.

"What?!" Pancras exclaimed, his spirits suddenly plummeting. "Why will you not be here?"

The old soldier, looking ever more grey and weary, avoided the boy's gaze. "I must share something with you, Pancras. This night, a ship will be arriving from Rome, bearing supplies for the island and for the Christian community here. When it leaves on the morrow, I will return to Rome. But Aquila and Achilleus will stay here – they will be your family now."

"Why must you do such a thing?" Loss haunted him eternally – not even this new faith could remove its specter.

"By now, Galerius has realized that I did not execute Domitilla as I told him I would. He has likely been sending emissaries across the Empire to search for me. I have a death warrant on my head. If these soldiers find me here, it would be danger for the entire community – certainly Domitilla and my wife and Achilleus would be the first ones to be killed. Even you, perhaps. Tomorrow, I go to Galerius to surrender, so to spare this entire island."

No! This could not happen!

"But Nereus..." he objected.

Nereus smiled and gripped the boy's shoulder. "Pancras, I can die a happy man knowing that you are embracing Christ. You have been like a son to me – the answer to many, many prayers. Aquila and I...we could never have children. And how we desperately prayed for one! Yet God had a finer plan, when he brought you into our lives."

"But I have been fickle, stupid..."

"At first, you were immature. But I have seen the kind of character you have developed these past few months...you possess true courage and have learned how to sacrifice. And God will mold you into a man pleasing to Him, as you yield your life to the Lord."

Were those tears running down the lad's cheeks?

"Dominum, I cannot find words," he replied, choking on his voice. "I am humbled by your kindness, but saddened by this news. I have lost my father, over and over again – first the father of my flesh, then my uncle. Your departure would be more than I could bear."

"But you will have a father – a new Father, one in Heaven, who loves you more truly than we ever could. And He will provide you with men to guide you – Miletus, Achilleus."

"I believe that now. I truly do. But...I will miss you." He could think of nothing more profound to say.

"And I will miss you. But we have hope, do we not? We will see each other again. And on that day, there will be no more sorrow, no more separations."

"How I long for that day!"

"As do I, Pancras. As do I."

~~~

The morning of the departure dawned. Nereus took only a few belongings with him – a skin of water, a change of tunic, a thick cloak, a scroll containing the words of life. The pack was hoisted upon his back, as he stood outside of the cave that had served as a home.

Several members of the community had assembled to wish him well. The gathering on the beach was a tearful one. Every man gave a promise of prayers, with a manly embrace and Godspeed.

Miletus was the last of the community to step forward. His eyes moist, he shook the soldier's shoulders as a man of equal stature. "Your leadership was a great blessing," the presbyter said. "I will look out for your family in your absence. This island will not be the same without your steady presence."

The presbyter raised his hand and offered a Trinitarian blessing as the soldier bowed his head.

When his head was raised, all could see tears flowing freely. Turning to his wife, he managed to whisper her name.

"Aquila."

She could not speak, overcome with emotion, for they would not see each other again in this life.

The lumps in their throats prevented further speech. Through watery eyes, Pancras tried to burn this scene into his memory. Here was his mentor, his friend, his father. He had provided a greater gift than the father of his flesh, for what was the gift of life without the hope of eternity?

The embrace of husband and wife seemed to linger on, but no one was anxious to see it end. It was a sendoff to the gates of death, as the soldier prepared manfully to storm those gates and claim the paradise on the other side.

The boat awaited – but let it wait. Delay the inevitable. Life is short, and this moment would be treasured for years to come.

Nereus tore himself away from his wife, wiping the streaks from his cheeks. He smiled. Hope sweetens even the bitterest of life's tragedies.

The tender scene was interrupted suddenly by cries from a young man, dashing down the cliff trail, his toga whipping in a frenzy.

"Miletus! Nereus! We have spotted ships!"

All attention was directed to the man, who stumbled the final few paces until, dashing across the sand, he stood doubled-over and struggling to catch his breath.

"What is it you are saying?" Miletus asked, his face darkening with anxiety.

"I saw…I saw them myself. Two Roman frigates…they were sailing towards Pontia."

"Are you certain?"

"Without a doubt. They were large – perhaps *quinqueremes*. The flag was unmistakable."

"Why would the Romans waste such manpower on a tiny outpost?" Miletus wondered aloud.

"They are in search of prey," Nereus growled. "Galerius' anger has been stoked; it will only be quenched when my head is hanging from his palace gate." He closed his eyes in frustration. "I am too late," he murmured.

"We must fight, then!" the young man exclaimed.

"We will do no such thing," the old soldier rebuked sharply, snapping to attention. "We will all be slaughtered – we are no match for their swords. Rather, we will outsmart them. From which direction are they coming?"

358

"From the north. They are perhaps two stadia away by now; I spotted them an hour ago."

"Due north, or slightly askew?"

"North-west, as if they were coming directly from Rome."

"Good. If they come down the west side of the island, they will completely miss the eastern port. The ship for my journey is docked there. Miletus, gather the community – as many as you can – and load that ship. Have them set sail immediately. No one is to bring anything – time is of the essence. Escape to the mainland and wait three days; then return here. It will be safe by then."

"What if they come around the east side?"

"It is a risk we must take. Watch the seas, Miletus – if you see them anywhere near, do not set sail. They *will* pursue you. Now, go!"

The men from the community hastened up the cliff trail, heading to gather their families and flee for their safety.

But Miletus hesitated, looking curiously at Nereus. "They desire your death so fervently?"

"I am not their only quarry," he replied, casting a glance at Domitilla, standing demurely against the cliff face.

"The two of you will stay, then?"

"We are prepared for this day."

"You understand this will lead to death."

"I am already dead, Miletus," he replied gravely. "I died on the day I accepted Christ."

Miletus looked at him somberly, and then cast his gaze upon Pancras. "None of us may live to see another day. Yet this lad here has not yet died in Christ."

Only indistinctly could Pancras understand their symbolism.

"Yes," Nereus affirmed. "Yes, he must be baptized, at once."

Addressing Pancras, the presbyter asked, "Are you ready?"

The tearful goodbye had quickly transformed into a preparation for death. "I...I suppose..." he stammered. Was he prepared to die?

Die he must, whether on this day or in his bed when his life had passed. But he could no longer face death without Christ. On this point, his heart was firm.

Shaking himself from his shock, Pancras confidently declared, "Yes. Yes, I am ready."

"Good. We must make haste. Come, let us step into the sea."

The presbyter and the boy waded in knee-deep. Miletus bent down to gather a handful of water, but stopped. "You must remove your amulet."

Pancras looked down. Upon his breast hung his bulla, the very medallion that he had never removed. He gripped it, feeling once again the hand of his father who gave it to him.

"It is dedicated to a pagan idol. It must be abandoned if you are to receive new life."

Slowly, reluctantly, he took it off and held it in his hand. Oh, how it ached to do this! Could he discard the very memory of his father?

Eyes wide with anxiety, he looked at his mentor, and then at his master. They stood unwavering, insistent.

No! How could he! It would betray his father...

"Pancras," Nereus said, wading into the water to stand beside this orphan. "Your father would be proud of you. For I am confident that he would have embraced the Name of Christ, if he lived to see the day."

He shut his eyes tight, clutching the amulet. It held every last memory of his father. He wished to extract the memories from the leaden charm, to store them within his mind.

"Make haste, Pancras," Miletus encouraged. "We must not dally. Christ awaits you."

With a heaving sigh, he threw back his arm and launched the bulla into the depths of the sea. It fell with a splash, sinking to the fathomless pits of the underworld from which it came.

He noticed Nereus' broad smile as he was immersed once, twice, three times into the placid water.

They arose from that font of life, allowing Pancras a moment to change into a clean tunic as his baptismal gown. The donning of the new clothes felt richly symbolic – for a moment he forgot the crisis that threatened his life, and instead felt as if he was putting on a new life. Come what may, he was clothed in Jesus Christ.

Coming forth from the cavern-home as from a tomb into the light of day, Aquila gave him an embrace.

"Welcome home, my son," she whispered into his ear.

"I wish we could properly rejoice," Nereus interrupted. "But time is greatly of the essence. Aquila, Achilleus, Miletus, Pancras – your ship awaits you. Make haste."

Aquila sequestered a few items into a bag, and Miletus offered to hoist it upon his shoulders. In a tearful silence she embraced her husband, lingering and exchanging their hearts in a single glance. At length she was able to tear herself away, and joined the fisherman as they headed to safety.

They set off a few paces, but noticed that the others had not moved.

"Achilleus, Pancras, come," Miletus ordered, his voice lined with urgency.

"In a minute," Achilleus called out in return. "We shall catch up to you."

Satisfied, Aquila and Miletus headed up the cliff trail.

When they had disappeared from sight, Achilleus gripped Nereus' shoulders with a surprising intensity from the genial man. "We have been friends for many years now. United in life, we will be united in death. I will not abandon you at this hour."

"You do not know what you are saying," Nereus replied. "You have much to live for. Go, and watch over my wife. She will need you."

"She has Miletus and the community," he replied earnestly. "I will not leave you!"

Nereus shook free. "You may do as you please. I am grateful for your friendship."

They scanned the horizon for a moment, on the watch for ships, before Domitilla spoke up. "But as for Pancras?"

It appeared that the soldier had forgotten his adopted son. "Pancras?"

"I will not leave you, either."

"Do not be foolish, Pancras. You have so much to live for…"

"I have finally discovered something to die for!" he exclaimed defiantly, his face set like granite. "Do not take this away from me!"

"Your youthful zeal is impetuous."

"Do not disrespect me! You have prayed for me to embrace the Lord Jesus, have you not? Then let me give it all for Him – every drop of my blood! I have lost everything else in life: my father, my future, my friends. I will not lose this chance for life eternal!!"

Nereus stepped back, a bit dumbstruck by his vehemence. The baptismal water still moistening his hair, the sun glinting off of his furrowed brow, his lips set firmly – this stubborn young man would not back down.

"Well, then."

Pancras' heart was thundering within his chest, but he could not deny the hope that grew within him. He looked over to Domitilla, who smiled so sweetly and nodded, approving of his courage. For if she could face death with confidence in the Lord, he could do the same.

The boy could tell that his master was secretly pleased. Master? No, Nereus was not his master. He was a father, a friend – and now a fellow believer in Christ.

Achilleus intoned softly, "They are here."

And so they were – the ship came around the crescent cliff, setting course for the beach.

~~~

Swords drawn, the detachment of eight soldiers circled them. A man stepped forth, dressed in a centurion's finery, plumage bristling in the breeze.

"Nereus, my old friend," he began, his own sword sheathed but at the ready.

"Gaius," Nereus nodded bluntly.

"It pains me to see who you have become. Dwelling here, as an outlaw?"

"Do not mock me," he snarled. "Do what you have come to do."

"I shall take no pleasure in it," he replied with a sigh. "But Galerius' anger must be appeased."

"I do not seek your mercy. I am prepared to die."

"Yes, yes, I know about the promises you cling to. Eternal life and all those myths. But I cannot dispatch you here – I will bring you back to the mainland and await orders there. It may be that Galerius wishes to make sport of you for the hungry eyes of the populous. They have not had games in a fortnight."

"Then do as you wish. I will come."

"And these others?" His eyes fell upon Pancras, and recognition dawned. "Ah, you must be the lad of which the Emperor had spoken. He has given orders to protect you and bring you back alive. A special role for you, lad."

Pancras returned the even gaze, his face not betraying the angst within. *O Lord, make strong my hands in the sight of my foes…*

"And where is the virgin?"

Domitilla stepped forth. "I am here."

"And what a prize you are!" Gaius commented, his eyes lustily devouring her figure. "I see why your hand in marriage is coveted by all the nobles. What a pity you chose the bed of pain over the marriage bed."

"What is your purpose in such drivel?" Nereus demanded, stepping forth. "Fulfill your task. If you are to dispatch us, do so quickly."

"Nereus, old friend," Gaius retorted, his tone chilled. "We have been comrades for years now. Where was it that we fought side-by-side, you and I? Was it in the Gallican campaign? Or against those Noricum rebels in the north, in those mountain passes? You and I have shed blood together. We were brothers. And I wish only to treat you with the dignity you deserve as my brother."

"We have taken different paths," the old soldier, now shriven of his weapons, replied.

"I see that we have. And a pity, too, for you had earned a quiet retirement with full military honors and pension. It would have been a fine way to end a career with distinction. But now your current path leads only to the arena…and to the sword."

"I have no regrets."

"But surely you regret being a traitor to the Empire."

"Galerius is the one who has betrayed the Empire, not I."

"Treasonous words you speak."

"I fear not, for I belong to a different kingdom."

"And this is precisely why the Empire despises the likes of you," Gaius replied wistfully, with a derisive shake of the head. "Well then, let us be off. Weeks of diligent searching has netted us the prize. Men, apply the shackles."

The captives were chained, their wrists bound behind their backs, and led into the beached ship. Under guard, they were instructed to stand on the deck as the men heaved the craft off the sand and into the water. The sail quickly caught wind and they began to leave Pontia to their memories.

"Nereus, two ships were reported," Achilleus murmured under his breath. "And yet where is the other?"

The four stood at attention, scanning the horizon for some time.

"Pray, Achilleus," Nereus responded. "Pray that our brothers are safe."

And thus began their captivity.

This was the beginning of the end, Pancras realized. Stock-still as the Neptunes he had seen affixed to the bows of warships, his hands gripped the chains that held him bound, turning them over and over in tremulous anticipation.

Was his refusal to leave the beach too rash? His seminal faith was already being tested with fetters – it would soon be tested with the sword. The blood and fire would step out of the shadows and into the daylight.

No, he reminded himself. He is different now. He has Jesus. He has faith.

But these words were as hollow as the wind, as the cold metal rubbed his wrists. Faith – as fickle as a cloud on a blustery day, the residual wisp of smoke from an extinguished flame. It was a philosophical concept, set against the very real metal blade that awaited them.

No, he fought within himself. Jesus died and rose – I will rise with Him.

But that faith, which seemed so solid upon the island, was being shredded upon the waves, as the machinery of death had begun to turn its hungry gears.

The ship floated around the southern side of the island, making a turn portside and heading north. It was an interesting choice of route to return to Rome, Pancras thought…

Nereus noticed the oddity as well. Without the minutest change of affectation, his eyes examined the horizon.

The wind blew, and they cruised abreast of the island, its alabaster cliffs and lush greenery standing sentry. It was beautiful but melancholy, as Pancras recalled the many delights of their stay.

In the distance a thin column of black smoke began to rise. First a wisp, then a pillar, then a cloud ascended – the thickest, oily black smoke went up from some unknown location on the island.

They could hear Gaius call out to his men, "Set course for the eastern bay. I have always wanted to see it clearly."

The frigate drifted closer and closer to the shore, still creeping northward. The peninsula jutted out before them, and as they rounded the outcropping of land, they beheld a shocking sight.

A ship was ablaze with an all-consuming fire. From the mast to the stern, flames engulfed the entire craft. It anchored a stadium from the shore, a torch in the center of the bay.

"What is this?" Pancras asked, afraid to know the answer.

Their own ship began to sail closer and closer, until they passed by close enough to feel the heat emanating from the burning wooden beams.

"Let us take a moment of silence, remembering the dead," Gaius shouted to all. His crew fell silent in a moment and the only sound they could hear was the sail snapping to attention in the wind.

And then they heard voices. Muted screams, banging on wood. Shrieks of a woman, the calls of a man. Amplified by the water, the desperate cries of those condemned to a fiery demise. The bowels of the ship were alive with people roasting to death.

It was a scene from the very pits of Hell.

Aquila! Pancras cried out, though the cries failed to find voice. *Miletus! God be with you all! May these accursed fiends who set you ablaze suffer the same fate for eternity!*

All aboard were fascinated by the scene – some with horror, others with glee. Nereus, for his part, was stoic, though he surely recognized his wife's voice blending with the others.

The cries and prayers became as a holocaust, mingling with the smoke as it rose to Heaven.

Those who stood upon the prison-ship added their interior prayers to the condemned. Pancras wished that the tears flowing down his face might be used to quench the flames, to cool the tongues of the burnt offering.

A gust of wind blew sparks towards their own ship, and so Gaius gave the orders for them to set sail again into the endless blue, headed to the mainland.

As they sailed away, Pancras cocked his ears to try to hear the last words of the condemned. But they had fallen silent, overcome by the flames.

They were some distance away when a loud crack echoed across the sea, the charred skeleton of the ship collapsing under the fire and burying its occupants in a watery tomb.

"It is not personal, Nereus," Gaius said, startling those on the deck. When did he slink beside them?

Nereus slowly turned to face him. "What is more personal than the death of one's wife and friends?"

"I am sorry," he apologized. Was the contrition on his face genuine? "Galerius, you know…"

"Carrying out orders," Nereus spat bitterly. "I pray that someday, Gaius, you answer to a higher power than a monster."

"That 'monster' had promised me a seat on the Senate."

"Where you will be yet another sycophant to a tyrant."

Gaius looked wounded; he turned away and pretended to adjust the mooring rope.

Nereus too looked back across the sea, as the island faded into the distance. "When a man compromises himself, he is capable of the most wretched deeds."

Pancras observed all this without speaking. What was the greater horror – a ship torched and men burned alive, or a man who had sold himself to evil?

~~~

The sun was dipping further towards the horizon, appearing to engulf the island of Pontia in unquenchable flames. They sailed into an unfamiliar port, docking quickly. The prisoners were led off the ship at the edge of the sword, into the small seaside village.

"Why here, Gaius?" Nereus demanded, recognizing the town. "Take us to Caesar. Why parade us through Terracina?"

Gaius regarded him thoughtfully as he walked astride of the condemned four. "Here you will overnight until I receive orders from Rome. Terracina has a prison that will serve as your shelter."

"And a brothel to serve as yours, Gaius!" one of the soldiers called out coarsely. Rough laughter all around, while Nereus looked disgusted.

The stares of onlookers were a constant companion as they walked through the small town. Merchants gave them a curious glance, patrons stopped their exchange and gazed pitiably, and small children looked up from their games to notice those headed to the gallows.

At length Nereus spoke again. "I forgive you, Gaius."

"You forgive me?" the soldier replied, with the slightest hint of mockery. "You forgive me for forcing me to sail halfway across the Empire in a frantic man-hunt for your pathetic corpse? You forgive me for being away from my family because of your delusions?"

369

"There is One who can forgive you for the man you have become."

The soldier dismissed the idea with a wave of his hand.

And the prison-march continued through the town, amidst the curious onlookers. There was very little shame for Pancras – no, his thoughts were elsewhere, on a precipice and looking over into an abyss. He wondered: when he fell – committing his life and his eternity into a Hand he could not see – would he be caught? Or will there be nothing there?

His faith, now in tatters from the journey – *why do the evil prosper while the good are consumed in flame?* – was his only hope as he teetered on the cliff of nothingness.

Miletus – Aquila – the others: where are they now? Their bodies were at the bottom of the ocean, awaiting the end of time – but where did their souls reside? Are they safe within the hands of their loving God, as they hoped? Pancras fervently hoped so, as well – and, in a strange way, anticipated their reunion in the next life.

They were led along a dirt trail outside of town which reached its terminus at a small stone building built into the side of a rock outcropping. It was tiny, befitting such an insignificant town. There was barely the space to lie down flat within the structure.

Unceremoniously, they were shoved inside, an iron grate locked behind them. There were no sentries, as there was no hope of escaping.

As Gaius turned aside without a parting word, Nereus called out to him. "Gaius! My old friend!"

He stopped and faced them, an old irony in his face.

"Will you do me one favor? For our brotherhood?"

The young centurion did not respond, so Nereus went on. "Will you alert Julia, daughter of Julius, that we are here? She lives in Terracina, though I know not which street."

A noncommittal shrug was the only response before he disappeared into the twilight.

~~~

What does one say to his fellow condemned? He feared to make light of their dire straits with mundane conversation. And so they sat in silence, entombed with their own thoughts. Hunger and thirst accosted them, but it mattered little when their death awaited.

After a while, as torchlights began to be lit in the town before them, Domitilla began a hymn.

Her pure voice was water to their thirsty ears, an oasis of life in the most parched desert. In a moment, Nereus and Achilleus joined in, with words that both haunted and consoled.

> *He emptied himself, and took the form of a slave*
> *Being born in the likeness of men*
> *And it was thus that he humbled himself,*
> *Accepting even death,*
> *Death on a cross!*
> *Therefore God exalted Him,*
> *And bestowed upon Him the Name above every other,*
> *That at Jesus' Name, all knees must bend*
> *In heaven and on earth,*
> *And every tongue proclaim to the glory of the Father:*
> *Jesus Christ is Lord.*

Pancras recognized this as the same hymn he had heard in another prison, a lifetime ago. How much had changed since then – how much had changed in him!

Yes, he was ready.

371

He was ready to proclaim the Name, even unto death.

For nothing else mattered. Not the temptations of a future in the Emperor's palace, nor the memories of his past family and friends, nor the fear that threatened him in the present. Nothing else mattered but this – the eternal life held out to him. Even as he peered into the abyss of death, he had taken the Hand, and would not let it go.

~~~

He dreamt of blood and fire.

Awaking with a violent trembling, he sat up, panting. His heart racing, breathless, he stared into the darkness. Where was his faith now?

"Nereus!" he called out, in a darker fear than he had ever felt.

The snoring man gave a snort and came to life. "Pancras?"

"Nereus! What if this is a myth?"

"What? What are you talking about?" he grunted.

"We are going to die, Nereus. What if there is nothing after the blade falls?"

The man sat up, leaning against the cold stone. "Pancras, I have hope."

"But do you have proof?"

"No, I do not. But I have hope and I have faith. Sometimes that is all we need."

The boy drew his knees to his chest. The reality of it threatened to overwhelm him. "But I am afraid."

"I am afraid, as well," he admitted. He coughed, and cleared his throat. "Pancras, I know you loved your father. Did you trust him?"

"Of course."

372

"And did he promise you things?"

"He promised me many things…"

"Because he was a good father. I believe that our Father, He who created all things – yes, even you and me – He is a good father. And He has promised me eternal life. So although I do not yet possess it, I trust Him."

"My father…most of all, he promised me that I would inherit everything. He would tell me all the time that *all this will be yours.* I placed my trust in him, and here I am, in a prison cell awaiting execution."

"Your father wanted to give you everything he had. But our good Father *has already* given us everything He has, including His Son. Will He not give us eternal life as well?"

Pancras remained silent. Yes, his earthly father was a good man, the best there was. But he was mortal, and thus subject to the limitations of all flesh. To have a divine Father, though…

"Besides, Pancras," Nereus continued, "You will be spared. *We* will be executed. You will remain in the Emperor's service."

"A fate worse than death!"

"Perhaps. But who knows the plans of the Almighty. Remember His love always."

"I am trying…but I have had so much sorrow…"

"And so much strength."

"No, no, no! I am not strong."

"Then let Him be your strength."

Here was a man who was a paragon of strength, and yet his strength came from above. For the briefest moment, Pancras saw that beneath the surface of this great man was a child, in the arms of his Father.

"Do you miss her?" Pancras asked quietly.

And Nereus could not answer for the tears flowing down his face.

"I miss them, too. And I miss my father."

"We will see them again," Nereus choked out.

"This I hope. This I hope."

~~~

But hope is a fragile thing, quickly dissipating in the night. He listened as Nereus' breathing became rhythmic, then snores. How could a man sleep in peace the night before his execution? Pancras was wide-eyed, staring into the darkened cell.

He tried to pray, but was unable to remember those beautiful words Miletus tried to teach him.

Our Father, who art in Heaven...oh, what was next?

Something about His Name, and then a Kingdom and daily bread. But he could not remember the words.

Nevertheless he tried to lift his heart and mind to higher things, to an eager anticipation of everlasting life. But as high as the thoughts rose, they inevitably came crashing down with the weight of his weak humanity.

He heaved a sigh as deep as the ocean.

"Pancras." A whisper in the dark.

"I am here."

"I have heard your fears," Domitilla replied, her voice as music. "And I wish to console you."

He looked in her direction, for they lay beside one another on the cold ground. "With what?"

"I wish I could give you a share in my own faith. As I cannot, I have little to offer you. But I have confidence that the seed of faith within you will grow and flourish and bear fruit a hundredfold."

"It is in danger of being destroyed before it comes to birth."

"Perhaps. Or perhaps the grain of wheat must fall to the ground and die before it can germinate."

Why this poetry before the gallows?

"You said you wished to console me. What words can bring comfort to my heart?"

"Only this: all is gift, Pancras. All is gift."

It was a beautiful thought and he felt a stirring in his heart. He wished to reach out and touch her, to caress her face, to hold her hand in gratitude. But she was a temple inviolate, a bride spoken-for, so he merely replied, "You have said this before."

"And yet how easily we forget that the cross is as much a gift as the resurrection."

"What sort of Groom requires this of His bride?"

"A Groom that seeks union with the Beloved. For the Cross is the meeting-place of God and humanity."

He was silent for a moment, reflecting. The crosses he had so often seen on the Via Appia seemed to be the very antithesis of love and hope. But to accept this new faith in the Lord required him to believe in a God who chose to die upon such a horrific symbol.

"I still struggle with this, Domitilla."

"That is because you see the Cross, but not the love behind the Cross. It is not that God desired a bloody death for its own sake. No, He desired to give Himself completely. And so He chose the most ignominious death to show the depths of His love. For the Cross symbolizes the shame and the torture and the death that we deserve because of our sins."

"And this, too, is a gift? The embrace of the Cross?"

"It is the greatest gift, given to Christ's intimates."

He came as a beggar, receiving only the gift of the Cross. With faith, there was a joy in the Cross, for with it came the Lord.

"Domitilla? May I ask you a question?"

"Of course," she laughed softly, the sound of bells chiming in the night.

"Why did you forsake marriage? How can one fall in love with an invisible God as one falls in love with a man?"

"I was brought up to love the Lord by my wet-nurse. She secretly taught me all about the things of God – a true *hagia* she was! When I was older, she and a fellow slave would smuggle copies of the Scriptures into the palace. I hungered for these words. They became my daily bread. Through them, I learned of this tremendous love of God for us. It was He who called me, in my nothingness, to return love for love.

"When I was your age, I would escape the palace for the breaking of bread in the homes of the faithful. When I tasted the Bread of Life for the first time, a burst of joy filled me, unlike anything I had ever felt. The sweetness of that *eucharistia* has stayed with me. It is renewed every Lord's day, and through every prayer."

"I have never felt Him like that," Pancras lamented.

"Oh, but you have! When your breath was taken away by beauty, did you not sense Him? Surrounded by the love of friends and family, was that not His embrace?"

"Yet my life has seen much sorrow…I have felt His wrath more than His love."

"It was not His wrath, but the hammer-blows that have shaped you into a vessel to receive Him."

"I feel like nothing more than a clay pot."

"One that holds a treasure."

"Must you always see the world in a positive light?"

"I could say the opposite about you!" she replied, and they both acknowledged the jest with a brief whispered laugh.

"Domitilla, this is indeed a consolation. I thank you."

"My dear Pancras, you will be called upon to give witness to the Emperor. It may or may not lead to your death. But on that day, when you stand before the lord of darkness, recall this: all is gift."

"All is gift," Pancras mused, and waited for the dawn.

~~~

It was the fourth watch of the night, the sky warming from ink to heliotrope purple. The beginning of the last day on earth.

The stillness was interrupted by scratches on the raw earth. A person approached, but whether they were friend or foe remained to be revealed.

The dim morning light revealed a cloaked figure, stooped and bent.

"Dominum! Nereus!" called out the shaky voice of an elderly woman.

There was a stirring in the jail cell as all awoke and came to attention.

"I heard the news." She knelt at the grate, setting down a covered basket.

"God bless you, Julia," Nereus rasped. "God bless you."

A solitary loaf of bread was quartered and shared. She plunged a dipper into a bucket of water and passed it through the grate. It barely slaked their pressing thirst.

"Please ask the brothers to pray," the soldier requested. "Pray that our courage will not fail."

"I will. We will meet this morn, and intercede for you with the Father."

He had abandoned all hope of release, Pancras realized. And this is how it ends…

Domitilla spoke up. "I have a plot of land outside of the city, on the Via Ardeatina. Will you bury us there?"

"I will have it done."

They exchanged greetings and promises of prayer, before the older woman fled, lest the dawn expose her as a believer.

~~~

They were led to the town square at the break of dawn. Gaius met them there, his face set as stone. He did not seem to relish the deed he was tasked to perform.

A small crowd had gathered, excited by the commotion of these men from Rome.

Unrolling a scroll, the centurion read from it. "Let it be known that these men are charged with the following crimes: conspiracy against the Empire, flagrant disregard for an order of the Emperor, insubordination, dereliction of duty, and belonging to the forbidden sect of the Christus. They are condemned to the penalty of death, to be executed this day with haste." Looking up, he added, "I suppose Galerius wishes to never see your face again – we are to execute you here."

The condemned men nodded solemnly.

Pancras' heart thundered. Though the order was only for Achilleus and Nereus, what horrors would transpire before his very eyes?

The four were led out of the forum to the nearby amphitheater, joined by a few townspeople eager for blood.

They stood at a respectful distance, along with Julia and a few whose sympathy prompted their attendance.

"Do the condemned wish to speak?" they were asked.

Nereus stood tall, at the center of the motley crowd. He was uncowed by the threats that lay before him. "I wish to speak."

At Gaius' gesture, the old Christian soldier began. "The Rome of yore was a city built upon the noble virtues of our forefathers. It is to this Empire that I am loyal. This Rome still lives within the hearts of the righteous, and I am confident that it will rise again – transformed by the grace of God. For the Kingdom of God has come, for those who believe in the Lord Jesus. And this King will reign, forever and ever."

With a sarcastic shrug, Gaius signaled that the executioner should perform his task.

Oh, Pancras had seen much death in his fourteen years, but this time was different. The fear was still present, seeing the well-worn sword leaning against the pillar. The ache of sorrow reached into the very pits of his bowels, wringing his heart, twisting the knot in his throat. But though the blood-stained column stood sentry as an icon of death, it was not the harbinger of oblivion.

In a short moment, two men will add their blood to the crimson stains, cascading down the pillar.

Oh Lord, accept this sacrifice. Let it be pleasing in your sight.

The executioner wielded the heavy blade, awaiting the moment to apply it.

Nereus was first, kneeling down of his own accord in silence. The old soldier, at peace, cast a penetrating glance to the boy – a final wordless goodbye.

And Pancras had to shut his eyes, his head hanging against his chest in an agonized grimace. He could not bear to watch. Let this not be prolonged! His heart was being torn out, destroyed.

A hand reached out to his – Domitilla's gentle fingers gripped his with unspeakable anguish.

A slice through flesh, and the deed was accomplished.

It was finished.

The sacrifice was consummated.

Pancras was numb, demolished. He was merely enduring until the end.

The butcher procured his next victim, and the sounds ensued of another offering.

Through a blurry squint, Pancras could see an emotionless Gaius observing the corpses that lay at his feet. The young soldier was completely detached – it was another routine execution in a career full of death.

But no! It was so much more! It was the death of a father, a saint. That pool of blood was sacred, a holy ransom, sanctifying the ground and redeeming this accursed nation.

Take my life, O Lord. Let my blood be mingled with the blood of the martyrs, watering the ground that new life may grow.

A spark of courage began to galvanize him. Seeing their heroic witness, Pancras ached to join them in the eternal life they now enjoyed.

Gaius gave instructions to his men to pile the corpses outside of the city wall, in the trash heap where the refuse of humanity found its resting place. Two jewels amidst the ashes.

"As for you," he instructed the princess and the slave, "Make haste. I wish to be at the gates of Rome by nightfall."

PART SEVEN: *The Final Witness*

Their feet were aching by the time the gates of the
imperial city came into view. Without food or water or rest,
the ragged travelers were propelled onward only by
swordpoint. And the knowledge that it was their destiny to
bear witness to Life in the city of death.

How the city had changed! Oh, to human eyes the
streets were the same, with their soot-caked walls and
sewer-river cobblestone streets. But now Pancras could see
clearly the darkness that cloaked the city, the sin that
pervaded every alleyway. The light was within him, and it
illuminated everything now.

*Oh, my city! My beloved Rome! How I have desired your
pleasures, sought your glories – and now I will die within your
gates!*

The ache within him had been dulled by exhaustion
and the journey, but as they passed through the gates, hours
after sunset, a different yearning arose within him. It was a
desire to speak the words of Life to this city, to tell of the
hope that can only be found in Christ.

Pancras was shivering, but whether it was the
temperature or the anxiety, he could not tell. It was quiet
upon those familiar streets. Only memories echoed in the
cold moonlight.

There was the Forum where he was sold as a slave,
and then later freed by his master. Up ahead was the Temple
of Jupiter, where his uncle had showed him the glories of
Rome and promised that all things would be his. Oh, to the
left was the entrance to the Tullianum prison, where he said

381

his last goodbye to his closest friend. Over there, yes, under that awning flapping in the wind, was a wonderful conversation with Daphne, and around the bend – there it is! – the baths where Decian played a trick that day, yes, how carefree they were!

It was as if the entirety of his life was being played out before his eyes. Somehow he knew that this would be the last time he would see these sights.

The palace gates loomed before them, imposing and dark. A few lanterns glowed in the windows.

Gaius brought them up to the palace steps, where they encountered the guardsman.

"I have orders from Galerius to bring these captives to him."

They received a cursory glance, as the guard was more interested in the document the soldier produced.

"Of course. Come with me."

The striking elegance of the palace, with its fresco-lined walls and intricate mosaics on the floor, with tapestries and gold-plated oil lamps, was a shock to the senses. Having lived in a cave for the past two months, this opulence was entrancing, enthralling, enticing...

He shook his head to regain his bearings, for the beauty and civilization had an intoxicating effect. His old heart, with its desires and cravings, sought to wield its influence.

The guard had disappeared to inquire of the fate of the two prisoners, and returned with haste.

"The girl is to come with me, while the boy is to be taken to Galerius. He is eager to see him."

For the first time, Pancras saw a flash of fear in Domitilla's eyes. But humbly like a lamb she submitted, following him meekly without need of shackles.

Gaius led Pancras away, through the labyrinthine hallways. "You must have made quite an impression on the Emperor."

The lad was silent. For what purpose was he being saved? He dreaded the thought of even seeing the face of this murderer.

They passed through a doorway, and there he was.

It was in a room Pancras had not yet seen. Dark mauve walls, with numerous hanging oil lamps casting dark shadows everywhere. Several busts and nudes stood mutely upon low columns – the faces of the dead, frozen in marble. A series of low couches formed a rectangle in the center of the room. Upon one of them reclined the Emperor, dressed in his finery.

"Ah, Pancras!" he whined with enthusiasm. "It is so good to see you. You have been on my mind ever since you were kidnapped by that traitor."

Should he contradict him? And risk hastening his death?

"Please, please. Sit down. I am sorry to see they have not treated you well on your journey. You must be hungry. Gaius, please have the servants bring food and drink, and have them wash the boy's feet."

The soldier nodded crisply before departing.

"Now, please, sit. I insist!"

Pancras reclined uneasily.

"I must apologize to you, Pancras. I was not hospitable when you came by during the party. I was not exactly sober, I must admit, and my manners had slipped terribly. You deserved a finer greeting. Please accept my apologies."

He was one of the statuary, immobile, silent.

Sensing the resistance, Galerius sat up and smiled, making friendly gestures. "Ah, Pancras! You need not fear me. I do not intend to kill you. No, not at all. You are far too precious to me."

"Why? You know nothing about me."

"On the contrary! I know you are well-educated, intelligent, principled, and you desire the finer things in life. You have a fine destiny ahead of you…though I fear you may have been corrupted by the lies of that soldier. But that is a trifle – and we will not discuss him here."

The food was brought in on platters, with a tall goblet of wine. Roast chicken, hot and tantalizing, stared back at him, with bread and cheese, olives and figs. He had not seen such a meal since before their exile, and his mouth watered against his will.

"Please, do eat," Galerius urged, as a servant began to remove the sandals from the boy's feet and rub the weariness out of them, washing them with water and anointing them with oil.

Such treatment – he could have this forever…

No! He was different, he was new. He would not forget the face of Nereus, peace emanating before the axe separated head from body. This was the murderer – he must not make peace with him.

Galerius observed this internal struggle with amusement. He lay back on his couch, his ringed fingers gently caressing his face. "You have been through many trials and sorrows, have you not? I can read it in your eyes. You have lost many friends."

This was disorienting – the food, the warmth, the civilized treatment. His courage began to falter as sadness and despair fought for dominance. All of a sudden the memories washed back in, the memories of everyone he had ever lost.

He nodded sadly.

"But I can promise you: that can all be over. You can live a life beyond the reach of death's sinister grasp. Here in the palace, I can assure you that you will be safe. No more sorrow, no more loss, no more death."

"What do you want from me?"

"For now, I want you to eat! You are wasting away!"

The hunger overcame his flimsy resolve, and Pancras tore into the chicken voraciously.

Galerius was bemused to watch him devour the meat.

"My boy, I do not want anything from you," the Emperor clarified. "Nay, rather, I wish to *give* something to you. You have impressed me from the first time I met you. I wish to renew my offer to you. I have been deserted by all – my son, my wife. I am alone, Pancras. I trust that you know how it feels to be...*alone*."

The boy ceased his rabid feast long enough to stare at the Emperor blankly. Yes, he knew what it was to be alone. He had wrestled with that demon many a day.

The Emperor continued wistfully. "And I know that you, too, are alone. You have no family. Your master is...passed on to the next life. What will become of you if no one looks after you? What will become of *me* if I do not find a worthy heir, a young man I can trust and love like a son?

"You think me mad," he continued. "But it is the madness of isolation that prompts this offer. Do not think I will abuse or mistreat you. I have not summoned you here to make sport of a lonely orphan like yourself. Nay, I am not heartless! I merely recognize your good qualities. You are a fine, handsome, strong young man."

385

Such praise was dizzying. He needn't suffer alone any more...

No! Stop this nonsense! He belonged to a new Love, and was never alone with Him at his side.

But this new faith seemed a paltry consolation compared to the offer of companionship, power, comfort. Now stripped of his fellow Christ-followers, he felt acutely his loneliness as never before, and all of this seemed tempting...

"But I...I am now a Christian," he rebutted weakly.

"A minor matter," the Emperor reassured. "A grain of incense burned to the Lares is sufficient to wipe away that cult."

A grain of incense was all it took to have all this...

"Pancras, the plebeian classes look upon us Emperors as gods. And so we are! You can join us in the caste of divinity, here on Mount Olympus itself."

"There is only one God..."

"A demigod, then. Let us not quibble over theological technicalities."

"But I am nothing, just a poor man."

"Even your humility bears testimony to your greatness!" Galerius exclaimed. "You are far more than a poor man. Your virtues and beauty make you a god, as fine as Hercules."

"I do not wish to be esteemed too highly."

"If praise does not entice you, I can offer you much more. You will never be hungry again; the subjects of this realm will bow to your will; you will command armies and rule over nations; you will inherit the very villa of Hadrian! This palace will be your home; riches will be your lot."

"Why such an offer? Can you not find another lad in the realm?"

The Emperor looked at him archly, his crown shimmering in the flames. "I am the master of this realm, and I have chosen you!"

The boy was reduced to silence, confused and dazed.

Contradictory thoughts raged for dominance. He longed for such security, comfort, love...but he had found that in the Christ, had he not?

Perhaps not. Perhaps that three-fold immersion did nothing but soak his body with ordinary seawater – he felt nothing different in his soul. The bandage of faith had been torn away, leaving his wounds exposed and raw. He had thought it was a solid rock, but instead it was merely sand, washed away by the tumultuous ocean.

The promise of eternal life was distant, unseen. The promises of life in the palace were close enough to reach out and touch, if he would but say a word, burn a grain of incense, and consent.

But no. Had Nereus died for no purpose? Had Miletus become a holocaust for an empty myth? Their deaths bore witness to an invisible reality. All things concealed will be revealed, in their proper time.

Galerius dispassionately observed his inner struggle, unblinkingly staring at the boy for some time. At length he stood up and said, "Pancras, I must show you a fine thing."

The boy followed him out of the room and through the palace, lost in his own thoughts.

The old man brought him up a flight of stairs, through a door and a hallway, until another flight of stairs deposited them on the roof of the palace. From such a perch, the entire city of Rome stretched out before them, dimly illuminated by the full moon.

From this perspective, they could see a thousand lights, lamps lit in the hundreds of *insulae* that dotted the seven hills. Like fireflies on a summer night were these man-made luminaries, in the city of a million inhabitants. The streets stretched out in an endless web. There were the landmarks – the Colosseum, the Temple of Jupiter, the Forum – rising from the sea of the common horde as islands of civilization.

"Do you see all this?" Galerius declared, sweeping his arm as they took in the view. "All this will be yours, Pancras. All this will be yours."

Such words were salt in the wound.

Oh, Father! Father! What would you have me do?

"My father used to say that," Pancras whispered into the night.

"As did mine," Galerius added softly, wrapping his arm around the boy's shoulders.

Pancras looked up, astonished.

"My father was a herdsman in the mountains," the Emperor explained. "He was not an aristocrat. But the little he had, he wanted to give to me – the flocks, the small cabin in the mountains. I spurned it then, with bigger dreams. And though I have achieved far more than I could have ever imagined, there is still a longing…I wonder if I would have been happier with my father's flocks than with this palace, these royal robes."

Who was this man? A tyrant, or a child playing dress-up in fancy costumes, longing for a Father?

"So you see, Pancras, I am a simple man, beneath these robes."

"But what of the bodies? The blood? The severed heads?"

He sighed. "I long for the days of old, for the glories of the Caesars. We were a proud Republic, governed by decent men. We can return to those days! We can bring back the nobility of this nation! But we cannot have rebels in our midst, whether they be political or religious."

"And those who profess the Name of the Christ…"

"We cannot have unity when dangerous sects seek to divide us. We have our gods – let them suffice."

They stood in silence for a while, observing the nightfall. One by one the lights were extinguished, as the city began to sleep. Pancras, too, could barely keep his eyes open and was in danger of tottering over the railing from exhaustion.

"Pancras, I beg you, consider my offer," Galerius said. "It is good for you, and it is good for the Empire."

"I thank you," he replied, bleary-eyed. He was too tired to think clearly.

"Come, you must be growing cold. My servants have prepared a bonfire in the courtyard. You may warm yourself before I send you home."

Home? Where was home? Did he have a home anymore? He wished to object, but lacked the energy.

Galerius led him down the stairs and through a part of the palace previously unseen by the lad. They approached the courtyard and could see the roaring blaze in the middle. It was a fine bonfire, a tower of interlocking logs.

They approached to grow warm, when Pancras stopped, alarmed.

Atop the logs was a body, a virgin making her final offering to the Lord.

Pancras was so startled by the sight of Domitilla's body, bound and aflame, that he could not react.

The Emperor turned halfway around, so that his face was half in shadows, half illuminated by the flames fed by human flesh. "I wish you to remember, Pancras, that I do not take refusals lightly."

The body – his face – the body – his face – both scenes of horror.

"Guards, please escort Pancras to his home for the night. I will expect an answer from him in the morning."

~~~

His feet moved, but his mind was too weary to think. Drowning in drowsiness, he paid no attention to where they were taking him. The second watch of the night quickly slipped into the third.

The guards led him up the steps leading into a small villa, and it wasn't until he was at the threshold that he recognized where he was.

Empty, without life, stood Nereus' house before him.

Was this an attempt to break him down further? A mockery of memory?

He was roughly shoved inside with a gruff reminder from the guards, "You are under house arrest. We will be posted all around the house, so escape will not be possible. Sleep well!"

And the door shut behind him, and Pancras was alone.

The warmth and familial love that so often filled that space was absent, making the darkness even more vacant, the absence more lonely. But he had no energy to ponder such deep things, as his feet led him to an abandoned couch, where he collapsed and closed his eyes, waiting to drift off – from one nightmare to another.

He was on the shores of the land of dreams when a pounding at the door woke him.

Let the intruder force their way in, he grumbled interiorly.

And then he heard his name: "Pancras!"

His heart beat hard, for he recognized the voice. He shot upright, watching the door slowly swing open. Into his solitude stepped the only one who could rescue him.

"Oh, Pancras!" Daphne cried out, tears of joy streaming from her eyes.

They raced to one another, embracing in a joy that joined the two into one heart, one love.

Words failed them at this jubilant reunion. Their tears mingled and flowed, until they formed a single river upon both cheeks. It was impossible to tell where one ended and the other began, so tightly did they enfold each other.

Laughter began to spill out, a wordless exultation at a love so long denied, a passion finally released.

"Oh, how I have missed you, Daphne!" Pancras exclaimed. Her name was honey upon his lips. Suddenly his exhaustion evaporated in the overwhelming felicity.

She could not stop kissing his cheek.

Eventually they had to surface for air, and they both collapsed upon the couch, still giddy in excitement.

"How did you know I had returned?" Pancras asked, unable to take his eyes off his beloved.

"It was a mere hour ago that the news was brought to my ears," she replied, stroking his cheek. "A guard from the palace appeared at our insula door with the glad tidings."

"From the palace?"

"The very one. You have friends in high places, it appears."

Pancras averted his gaze. "It would not be correct to call him a friend."

"Whom?"

"Galerius."

Daphne's face registered surprise. "You know Galerius?"

"Unfortunately."

"Why do you say this? It could be greatly to your advantage to have such a friendship."

The boy searched the girl's eyes for something inexplicable. Not finding it there, he rose and began to pace the room.

"Much has happened to me since we had last spoken. You may have heard that I fled Rome with Nereus – that rumor has certainly made its rounds of the city, I am sure."

"Yes, it grieved me endlessly when I heard. I was sick for days – I thought I had lost you forever, and wondered why you did not send a message."

"We had to hasten, for Galerius' bloodlust would not be satisfied until he killed every good and innocent soul in this Empire. But Galerius took a liking to me and invited me to become a member of his household."

"That is wonderful!"

"I thought so as well, but I have seen his evil. I refused his offer."

"Why?"

"I am different now, Daphne. I have followed the way of Love, not the way of the world."

"Why can you not have both?"

"The world is bloodthirsty," he lamented. "To dwell with Galerius is to become him."

"Nonsense!" she exclaimed. "You are strong, you are pure. This is what drew me to you, all those years ago. You could sit upon high places and accomplish such good!"

"I cannot accept it, Daphne. If you have seen the things I have seen…"

"But consider what a rare opportunity this is! He truly wishes for you to be his heir?"

Pancras nodded, sick at the prospect.

Daphne clapped her hands, excited. "Wealth, power, comfort…all the things that make life rich!"

"What I once considered riches, I now see as filth."

"I do not understand. You could have everything!"

"And now I do not want it."

"Pancras, are we still a *together*?"

The lad was taken by surprise.

"I…I don't know…"

"Well, I do. I want to spend the rest of my life with you. And what a beautiful life it would be for you and me to live in the palace! I could be the wife of an Emperor!"

All the gold, all the power, and his beloved as well!

But only a profound sadness filled the atmosphere between them. No, she would never understand.

The stars continued their course across the heavens, the silent heavens that remained mute before his needy pleas.

"You have changed," she observed at last.

He nodded. Reveal the soul, and let the axe fall between them. "I now believe in the Christ."

"The Christ?" she said with disgust. "That devastating myth…"

"I do not expect you to believe, Daphne," he interrupted sharply. "But now I have a hope that I never had before."

"You have always wanted to run away from death," she sneered, her love and joy disappearing behind a cold countenance. "And now you are running headlong into the arena?"

"But He has triumphed over death…"

"Ah, so you turned to this Jesus because of your fears? You are not a little boy anymore, Pancras. We have all had our deaths. But we must not let them cripple us, for we have a life to live."

"I saw what life was when my friend knelt before the executioner's sword."

"Men die for all sorts of causes. Are you willing to throw away our *together* because of a myth? You would rather seek some hidden afterlife than a beautiful life of joy here, together, you and me?"

"I wish for both, Daphne. But I..."

"Do you love me, Pancras?"

He had never made such a declaration explicit; didn't she know that their love was the most fervent love since the creation of the world?

"I do!"

"Then why would you refuse the Emperor's offer? Why would you cling to this dangerous cult? You will ruin our love!"

He sighed and shook his head. The few paces that separated them were an uncrossable chasm.

"I love you, Pancras," she purred, her eyes filling with tears.

Every word was another nail into his heart, another reminder of all that he was giving up. All of his hopes and dreams were being wrested from his clenched fists – for what? For an unseen promise?

"Daphne, I am afraid," he admitted, seating himself beside her once again. "I am afraid of losing you. I am fearful of being killed. But most of all, I fear losing the hope of eternal life."

"Do you not fear that all this is a myth?"

"Nereus did not fear. Domitilla did not fear."

"But can you not cling to your religion in the palace? Think of *me*, Pancras. Your decision takes these joys from me, too – and most of all, they take away *you*, my one and only joy."

"Galerius will not tolerate this new religion. You remember what they did to Antonius. We have already lost friends to it – and I fear that I may be next."

"You? You might follow in Antonius' footsteps?"

"I cannot say what the future will hold."

The tears flowed freely now. Pancras ached upon seeing her sorrow, but unlike the sorrow that flowed from her soul when they were young, he could do nothing to comfort her.

"I do not understand…"

"This is much to grasp, I know. And I fear I cannot explain it adequately, for I do not fully understand my own faith. All I know is that I faced death, and found that all my strength is nothing. I needed the strength of God."

"I have already lost you once! I cannot do so again! It would be more than I could bear!"

He yearned to give a word of consolation, to draw her to him and take her grief upon himself. But no, he was the cause of it – it was his faith that was destroying their mutual dreams of a future together. So he sat in silence, absorbing the tears and the sobs, feeling them acutely as blows upon an already-scourged heart.

"I urge you, Daphne," he began softly, knowing his words could cause an eruption. "I beg you, come to know the Christ. He is not a myth – He is alive forever and ever."

Abruptly standing, she glared through tears. "You are mad," she seethed softly. "Utterly mad!" Two rapid strides led her to the door, where her parting words were lances to obliterate a soul: "You are not the Pancras I once loved."

When the door shut behind her, the house echoed with the horrible finality of loneliness.

For a time, Pancras sat trembling upon the couch. The cold penetrated through his skin to his very soul. This temptation was too great to bear! His very heart and flesh cried out to the girl, and he ardently wished to run after her, give her a word of reconciliation, seek to find understanding. But no – his fate was sealed. He had lost her…forever.

He was numb beyond tears, aching beyond mere pain, exhausted and spent in every way. Every form of doubt and despair drowned him. Was he doing the right thing? Or was he rushing to a blood-soaked arena in a suicidal frenzy?

With the little scrap of will he still possessed, he fell to his knees and whispered aloud, "Oh Lord God, Jesus Christ. I do not have beautiful words or good deeds, but only my own misery to bring You. I am alone with no refuge but You. I fear the loss of all things, for I am still attached to this girl and to my own life, and I know that these too will be required of me. My faith is weak, and I feel that You are nowhere to be found. I need help, O God. Let me not fail or falter in the time of my deliverance."

And then he fell into silence, the silence of a living sacrifice consumed on the altar of the heart.

After a minute, he heard a voice speaking to his soul, clearer than he had ever heard anything in his life:

My son, My beloved, you are on the very shores of Heaven.

~~~

That night, he slept soundly, at peace.

~~~

"The Emperor awaits a response," barked the florid man, well-decorated and imposing, who towered over the sleeping figure.

Pancras rolled over and rubbed his eyes. The sunlight streaming through the windowpanes indicated that he had slept late into the morning.

"The Emperor can wait until I wake up," he replied, yawning immensely.

"He does not take kindly to delays."

"Then tell him that the answer is no. I am not interested in his offer."

"Do you understand the consequences of your decision?"

He nodded. Yes, he understood. He was going to die.

The soldier helped him up. "Then on your feet, lad. There are games this morning, and we must meet the Emperor there."

Games. Death in the Colosseum. Although he had prepared for such a fate, the prospect still stirred the old fear within him.

O God, Savior of all, make my life into a holocaust for You!

He rose and was bound, his hands behind his back. With a confident step that belied his terror, he followed the guard out the door and onto the street.

It was a beautiful autumnal day, the sun shining brightly as leaves began their annual metamorphosis from green to brown. The bustle of the streets was familiar, comforting on his last day of life. Merchants continued with their business, patrons purchased the fixings for the midday meal, and Pancras prepared to give his final witness to the world.

The Colosseum rose from the surrounding buildings, a gleaming testimony to the glories of Rome. The glories that were in his grasp – but spurned.

The guards led him through the bowels of the edifice, through hallway after hallway, up several inclines and staircases. Pancras had thought that the condemned were held underground, in the underworld, but here he was being led upward, upward!

There was another burst of terror as he stepped out of the shadows into the bowl of the arena. He could see the sandy floor that would receive his blood. But despite the terror, there was also a peace, a peace the world could not give.

But he was in the wrong part of the arena – he was not on ground-level but high up in the stands, far from the action.

Confusion reigned for a moment until he heard the sickly-sweet voice call his name.

"Pancras, I see that you have made your choice."

He had come out of the tunnels next to the Emperor's podium.

"Yes, I have chosen to join my fellows in death, and thereby claim my reward," he answered with courage.

"Ah, Pancras, Pancras. You think I have brought you here to kill you? Nonsense. I promised that you would either be my son or my slave – either way you would be mine. You have made your choice, and slavery it will be."

A deeper terror filled him. No longer on the shores of Heaven – he was now facing a lifetime of Hell.

"Come, sit by me."

Pancras was led – forced – to sit beside the Emperor on the marble bench, overlooking the arena. The crowd murmured in anticipation of the games that would begin momentarily.

"Untie him," Galerius ordered a servant, who did so. "And tell the ringmaster to bring out the spectacle first." The servant hastened to execute this command.

Pancras rubbed his wrists and scanned the horizon for a means of escape.

"You shall find that all exits are occupied, slave," the Emperor said, bitter at being spurned. "You have nowhere to run – from now until the grave."

Indeed, behind him was a phalanx of Praetorians, alert with swords and pikes at the ready. He could see no way to leave the arena, nowhere to run that would lead to freedom.

Galerius ignored him and began a cordial conversation with the man on his left, exchanging laughs and lighthearted remarks.

The boy was sick to be there. He longed to be with the condemned, for surely his fellow Christians were among the living dead. This perch, with its fine view of death and surrounded by the mocking laughter of the crowd, was a source of shame and horror.

After a few minutes passed, a roar of delight rose from the crowd as the grate was withdrawn, signifying the beginning of the games. A charismatic legionary served as master of ceremonies, addressing the crowd and announcing the day's contests. The assembly laughed and cheered appropriately – the cackling of demons, it seemed to Pancras.

Presently the first victim came forth from the underbelly of the Colosseum – a fat man, dressed shabbily in a filthy tunic, with months of unshaven growth on his chin.

"Oh, you will enjoy this one, Pancras," Galerius teased, pointing to the obese man.

The victim was led, bound, to a stake in the center of the field. He was fixed to it with thick ropes, before slaves piled up firewood at the base. The crowd delighted in the horrors to come, cheering and laughing as the fire was lit and began to climb onto the man's tunic.

His screams grew and grew, his face writhing in pain. Pancras could no longer look, as he cast his eyes downward in shame and disgust.

And then he heard his name. "Pancras! Pancras!"

The boy looked up, shocked. The man in the center of the arena was staring at him, contorted in agony but glaring with pure hatred.

"Pancras! You did this to me!" he screamed, shrill and hoarse. A shiver ran down Pancras' spine – he recognized this victim.

"Ah, a friend of yours?" Galerius scoffed softly, into his ear. "I found him languishing in a mine up in the north. He knows all about your decision. If you had chosen to be my son, he would have been freed, as a wonderful present to show my esteem for you. But alas, you have become his judge and executioner."

As much as he wished to turn away, the lad was frozen in place, watching his uncle be roasted alive.

"You did this to me!" Dionysius cried out, the flames turning his flesh black. Oily smoke from burning skin and sinew and fat rose up as unholy incense. "Cursed be your God! Cursed be this Jesus you follow!"

The whole of the arena cheered appreciatively, but the victim's bitter words carried over the raucous crowd.

"I hate you! I have always hated you!" spat the vitriol from the burning man. "You will burn! You will follow me to the pits of Sheol!"

You will follow him to the pits of Sheol, taunted a mocking voice. And everything began to crumble in his soul.

Faith? What was that? It leads only to death, death, death!

And the man was silent, hanging his head as the fire overtook him, turning his once-ruddy face to black.

And black was Pancras' soul, as he watched the corpse removed once the fire was extinguished. He was responsible for this travesty! He knew that such travesties would be the fabric of his life forever as he served this wicked tyrant.

The tears remained dammed-up within him, for he was beyond weeping. If this was Galerius' way of forcing him into submission – he would forever be a slave.

A scrap of a phrase came back from one of the many lessons he had shared with Miletus: *If the Son sets you free, you are free indeed.*

"Free indeed," Pancras muttered, trying to transmit this thought to his heart, that he may believe it with every fiber of his being.

"I'm sorry, did you speak?" Galerius ridiculed.

"I am free indeed," Pancras replied, interiorly begging for courage.

"Ah, the dream of every foolish slave," the Emperor answered, unconcerned. He drained his cup and held it out to the young man. "For your first task, my dear slave, you can refill my cup. You will find the tables behind us, with the food and drink."

Would he acquiesce? He reached out his hand, but did not grasp the chalice. Intuitively he knew this would seal his fate – forever.

He withdrew his hand.

The Emperor regarded him with contempt. "We shall address this later."

Gladiators came forth to battle to the death, with copious bloodshed. Despite the raucous crowd and violent spectacle, Pancras paid no heed. His heart and mind were on a peaceful island, surrounded by the *hagioi*.

The contrast was stark – the memories of the beautiful life of those who followed the Lord, and the misery of this exhibition. There was a happiness there, an order, a peace. Here, there was only destruction. He wished he could accompany those great souls; the memory of the martyrs strengthened his wavering faith.

Amidst the cacophony, he happened to glance up and across the arena. Among the assembled throng was the face of his beloved. Ignoring the action upon the floor, she penetrated him with a somber gaze, tears streaming endlessly down her face.

As much as her tears moved him to sorrow, he had found a higher love. She could not offer him the Life that he now possessed. The sorrow of his loss was duller now, but could not be avoided entirely.

Several gladiators fell, offering their life for nothing more than the entertainment of the masses.

Time dragged forward slowly, agonizingly slow. Pancras sat immobile, blocking out the sounds of hatred, the sights of violence. Will this ever end? Or will such hatred and death follow him until he became a victim?

Slaves dragged off the bodies of the deceased, combing the sand again to bury the evidence of their struggle.

"Oh, you will enjoy this next one," Galerius commented to him, trying to make cruel sport of the young man's suffering. "*Damnatio ad bestias.* I believe these are some of your co-religionists, are they not?"

He looked up numbly to see the good and the holy, stripped and mocked and laid bare for all to see. The jeers chorused around him, screeches of pure evil. The Emperor joined his voice to the crowd, pointing out this one or that one in derision.

There comes a time in a life when evil becomes intolerable. Pancras, horrified to the core, cast one last gaze at the Emperor. All of the evils of Rome coalesced in this one man, the symbol and sign of death itself.

He could not remain the servant of Death.

I came that you might have life, and have it abundantly.

Frantically, he looked around for an exit, near or far. But every single one was guarded securely.

One by one, the Christ-followers spilled out of the underworld, to take their place in the sunny arena and offer their blood for sport. A group of about twenty stood huddled in the center of the arena, fearful in their weak humanity but made strong in Love. A metal grate rose, and jungle animals began their prowl.

If the Son sets you free, you are free indeed.

Abruptly, instantaneously, Pancras leapt to his feet and bolted down the stairs, heading towards the arena floor.

"Pancras! Where are you going!" the Emperor cried out, and Pancras could hear the tromp of Praetorians following in pursuit.

At ground level, Pancras leapt over the wall that separated spectators from sport, his sandals landing softly in the arena sand. Dashing a few paces away, he turned and faced the Emperor.

The crowd, by now, had fallen silent at such an unexpected display. Who would willingly bound into the death-cage? Forty thousand pairs of eyes inquired as to the identity of this bold young man.

"Pancras! What foolishness is this!" the Emperor demanded.

The Praetorians stayed safely behind the wall, not wanting to tempt the beasts.

But the beasts themselves seemed struck with wonder, as they approached the young man at a distance, curious at his courage.

"Emperor! People of Rome! I am a stranger in this city," he began, his young voice confidently filling the Colosseum. "I belong to a kingdom that has yet to come. You have mocked these Christians, but I am one of them. The Son has set me free and promised me everlasting life. I have come to claim that prize."

"This is suicide!" called out a voice from the crowd.

Was it foolish? To see the leering face of the Emperor, a wicked smile playing upon his lips, convinced Pancras of his conviction.

"I am not afraid. Let the beasts tear me to pieces – I will no longer serve the Emperor, or any other man. I am a servant of the Lord alone."

His vehemence seemed to entertain the crowd. Many smiled, and tittered to their neighbor. The Emperor himself chuckled, then raised his hand to regain order.

"Well, then," he declared, "You are very daring, my dear Pancras. Clearly, you are not worth my time – let it be done as you said. At least you may provide some entertainment for me with your dying breaths."

All attention was on the young man, his face like flint in unflinching hope. Pancras turned his gaze across the stadium, taking it in. He knew it would be his last glimpse of the city that had betrayed him.

The Emperor sat down, gesturing with his hand to allow the beasts to perform their vicious duty.

But the beasts seemed fearful to attack.

"Come, make quick work of me," Pancras encouraged, his hopes already set on the world to come.

Slowly, reluctantly, the beasts came forth.

But the roar of the crowd slowly died in Pancras' ears. The thousands of mocking faces faded into a brilliant white light, and he could see people coming forth, processing with white robes and palm branches. Those who had won the victory, whose souls had been covered in the Blood that Saves, came to greet him with open arms, in an embrace that would never end.

And first in this procession was a man that Pancras recognized immediately, greeting him with joy.

"Come, Pancras," said Cleonius. "All this will be yours!"

THE END

Finished November 27, 2019
Edits Completed June 24, 2020

POSTSCRIPT

"Church historians know little about the 14-year-old orphan boy who was martyred with Sts. Nereus, Achilleus, and Domitilla." This begins the short entry for Saint Pancras from "The Encyclopedia of Saints" by Rosemary Ellen Guiley. This was also the sentence that changed my life.

In January 2019, Mr. Ernie Bourcier gave me Guiley's book. Paging through it, I encountered St. Pancras and his sparse story. It intrigued me so much that I thought about his story non-stop for the next several days. I felt strongly called by God to expand upon his story, and the plot of this novel – based on the true facts of his life - coalesced in my mind in its entirety all at once.

But my relationship with St. Pancras goes back further than that. During the 2006-2007 academic year, I had the blessing of studying in Rome. Throughout that year, I got to know the city quite well, and always enjoyed visiting the religious and historical sites. There was a church of San Pancrazio (St. Pancras) right around the corner from my favorite park. I would frequently pass by the church, but in a city full of beautiful churches, it didn't catch my eye...until I realized that there were catacombs underneath. Unfortunately, the catacombs were closed to the public every time I went.

But on St. Pancras' feast day (May 12), I tried one last time, and lo and behold – the catacombs were open! Since these catacombs are small and not well-known, I had the subterranean tunnels all to myself. It was a sacred and mystical experience to stand in the ancient Christian burial ground, connected with my brothers and sisters across time. I felt a closeness with St. Pancras, even though at the time I literally knew nothing about his story!

So what is his story? The details are fuzzy, but we know some general facts. He was born in Synnada in Phrygia, which is in the western part of modern-day Turkey. His mother died in childbirth and his father Cleonius died when he was eight, leaving his uncle Dionysius to take him to Rome shortly thereafter where they both converted to Christianity. Somehow (no one knows exactly how) he became associated with Saints Nereus and Achilleus, who were both part of the Praetorian Guard. Along with Nereus and Achilleus, Pancras was sent to Pontia to execute the niece of the emperor, Domitilla, who, as a Christian virgin, had refused to submit to a marriage proposal with a pagan man. But Domitilla's example so inspired the soldiers that they abandoned their plan and protected her instead. They were all captured together and put to death by beheading in 303 during the persecutions of Diocletian. Before his death at age fourteen, Pancras was offered great riches and power by the Emperor, who was impressed with his courage. But spurning them all, he chose to follow his mentors to martyrdom.

But this straightforward story contains many historical gaps and problems. For example, some historians have found evidence that Nereus and Achilleus suffered, not under Diocletian, but under Domitian – who reigned in the 90s AD. One story says that Nereus and Achilleus were not Praetorians but rather eunuchs who served Flavia Domitilla in her palace. Later on, when the Catholic Church reformed the calendar of saints in 1960, they removed the name of St. Domitilla, citing lack of historical evidence for her existence. Our only evidence for the existence of Domitilla is the fifth-century list of martyrs that was later compiled into the Roman Martyrology. The other saints have a bit more – but not much more – historical evidence, including inscriptions in the catacombs, inclusion in the Sacramentarium Gelasianum (one of the earliest liturgical books), and evidence of a church built to honor Sts. Nereus and Achilleus in the late fourth century. For his part, Pancras was honored with a basilica built in the sixth century, over the catacombs that bear his name.

St. Pancras is particularly venerated in England, where his relics were brought by order of Pope St. Gregory the Great. There is a hospital, school, several churches, and even a railway station that bear his name in England.

Many of the characters in this novel, admittedly, are fiction. Daphne, Antonius, Miletus, Aquila...these characters came to life only through imagination and prayer. But other historical situations and characters are quite real – Galerius, for example, really was one of the tetrarchs who was bloodthirsty and virulently anti-Christian; he came to Rome in 303 and intensified his persecution of the Church there. It is almost certain that Pancras and Galerius had several interactions, and it was Galerius who ordered his death.

In sum, I hope that these saints would approve of – and delight in! – what I have written. I write in their honor, hoping in some small and unworthy way to follow in their footsteps. For we walk in the footsteps of the hagioi – and bloody footsteps are they. But I pray that these footsteps lead to eternal life, where someday we will meet the real St. Pancras, St. Nereus, St. Achilleus, and St. Domitilla on the shores of heaven.

AFTERWORD

One person puts the words on paper, but many others help in the crafting of a novel! I am thankful in a special way to Ernie Bourcier, for giving me the book that inspired this novel. Many thanks to Josh Garrels, a fantastic musician whose albums "Love, War, and the Sea In Between," "Chrysaline," and "Home" were the constant background to my writing (in particular his song "Odysseus" was an inspiration to me!). When I would run out of Josh Garrels, I would turn to the ethereal and beautiful music of Kai Engel, Ean Grimm, and Adrian Von Zeigler – thank you for sharing your gifts with the world! Thank you to my parents for their helpful feedback. Thank you to my editors: Maureen Kuroski, Caitlin Stote, and Joe McAleer, and to those who wrote kind words about this book, Ryan Young and Noelle Amann. Many thanks to those who inspired a character, and thanks to those who read my first novel "Days of Grace" and offered positive encouragement and constructive criticism. Finally, though, I must thank God, and I thank His many saints – especially my new friends, St. Pancras, St. Nereus, St. Achilleus, and St. Domitilla. I can't wait to meet you all.

GLOSSARY

Aeaea – mythological island in Homer's "Odyssey", home to the sorceress Circe.

Ager Romanes – the fields outside of Rome which provided much of the grain for the public dole. The territory was governed by the municipality of Rome.

Aphrodite – ancient Greek goddess of love.

Bulla – a small amulet worn by Roman boys, usually made of gold or lead. It would be given to them at nine days old and worn until they took the "toga of manhood."

Caldarium – one of the rooms in the public baths that featured a hot plunge bath and steam treatment.

Caryatids – a stone carving of a draped female figure, often used as a pillar to support a building.

Cena – Latin for "dinner".

Cerberus – in Greek mythology, the multi-headed dog who was the guardian of Hades.

Charon – in Greek mythology, the ferryman who takes souls from the land of the living, across the rivers Styx and Acheron, and into Hades.

Cohortes Urbanae – legionaries who served as the local police force for ancient Rome.

Culina – Latin for "kitchen".

Curule Aedile – a magistrate responsible for the care of the markets and the economy of ancient Rome.

Damnatio ad bestias – condemned to death by being thrown to the beasts.

Delphic Oracle – in Greek mythology, priestess of the Temple to Apollo in Delphi, who was granted the gift of knowledge, wisdom, and prophesy.

Denarius (pl. denarii) – silver coin that represented an average day's pay for a laborer.

Di Omnes – a Latin swear word, roughly meaning "All the gods!"

Dies Natale – Latin for "birthday".

Domus – a single-family house for the upper-class in ancient Rome.

Ecclesia – Greek for "Church" (literally "called-out-of").

Elysian Fields – in Greek mythology, the final resting-place for the virtuous.

Evangelion – Greek for "Gospel" or "Good News".

Garum – an expensive sauce made from the salted and fermented innards of fish.

Gaul – The Latin name for the area that encompasses modern-day France.

Gnosis – Greek for "knowledge", often referring to secret or hidden knowledge that gives a person power.

Grammaticus – the second of three levels of Roman schooling, usually for boys ages 9-13.

Hades – in Greek mythology, the god of the Underworld. In time, it also referred to the location of the Underworld itself.

Hagioi – Greek for "the holy ones", often translated "saints".

Haruspex – a man trained in the art of divination from the examination of the innards of animals, particularly the liver.

Horrea Galbae – the major warehouses in the south of Rome, holding immense amounts of imports and dry goods.

Icarus – in Greek mythology, he sought to escape from Crete with his father on wings made of wax and feathers. Due to his hubris and arrogance, he flew too close to the sun, which melted the wax and caused him to plummet to his death.

Insula (pl. Insulae) – a multi-level apartment building in ancient Rome, often constructed of brick, wood, or concrete. The ground floor was generally shops while the upper floors were residences for the middle and lower classes. They had sanitation and running water but were frequently filthy, disease-ridden, and prone to fire.

Knucklebones – a game played by ancient Roman children, similar to modern-day jacks.

Lapsi – Christians who had denied their Faith under torture.

Lares – guardian gods in ancient Roman religion. Most Roman homes would have statues of the Lares at the entrance of their home, where they would be invoked upon entering or leaving the house.

Lararium – the small household shrine, usually close to the front door, in which the Lares would be placed.

Leviathan – a sea monster, originally mentioned in the Hebrew Scriptures.

Ludus – a Latin term that could refer to a "school" in general, or specifically to the first of three levels of Roman schooling, for boys and girls up to approximately age 11.

Lustratio – a Roman purification ceremony, usually performed when a boy was nine days old (or eight days for a girl) in which a sacrifice would be offered on their behalf and the boys would receive their bulla.

Mare Nostrum – literally "Our Sea", it was the common Roman term for the Mediterranean Sea.

Mensa – Latin for "table".

Mysterion – Greek for "mystery," this was the early Christian name for the Sacraments.

Neapolis – the ancient name for Naples, Italy.

Noricum – a kingdom of tribes north of the Alps in modern-day Austria and Slovenia.

Nummius – the man who served as Urban Prefect (similar to a mayor) of Rome in 302-303.

Paenulae – Large outer cloak worn by the Romans in the cold or bad weather.

Parentalis – Nine-day festival in ancient Rome, celebrated in February, which honored one's ancestors.

Paterfamilias – the father of a family in ancient Rome.

Pax Romana – the "peace of Rome".

Praefectus Annonae – Roman prefect in charge of the grain supply for the city of Rome.

Prandium – Latin for "lunch".

Pro Di Immortalis – Latin swear roughly meaning "Good heavens!"

Quinqueremes – A large Roman warship.

Sacramentum – a military oath of loyalty sworn by a legionary to his superior.

Senatus Populusque Romanus – Latin for "The Senate and People of Rome", a form of address used primarily during the Roman republic.

Sestertii (sing. sestertius) – a Roman coin worth about a quarter of a denarius.

Sheol – literally "the Pit", similar to "Hades"/the Underworld. Sheol is mentioned in the Hebrew Scriptures.

Stadium (pl. Stadia) – a unit of measurement in ancient Rome: approximately 600 feet.

Stultus – Latin for "stupid, foolish".

Styx – in Greek mythology, the river that forms the boundary between the earth and the underworld.

Subura – the crowded, crime-ridden section of ancient Rome, located between the Viminal and Esquiline Hills.

Tartarus – in Greek mythology, the dungeon of the afterworld which was a place of suffering and torment for the wicked.

Tetrarch – one of the four co-emperors during the reign of Diocletian.

Tiberim – the ancient name for the Tiber River.

Toga Praetexta – the toga worn by freeborn boys until they took their "toga of manhood". This toga featured a purple stripe to show that they were underage and therefore (theoretically) protected by law from predators.

Toga Recta – the toga (lit. "upright toga") worn by youths in ancient Rome beneath their outer toga.

Toga Virilis – the "toga of manhood" donned by those who had undergone the adolescent rite-of-passage ceremony in ancient Rome. This toga was pure white and signified that the wearer was now a full citizen with the right to vote, marry, and conduct business.

Trabea – a colorful mantle worn by nobility in ancient Rome to signify their role or profession.

Transtiberim – the area of Rome now known as Trastevere, on the opposite bank of the Tiber River from the main part of the city of Rome.

Triclinia (sing. triclinium) – the formal dining room of a Roman domus. There would be three *klinai* (low couches) that would be assembled for reclining while eating – thus, even if not a separate room, the triclinium would be the area in which food was consumed.

Tubilustrium – a feast of ancient Rome, usually held in March, to celebrate the military and send them off on campaign. At times, this feast would be celebrated multiple times each year.

Tullianum – a prison of ancient Rome, now known as the Mamertine Prison. Sts. Peter and Paul were held here.

Vestal Virgins – priestesses of the goddess Vesta, who took a thirty-year vow of celibacy to tend the sacred fire of Vesta and offer worship to her.